The Family Roots of Adolescent Delinquency

The Family Roots of Adolescent Delinquency

Joseph F. Perez, Ph. D.
Westfield State College

VNR VAN NOSTRAND REINHOLD COMPANY

NEW YORK   CINCINNATI   ATLANTA   DALLAS   SAN FRANCISCO
LONDON   TORONTO   MELBOURNE

Van Nostrand Reinhold Company Regional Offices:
New York   Cincinnati   Atlanta   Dallas   San Francisco

Van Nostrand Reinhold Company International Offices:
London   Toronto   Melbourne

Library of Congress Catalog Card Number: 78-7035
ISBN: 0-442-26535-2

Manufactured in the United States of America

Published by Van Nostrand Reinhold Company
135 West 50th Street, New York, N.Y. 10020

Published simultaneously in Canada by Van Nostrand Reinhold Ltd.

15 14 13 12 11 10 9 8 7 6 5 4 3 2 1

Library of Congress Cataloging in Publication Data

Perez, Joseph Francis.
    The family roots of adolescent delinquency.

    Includes index.
    1. Mentally ill--Family relationships.
2. Juvenile delinquency.   I. Title.
[DNLM: 1. Family.   2. Juvenile delinquency.
HV9069 P4JUI]
RC455.4.F3P47   364.36'3'0926   78-7035
ISBN 0-442-26535-2

*A hero effortlessly creates
expectations, dreams, and an ideal
self. This book is dedicated to
my natural hero, my father,
Antonio.*

Rispettu, rispettu fichiu miu, e tuttu che vulemu na chista vita.
Respect, respect, my son, that's all we ever want in this life.
Santina Senofonte

U rispettu chiu importanti e u rispettu toiu stissu.
Nun veni dei amici chi cambiano ca vichiania
Nun veni dei guverni, chi vannu e venunu,
Nun veni da chiesa chi e iterna,
Nun veni di diu propriu,
Veni, fichiu miu, da famichia.

The most important respect is self-respect.
That comes not from friends, who change as you advance in years,
It comes not from governments, which come and go,
It comes not from the church, which is eternal,
It does not come even from God himself,
It comes, my son, from the family.
Vincenzo Giacotto

THE FAMILY TREE

Francis and Maureen (Casey) Whiting

>   Francis Jr. (father)
>   Mary
>   Phyllis
>   Martha

John and Helen (Abbott) Conley

>   Thomas
>   Robert
>   Christopher
>   Kathleen (mother)
>   Helen

Francis Jr. and Kathleen (Conley) Whiting

>   Thomas
>   Francis III
>   John
>   Alice

Preface: Why This Book?

This book developed out of the author's work with adolescents adjudged to be delinquent by the courts. He learned early in his work that if he was going to be effective as a counselor with these adolescents, he needed to deal with the families of the delinquents as well as with the delinquent himself. If nothing else, he learned that a person termed "delinquent" is one who has been spawned by a "delinquent family", that is, a family which has developed neurotic patterns of interaction.

The story which follows is precisely about such a family. It is a family caught up in a web of destructive habits, attitudes, and values. As the story unfolds however, the reader begins to see that the family profiled here incorporates characteristics, behaviors found among many "typical" families. The problems with which they are beset are those with which any American can identify. They are the real family problems of today. They are the "au courant" problems—dope peddling, breaking and entering, illegitimate pregnancy, abortion, and sexual dysfunction. A prime object of this book is to explain how these contemporary neurotic behaviors are rooted deeply in the inherited familial patterns of interaction. And, it is in the process of telling the Whiting family story that the author shows how family life today can make a person sick.

Via social history the author shows how neither husband nor wife were prepared for marriage, they married because they were supposed to. He married her because it was the honorable thing to do. (He got her pregnant.) She married him because she felt she had no choice.

It was upon such a shaky foundation that their marriage was built. It was into such a family, too, that four children were born and reared. The book focuses upon one of the three children—John Whiting, a boy adjudged delinquent by the court. John is the central character of the book and the vehicle for profiling his nuclear and grandparental families.

From birth, John is steeped and reared in the family's neurotic pattern of interaction.   As he grows, John finds that his own pattern of interaction becomes inextricably interwoven with that of his family.   Like so many of us however, he only dimly understands the how, the why, and the general nature of his emotional disturbance.   As the story unfolds, the reader is taken step by step through the complex maze of familial dynamics.

Each chapter is preceded by "Focus Guides" and followed by Discussion Questions.   Both the "Focus Guides" and Discussion Questions were designed to help the reader glean the maximum amount of information from each chapter and also to help him develop insight into the complex interpersonal dynamics presented. These "Guides" and Questions serve another purpose too.   They help the author to achieve his purpose, namely: to show the reader how familial dynamics contribute to the molding of a delinquent personality.

The point of view here is that an adolescent delinquent is the product of interpersonal ways which are indigenous to a family. These ways are founded in the inherited familial values and attitudes and are interwoven with emotions.   And emotions and their expression are at the nub of individual personality.   They are the psychological life blood of a family.   How love, anger, and joy are communicated is a critical determinant for how a family will get along or if, indeed, it will get along at all.

As will be seen, the parent's emotional understanding and learning are acquired in their own childhood and, like the values and attitudes, are passed on to their children.   This is done subtly, unconsciously, and imperceptibly.   But it is done truly.

John Whiting was not born a delinquent.   He learned to be one. He was born to parents who themselves had never learned to communicate love.   Both parents were reared in homes where the value focus was not on rewarding familial interaction but rather on, "what will people think."

A social history of the grandparents will show how they created emotionally stultifying familial climates.   This was especially true of both maternal grandfather and paternal grandmother. The boy's father grew up socially inhibited, and an alienated man,

He never learned what it means to be a man, to be a father. The boy's mother is virtually unable to give or receive love, yet she desperately seeks to learn. The maternal role is not one with which she had identified because her own mother had been a passive-dependent, inept woman.

Finally, the grandparents, parents and delinquent described here, as well as the supporting cast of characters, are all real people. Names have been changed, of course, and incidents altered, to prevent the recognition of any person. Much research, discussion with colleagues, and innumerable hours in interviews were spent to explain how familial dynamics help mold a delinquent personality. I leave it to the reader to judge how successful the effort has been.

JOSEPH F. PEREZ, PH.D.

Northampton, Massachusetts

Acknowledgments

This book is the product of my professional experience as a psychotherapist. It is the product, too, of my observations and discussions with adolescents at their various stages of personal and social development. Several of these young people, via their talks and behavior with me and with each other, contributed to the development of the manuscript.

Specifically, I should like to thank my son, Christopher, who gave me the original idea; my daughter, Kathleen, and Aimee Collins, both of whom supplied me with much rich material; my son, Joseph, who read the first draft and gave me many constructive ideas; my daughter, Monique (9 years old) who provided me with an endless supply of sharpened pencils and delightful respites from my writing.

And most importantly, to my confidante and wife, Geraldine, who insulated me from phone calls and minor family obligations when I felt the need to write.

All these people were helpful and instrumental in the development of the manuscript. If there are any deficiencies in the work, however, they are my responsibility.

Contents

The Family Roots of Adolescent Delinquency

Chapter 1

A note to the reader regarding the "Focus Guides". These have been designed to help you better understand what follows. Used thoughtfully they should help you literally milk each page for every ounce of psychological and literary worth. Accordingly, as you read the "Focus Guides" and their respective chapters, keep asking yourself "why?" It is the author's firm conviction that only by asking "why?", sometimes "why not?", that we can get at the essence of human motivation.

FOCUS GUIDES

1. Consider Mr. Sortino's temper and its effect upon the school climate.
2. Reflect upon Dalton's pomposity and how students react to it.
3. Think about how Sortino and Dalton jibe as people and how they affect the emotional climate of the school.
4. How does John's adjustment to school reflect his emotional disabilities? His emotional health?
5. Consider the inability of Kathleen and Francis to talk to each other and what kind of an emotional climate this creates at home.

"Hey, John, ya' got any weed?"

"Yeah, Chris. What ya' want?"

"All I want's a nick."*

"All I got is lids."+

"Oh, shit, man, I don't got twenty bucks."

"Too bad, man, it's really dynamite weed."

"What kind is it?"

"Jamaican. See if ya' can find anyone to go in on it with ya."

"Yeah, that's cool. See ya' here at the end of 4th period."

---

* Five dollars worth, approximately one quarter once.
+ Approximately one once.

1

Two class periods later.

"Hey, John, I got the money. I'm going in on it with Mark and Pete."

"Sounds cool."

"Let me see the lid. Oh, wow, man, that's pretty good."

"Yeah. It'll get pretty screwed up."

"Far out. Hey, thanks a lot."

This second conversation and transaction took place in the Boys' Room on the second floor of Middletown High School. Neither John nor Chris could know that the 6' 3" and 230 pound Assistant Principal, Frank Sortino, would be the next person to push into the toilet via the swinging door.

He did. And Frank, who is famous for his instant temper and who has become not a little paranoid about marijuana selling in the school, digested the entire scene in a wink. His response was comparable to his split second enlightenment. In a flash and with a roar he thundered, "O.K. Let's go to my office." Both boys backed away. Donnelly started to speak but never did. Without another word Frank seized both thunderstruck boys by the napes of their necks, never releasing them, he pulled, dragged and carried them both to his adjunct second-floor office, three doors down from the toilet. (Frank had set this office up two months before precisely because he suspected most of the selling went on upstairs over the main administrative offices.)

Even before he reached his door he bellowed, "Martha!" Martha is his part-time secretary and a fifty-four-year-old maiden lady, with an almost stereotyped maiden-lady view of the world. She very much disapproves of the, "lack of discipline and horrendous manners of the high school students." The faculty has learned to avoid Martha. A younger member of the faculty observed that, "Martha is the only person I know who can give a very complete three minute lecture on how to be a complete bastard in the classroom." Martha hates kids. Like Frank, she gets messages instantaneously. Frank's bellow and complementary scuffling told her much.

He bombed through the door with his two terrified culprits.

"Look at this and at this!" he cried. Martha observed the this and this to which he pointed. The "thises" included the twenty dollars and the lid of marijuana, each item still clutched without any appreciation in each boy's hand. John dropped his twenty dollars (two fives and a ten) on the desk. Martha reached to pick them up.

"Christ, don't touch that money."

Martha, convulsed back in her chair, and her left eyelid, which always winked uncontrollably when she was in an anxious state, started blinking like a neon light. Lordy, she thought, Frank's acting like a madman, even for him.

Frank was in a very agitated state. Finally, but finally, he had nailed one of the little bastards. He had long suspected that John Whiting was pushing the stuff. He came to school stoned too often. But to nail him selling it! Too much! Hot shit!

"Martha, please note down, Whiting had the money, two five dollar bills and a ten dollar bill in his hand, in his hand, write that down." Martha scribbled furiously.

"And note, too, that Chris Donnelly is holding a lid of marijuana in his hand." Martha noted it dutifully.

"A lid of marijuana. What's a lid?" she asked nervously.

"A lid's an ounce."

"All that's an ounce? That whole package is only an ounce?"

"Yes, yes, yes, an ounce," he answered absent-mindedly.

Frank didn't know what to do next so he called the "Old Fart." The "Old Fart," whose more proper title is "Principal," is Thaddeus Dalton. Thaddeus acquired the undesirable appellative a long time ago. Significantly the laconic alias was appended not by the students, but by the faculty. Most of the teachers feel that it's a very appropriate designation. The feeling is that he has a positive talent for making "a stink" wherever he goes.

Whithin three minutes Mr. Dalton came bounding in. He is a bachelor and a fashionable dresser. He reads *Esquire* magazine religiously. Unfortunately, however, clothes are the only item about which he keeps current. The general opinion is that there isn't too much else that he knows about.

Physically he is a slightly built man (110 lbs.). He is also very short (5' 2"). When he stands next to Frank Sortino, he feels very undignified; and, since he's very concerned about his dignity, especially in public, he avoids being positioned near his assistant principal in the corridors, at teachers' meetings, and especially at assemblies. Mr. Dalton's most striking physical characteristic, however, is not his thinness nor even his shortness. It is his pallid complexion. Most people turn a little red when they get nervous. Mr. Dalton does not. He gets paler. And right now he was very pale. Frank thought he looked like death, warmed over.

"Well, well now, what's this, what's going on here, Mr. Sortino?" he asked pompously. Frank was sitting down and Mr. Dalton was pleased about that. Sortino had said something about dope, that damned Whiting kid selling it.

"Yes, well it's very simple. I caught Whiting here selling pot to Donnely."

"I see. I see. Martha, escort these two lads to my office." Martha scurried out with the two offenders. Thaddeus turned to his assistant.

"What's happened?" Frank, who was still in an emotionally disordered state, explained quickly and concisely.

"So what do we do now?" asked Thaddeus.

"I don't know, call the narcs, I guess."

"The narcs, the narcs," he echoed, puzzled. "Damn it, Frank, don't use this hippie language with me." Mr. Dalton was very upset. He almost never cursed.

"The narcotics unit of the police department."

"The narcotics unit. The narcotics unit. My God, Frank, have you taken leave of your senses?"

Frank thought, I knew it, I knew it. The son-of-a-bitch is going to cop-out on me. He looked at his superior with thinly veiled distaste. And despite his own agitation he could see that Thaddeus was really upset. No doubt about it. If it were possible he had turned another shade lighter. Thaddeus was so upset that he had sat down, and Frank knew he loved to stand when Frank was sitting.

"Tad," Frank figured that the familiarity was warranted by the circumstances. "Tad, they'll come down, scare the hell out of the two of them and maybe even find out where Whiting's getting the stuff. It'll all be very quietly done. It'll all be very discreet. No one downtown need know anything. Leave it to me!" (Dalton's fear of the downtown politicians was legendary in the school and downtown too.)

Thaddeus was sick. Sick of the whole mess. Until five minutes ago he had never really believed that his school was contaminated by this abominable plague of narcotics.

"Frank," he said in a weak but prophetic-like tone, "downtown will know. They always know. Believe me, I know."

"So what if they do?" Frank's characteristic impatience was starting to surface. This lily-livered pansy was starting to bust his Sicilian "cuglioni," balls for short.

"Frank, Frank boy, listen to me," he was almost whining.

Now the cop-out. The eternal political, proper, gentlemanly cop-out, Frank thought. Bullshit. No way. Not again.

For the second time in about fifteen minutes Frank exploded, "Thaddeus, you hear me and you hear me real good. And, man, you can turn ten more shades whiter. Your heart can stop for all I care. We are not, we are not gonna let these little bastards get away. They just broke federal, state, and city laws. For Christ's sake, Thaddeus, what the hell kind of a school are you running when you knowingly, knowingly let kids break the law? I don't know about you, *Mister* Dalton, but I won't sleep tonight, I won't sleep for a long time if I ever let you do that."

Frank finished. He was as surprised as Thaddeus looked to be. And Frank's face was real red, he knew that, as red as Dalton's was white, but he was calm now, almost serene inside. Finally, but finally, the "Old Fart" had learned how Frank felt about things. Frank looked to see just how painful the learing had been.

Thaddeus sat there stupefied. He couldn't believe it. Never in his forty-one years at Middletown High had he been spoken to with such acrimony, with such condescension, with such authority. And he just sat there. His mouth moved, jerked, but no words came out. Finally he sighed.

"Thaddeus, I'm gonna call a fella I know in narcotics, O.K.?" The "O.K.?" signified his continued deference to Dalton's authority. And it was pure Sortino for, whatever he is, Frank is not a cruel man.   He's tempestuous, he's loud, crude, even vulgar and everyone knows about his unfortunate penchant for braggadocio. But he's not unkind.   Thaddeus nodded and sighed in resignation.

Two hours later, John's parents, Francis and Kathleen, met with Frank and Thaddeus.   The two narcotics officers (also the city's truant officers, police department's Little League Sponsors and, in the summer, official "Dog Leash Officers") had left moments ago.   They had learned nil from either John or Chris.

Frank felt that the cops had been too damned gentle with the boys.   And that Whiting kid!   What a wise-ass little bastard he was; with those bored and at times affectedly incredulous looks.   The most he permitted himself to do was to grunt an "I dunno" to a couple of questions!   Damn!   Frank realized now that it had been a mistake to call in the narcs.   Narcs.   Ha!   What a joke they were.   They could care less about the whole incident.

Christopher's parents, meanwhile, were vacationing in Bermuda, a fact which did little to abate Frank's exasperation.   Thaddeus, on the recommendation of the policemen, had suspended Chris, pending the return of his parents.   A ten minute conference with the parents together with a pompous lecture to Chris in front of them would end the whole affair for the Donnelly family.   Frank knew that.

John, at this time, was still waiting outside.   And Frank knew that Thaddeus was going to have his way, not much of anything way going to be resolved with the Whitings either.   This was the way of Thaddeus Dalton, never deal with a problem, just smooth it over.   If things look good, they are good!   Damn.   Frank's stomach was beginning to churn, a sure sign to him that he wasn't going to leave this conference without being heard.

He turned his gaze to Kathleen.   He knew her.   She had grad-uated from this school when he was still a sophomore.   She was still a damned good-looking woman, still well built, he noticed. How'd she ever get tied to this creep?   Frank had never met Whiting.   He knew him only by reputation.   His other two boys, Tom and Frank, like John, had also been little zeros.   This guy had to be the reason, a real big zero, at least as a father.

Frank's greatest personal satisfaction came from his own

competence in the paternal role. He ran his home like a Sicilian despot, albeit a benevolent one. His two older boys were success- ful college students and the two younger boys, as expected, were following in the best tradition of the Sortinos. How could this Whiting guy permit his family to go to pot like this? He smiled wryly to himself. The "pot" analogy was most appropriate in light of the day's events.

Thaddeus cleared his throat. "Uh, Mr. and Mrs. Whiting, we want you to know, both of you, that this is a most serious matter." He cleared his throat again. Surprisingly, Thaddeus was no more wan than usual, a further indication to Frank that he was bent on smoothing over the whole matter. "Yes, you know why you're here. Your son, John, was apprehended with another boy upstairs in the Boys' Room," he paused dramatically, "selling marijuana. A most serious offense. Most serious. The Narcotics Unit of the Middletown Police Department were here investigating. Your son was not . . ."

Kathleen interrupted him. "What do you want from us? What can we do?"

Women in general and mothers in particular had always made this life long bachelor more than a little nervous. He nev- er even pretended to understand them. They were too emo- tional, too unpredictable. Thaddeus responded predictably, "Mrs. Whiting, it isn't for me, the principal, to tell you what to do. I am only the principal of this educational plant. I have hun- dreds of children here. I can't take each one under my wing, much as I would like to. Parents have a more rewarding task and a more sacred one to guide these young people to be our future citizens."

Frank thought idly that Thaddeus was at his supercilious best, or worst, depending on who was listening.

"Now," he continued, "John has been an incorrigible truant, as you know. This latest episode is another chapter, another chapter, in the continuing serial of his unfortunate life." Frank had heard Thaddeus utter that pretentious line too many times to be impressed. Kathleen seemed impressed, though. So did her husband.

Thaddeus continued his pontifications, even using the papal "we."

"We here seek only to help.   But please understand we cannot rear, we cannot be absolute guardians, but only gentle, interested, ancillaries [here he softened his tone].   We are only ancillaries to the parents.   'In loco parentis' is our guide."

The horseshit was getting a little deep, even for Thaddeus. The Whitings seemed to be mesmerized by the awful rhetoric. Especially Mr. Whiting.   He looked like he was in some kind of trance.

Thaddeus fully appreciated the parental reaction.   Now he would completely disarm them.   "What should we do?"

Silence.

Kathleen broke it.   "But that's what I asked you before, before you went into your, your incredible sermon."

Frank smothered a chuckle.   Good for you, lady, he thought.

"Eh?"   Now it was Thaddeus' turn to look inundated.   As expected, he turned a couple of shades lighter.   This woman reinforced all his anxieties about women.   "But, but . . ." he stammered.   "You two are the parents.   I'm not.   That boy is a constant source of dissension in this school.   Something must be done."

"Look, Mr. Dalton.   I've tried the very best I can with John and his brothers, too.   I don't know which way to turn.   I've just come out of a three-and-a-half-week stay in the State Hospital. Right now I feel like I'm shot to pieces.   I don't know what to do and I admit it.   I feel John needs help.   I know I still do.   Our whole family needs help."   Kathleen's eyes were very red and wet.   The tears were there, or about to arrive.   Frank lowered his head.

Thaddeus was getting very embarrassed.   The whole damned conference was going all wrong.   This certainly was not what he had intended.   And certainly not what he wanted.   He had never learned how to deal with a tearful woman.   They made him very uneasy.   He didn't know what else to do so he turned to his assistant principal.

"Mr. Sortino, you know the lad John better than I, what would you suggest?"

Frank became irked. Characteristically the "Old Fart" was copping out and passing the buck. What could he say? Dalton cleared his throat. That irked him more 'cause it was what Dalton had done too many times already.

"Mr. Dalton, Mrs. Whiting didn't address herself to John only, she asked for help for her whole family. I'm not sure that I can offer the kind of help that . . . what did you have in mind, Mrs. Whiting?"

"I don't know. I don't know." Kathleen was so obviously miserable. Frank felt sorry for her. Thaddeus was just embarrassed, and not a little bewildered by the turn of the conference.

Frank looked at Mr. Whiting. The poor bastard was an even bigger zero than he'd figured originally. Not yet had he even uttered a sound. Now he sighed. Frank couldn't stand it anymore. "What do you have to say, Mr. Whiting?"

"Nothing," he mumbled.

"Nothing," echoed Frank incredulously.

"Well, uh, what am I supposed to say?"

"I don't know, but the 'nothing' really bugs me. That's a big part of the problem, I bet," hissed Frank.

"What?" Francis Whiting asked perplexedly.

"Ah, forget it," Sortino murmured. He wanted to scream at the bastard. For Christ's sake, Mister. For Christ's sake, your kid's pushing dope. He was caught at it. This gorgeous woman of yours is disintegrating in front of all of us and you've got nothing to offer. Nothing to even say? For Christ's sake! That's what he wanted to say. Instead he said nothing more. Probably he'd said too much anyway. Listening to Dalton he knew it.

"Mr. Sortino is like that. A little temperamental, Latin type and all that. Ha, ha," he laughed, affectedly. Dalton sort of liked it when his assistant lost his cool with parents. It made Dalton look better. Sort of the reason *He* was the principal. The principal should always be the mediator, the arbitrator, the diplomat in control. Yes.

"Mr. Sortino is a man who cares," murmured Kathleen. She continued more strongly. "He flared up because he sees our family is in trouble. And he cares. A man who cares is rare today.

I can admire such a man." She gazed unabashedly at the assistant principal.

Frank is renowned for his male chauvinism. All his adolescent and adult life he'd assumed a benevolently patronizing attitude toward woman, any woman, including Angie, his wife. This woman now made him turn scarlet with embarrassment. He sat and hung his head now like a new freshman just caught smoking in the john.

The principal meanwhile dazedly stared at Frank who looked like an embarrassed schoolboy. Thaddeus had the uneasy feeling that there was a lot more going on than he understood. Dalton's only comfort was that he was more in control of the scene than Sortino. This bloody woman with her sniveling remarks, her tears, and her artfully remarkable candor kept him from exercising his rightful control. What made him feel even more queasy, however, was Frank's obvious discomfort. Frank, he had long felt, knew about women, at least far more than he did. Damn! This woman was a witch and an outspoken one at that.

"I care, Kath," said Whiting.

"Oh, Francis, what good is it if no one knows?"

"I, I just never show it."

"I know," she replied.

"But I care."

"Yes, Francis. Let's not fight here." There was a strong edge to her tone that only increased Dalton's discomposure.

"You know, Thaddeus," Frank said slowly, "I think we ought to bring the guidance director into this. What do you think?"

Dalton didn't like being addressed as Thaddeus in front of parents or, for that matter, the faculty either. However, he was glad Frank was tactful enough to have added the "what do you think." Right now all he wanted was to get the problem solved— that is, out of his office.

"Yes. Yes, a splendid suggestion." He buzzed the outer office. "Have Mr. Ballard come in here, please."

Allen Ballard is the director of Guidance and has a graduate degree in social work. He is intelligent, articulate and competent. Most of the time Dalton studiously avoided contact with him.

He entered the office and sat in the only unoccupied chair, next to Frank.   Ballard is a nondescript thirty-five-year-old man of medium height with dark hair.   His only visible distinguishing characteristic is the lower part of his face which is mildly scarred by adolescent acne.

"Mr. Ballard," Dalton began briskly, "you saw John Whiting outside, I take it."

"Yes."

"Well, this conference concerns an incident of several hours ago.   Mr. Sortino apprehended John while selling marijuana in the Boys' Room."

Ballard nodded in response.

"Yes, well . . . " Dalton always felt a little patronized by this social worker.   Most of the time his thought about him was, why wasn't he working in some ghetto, someplace?   Right now, however, he was glad he was here.   "Yes, well, Mrs. Whiting raised the question of, well, uh, help for the boy, perhaps for the whole family."

Kathleen spoke.   "I've just spent time at the state hospital as a patient and a psychologist there recommended some family therapy."

"I see."   He looked at the Whitings.   They both looked wretched. He knew about John.   The boy had been referred many times to his office.   Several of his counselors had made appointments with him but he'd never shown.   He addressed himself to both parents, "If you are willing, I'd be happy to arrange some family therapy sessions at Children Aid and Family Services."

"Splendid, splendid," chortled Dalton.

Ballard continued, "That is, if you're both willing, if John is willing—I understand a central concern here is John, in fact, if your entire family is willing."

Kathleen responded, "As I just said, I just came out of the hospital, the State Hospital.   I was told there that we should all go into therapy.   I think we should.   Frankly, I don't know what else to do."

"How do you feel about it, Mr. Whiting?"

"I don't know."

Frank rolled his eyes to the ceiling and sighed, but imperceptibly. "I don't know but I'm willing, I'm willing," he said in a not-too-firm voice.

"O.K.," Ballard said. "You should know that seldom does each member go into family therapy with a lot of verve. I appreciate your vacillation. Now how about John and the other family members? How do you think they'll feel?"

"John will come. We'll all come, I guarantee it," said Whiting. The response took everyone except Ballard by surprise. It wasn't the words only, but the steel-like tone with which they were delivered. It was all so incongruous with everything which had preceded.

Frank looked at him puzzled and thought, maybe there was more to this guy than met the eye. He "guaranteed it." He doesn't look like the type who had given too many guarantees over the course of his life. That's for sure. Yeah, we'll see. The kid had been out there now for a long time. What had he been doing all this time? Worrying? Nah! John Whiting didn't seem to worry about too much. What had he been thinking all this time? Frank often wondered what kids thought while waiting on the bench.

John sat on the bench outside gazing with unveiled interest at one of Mr. Dalton's secretaries. His experienced adolescent eye was captivated by what he perceived to be an enormous blouseful of bosom. "Christ, what a pair of knockers," he thought. For a few moments he gave full rein to his fantasies.

John is a blue-eyed boy who wears his dark blond hair to his shoulders. Although he's just under six feet, adults and even his peers do not find him to be especially imposing. He's too skinny (130 lbs.), even for the thin world in which we live. His general lack of weight is reflected in his face. John won't be handsome for a long time, not until he's filled out more. Presently his face is too fleshless, the contours are too sharp, too angular. His girlfriend, Dee (Diane), thinks he's real beautiful and a real "hunk," especially his blue eyes framed in part by the long light brown lashes.

The secretary glanced at John and caught his too obvious stare with the transparently associated thought. She blushed. He didn't. John's thoughts shifted to the events of the past hours. Sortino. Prick. "Let's go to my office," he had yelled. Yeah, John had figured him right. Sortino had put that office there just so he could nail kids for screwing up. Bastard. He was a stupid asshole to sell the stuff there, in the john right next to his office. Why had he done such an asshole thing? It definitely had not been the "cool" thing to do. Stupid. Shit! What bothered John most though, was not being caught, better if he hadn't been though. No, what bothered him most was his reaction to being caught, and the first few minutes afterwards. He had been really scared! That had surprised him as much as anything. He didn't think he'd be scared if he was ever caught. What would bother him even more was if Donnelly had seen his fear. Maybe, but probably not. Donelly was scared shitless himself. Ah, screw it. Screw them all. So what? What did it matter?

Sortino. King of the assholes. Know-it-all. John gingerly fingered what he knew were bruises on the back of his neck. Prick. He'd really hurt him. What right did the bastard have to hassle him like that? Who the fuck did Sortino think he was? Just a jock, a big jock with a big gut that stuck out, like a fag who was six months pregnant. Fag. Assistant principal. Ha! More like retreaded jock with an "in" with the downtown "pols." Everybody knew that. Even his father.

His father, ha! Now there was, what? Nothing. A big, nothing. Once he had heard his father say to his mother, "Ya' know, Kathy, I don't understand John." Christ, how could he? He never talked to him. John couldn't remember a conversation with his father. His didn't talk much. He didn't even yell much. Chris' old man, now there was a guy who yelled. His father didn't yell. Quiet man. Real quiet. He didn't even walk loud. He was like a ghost. Haunted the house. Lately his father gave him the creeps. He made John real uncomfortable. He just sort of looked at him. Looked at him. Stared at him. Then he would shake his head and walk away. Real quiet. He heard people say that he, John, was strange. Ha! They oughta see his father. Now, that was strange!

Sortino. He wasn't strange. What was the word? Predictable,

yeah, that bastard was predictable. Ya' always knew where you stood with him. Loud, know-it-all and a prick. Once, once he had seen the old' bastard at the bus station. One of his kids was coming home from school at Christmas. Sortino had yelled, "For Christ's sake, Nick, Nick," and then the old fag grabbed and kissed him! John had stood open-mouthed and watched. He'd never seen a man kiss a kid—*kid*! The guy must've been 20. He couldn't forget that.

His father never kissed anybody. Not him, not his mother, his sister Alice nor his brothers. Not his way. No. John sighed. What was his father's way? Didn't have any. John sighed again. Maybe that's why his mother had gone nuts. Flipped out. Bananas. He hadn't see the fight. John had got home right after. The car was gone and so was ma. When was it, last month? Yeah, at the beginning of last month. For once his father looked upset. He had looked at John and said only, "Your mother's left." That's all he said. John asked, "Where'd she go?" "I dunno," had been the response. Later the hospital had called. His father had said, "Oh?" That's all and then, "yes." "Yes." Never said much. You could never tell anything from a phone conversation if you were on his father's end! After he had hung up he said, "Your mother's at the State Hospital." Alice had cried. He remembered that his father looked sort of different. At the time he couldn't figure out why. Now he realized it was because he had been really upset. He looked different 'cause he generally didn't show his upsetness. He had then. Yeah. Alice had cried. His father had said, "It's O.K., Alice, it'll be O.K. You'll see. Mother will be back." The words were O.K. It was how he'd said them. It was, what do you call it? The tone. The tone had been finky, phoney, not real. Poor bastard tried. Even when he tried hard and it was serious, he couldn't pull it off. It was the only time he had ever heard his father try to comfort, and it came off almost funny. If the whole fuckin' scene hadn't been so awful, it would have been funny! John remembered thinking, poor ma, poor fucked-up ma!

Ma. Poor ma, poor screwed-up ma! How'd she ever, why did she ever marry him? Ma had her own troubles. She was as noisy,

as loud, as dad was quiet. If dad never talked, ma never shut up!
In the morning lying in bed, you couldn't even hear dad walking
downstairs.   Ma alone sounded like a herd of elephants.   John
remembered as a little kid at supper spilling his milk. Dad never
commented, maybe he didn't even notice. Ma ranted and went
bananas.   Supper was O.K. if ma was feeling O.K. If ma was
rippin' it was disaster time. Christ! He thought, ain't life a bitch!
As a kid my life was happy if my mother wasn't rip-shit! And
most of the time she was rip-shit.   My father wasn't alive to
notice! He sighed again.

John remembered things.   He remembered being little, four,
maybe five, and being scared of a dog two houses down, a Dober-
man Pinscher. Fuckin' dog! Once the dog had nipped him in the
heel and he'd run home, into the backyard screaming. His mother
was hanging clothes.   He remembered vividly.   She had a sheet
in her hands, one corner of it was in her mouth.   John had gone
slobbering up to her, scared as hell.   He had wanted to run into
her arms. He had wanted her to hold him. She didn't hold him.
Instead she had said, "Heaven sakes John, watch you don't dirty
the sheet!" Why didn't she drop the goddamned sheet! She hung
it up nice and careful, then responded irritably about being a
baby.   Yeah, he had been a baby, a four or five-year-old baby.
That's what he was. *SHE* hadn't been a mother.

Sometimes, however, she did hold him, even kissed him. She
did that often with Alice. He was pretty old when Alice was born.
He remembered wishing he were Alice, always held. That's what
he remembered about her, always held. And he wasn't. Ain't
life a bitch! Poor ma! Hey! Poor me! He didn't know why,
but she had always seemed so unhappy. Except maybe since the
hospital scene.   She'd been pretty good since then.   Ah, what
did it matter! How did the song go? "A teenage waste-land. I'm
livin' in a teen-age wasteland with poise and pot and piss 'em all!"
(John wasn't sure about the accuracy of the lyrics but it fit his
mood.)

The bell rang to signal the beginning of the last period of the
day.   It served to rouse John from his reverie.   Laconically he
began thinking about his current problems. The narcs. Ha!

Another joke. They could care less. John knew that. He didn't know the little guy. The big one had been his coach in Little League. The bastard hadn't remembered him at all, not even his name. That fit. His very first comments and questions had told John everything he wanted to know. "Now son, why would you want to do something like this? Don't you know how dangerous this stuff can be? What it can do to you?" Christ! Long ago John had learned that the best defense at disaster time was to put on one of two expressions, a blank one (tune out the world at the same time) or a puzzled one, if things got too rough. The blank expression had been sufficient today. Narcs, what a crock!

Again he sighed and looked at the clock.

What the hell is happening in there? And his next thought was, What can happen in there? What can they do to me? Nothing. Dalton didn't want trouble. And weed was real trouble. John had long suspected that school was the best place to sell. The best place 'cause it was the safest. School was the safest place because school is loaded with finks. Phonies. Bullshitters. Daltons. They don't care what's going on as long as they don't know what's going on. In fact, a kid was safe doing anything as long as the finks could pretend that you didn't know that they knew. School was finkdom. House of finks. One exception. That fuckin' Sortino. Bastard. The last, honest prick. An honest prick can fuck up the world.

The principal's door opened. Sortino stood in the doorway. He looked at John and murmured, "come in." John walked in. A cold, maybe embarrassed silence greeted him. Sortino nodded him to the only empty chair. John sat down. The atmosphere was confusing, even intimidating, so he put on his puzzled look.

Dalton cleared his throat. "Young man, you are indeed fortunate. If you cooperate with Mr. Ballard's splendid suggestion, which he will explain to you in a moment, you will be on principal's probation for two weeks, that's all. This, of course, means [John knew what it meant] that you will check in every morning and afternoon with my secretary, Miss Feltus. Principal's probation for two weeks to atone for this day's behavior. We seek here to temper justice with mercy."

John was sure now he had the right expression. He didn't feel scared or anything. He was genuinely puzzled. His expression fit.

Ballard spoke, "John, I'm going to try to set up a series of family therapy sessions for you and your family."

Silence.

"What that means is that you and your family will come once a week, maybe twice, for about an hour and talk about how you all feel about things."

Silence.

"How do you feel about that?"

John shrugged.

Dalton was exasperated. He'd been here for over two hours now and he had to go to the toilet.

Ballard continued, "John, your parents, anyway, feel that there are significant problems at home. They've agreed to attend. What we want now, especially Mr. Dalton, is an agreement from you that will cooperate with whatever I set up. What do you say?"

John was truly puzzled. What was the big deal? Why was it so important that he O.K. anything? Family therapy? Why not?

"Sure, why not?" he responded with just a hint of boredom.

"John," Mrs. Whiting spoke laconically but firmly, "for once, try to agree to something like you mean it."

"Yeah, I'll go," he said, tonelessly.

Ballard had hardly expected an enthusiastic response. "Fine. I'll set it up."

LATER

Frank and Ballard talked on the way to their cars.

Frank sighed, "There are days I don't enjoy my job. Today was one of them."

"Yeah," Ballard responded, "I'll bet."

"Do you think that this family therapy business will help the Whitings?"

"I don't know, Frank. A lot of the answer depends on them, on how much they want to be helped, on how much they want to change."

Frank was thoughtful. "Al, do you think people change?"

"If they're unhappy enough they do, sometimes."

"Seems like the Whitings are pretty unhappy."

"Yeah."

They reached their cars and nodded to each other goodbye.

Kathleen and Francis left the High School together. They lived only fifteen minutes from the school and had decided to walk. For several minutes they strode at a moderate pace without talking. So what else is new? Kathleen thought dejectedly. Since her return from the hospital they talked more infrequently than ever. Prior to her hospital admission she had raged and nagged a lot. She knew that and hated herself for it. So far she had been able to adhere to the secret vow she had made to herself on the last day at the hospital while walking on the lovely grounds. She promised herself that she would not scream, yell and rant anymore. To date she had done pretty well. She had slipped only once. With John. It had not been about anything important. He'd wanted some clean underwear first thing in the morning. Unfairly, she had shrilly complained about why couldn't he do his own laundry, blah, blah, blah. John had cried back, "For Christ's sake, ma. I'm sorry but I need underwear. Excuse me for livin'." It had been a good response, a perfect squelcher. She'd shut up on that one. A pair of clean shorts was not an awful lot to ask your mother for, especially if you have none! Anyway, her bitching, nagging and complaining was very much under control. She glanced at Francis. His head was down. He turned his head toward her, then in his usual way averted his glance and looked ahead, simultaneously stepping up his pace.

Why? Why? Why was Francis so mute? Didn't he realize how much his awful silence interfered in their relationship? Relationship? Had they ever had any? Could they ever have one? Her sense of dejection remained. His virtual muteness during the better part of the conference had been, well, embarrassing. If only he could have been a little more, what? Involved.

After all, the whole thing had been about their son, his son, too. Mute! He'd been mute! What could they have thought? Oh, what did it matter what they thought. What they thought really wasn't important. What was important was what happened to John, to Francis, to her, to them all. For a moment back there she'd been hopeful. "John will come. We'll all come, I guarantee it." He had sounded so firm, so masterful, as if he were in control or ready to take over. She broke the silence. "I was impressed, back there. I was proud of you, Francis."

"Yeah," he replied tonelessly.

"You really sounded like, like . . ."

"I cared?"

She reddened. She shouldn't have embarrassed him like that, in front of all of them. "I'm sorry, Francis. I didn't mean to embarrass you."

"It's O.K."

It wasn't O.K. Francis was inhibited. Embarrassing him was not the way to cure him, was not the way to get him to come out of his shell in front of people, that's for sure!

"I shouldn't have said what I did." She stopped walking and took his wrist. "I'm sorry, Francis. I know it didn't make you feel manly." He stopped and looked at her, open-mouthed. As soon as she said it she knew it was wrong, as wrong as it could be. He looked away and they continued walking.

For a long time, weeks? months? For a long time anyway, Francis had not made advances in bed. At first it didn't bother her. Now it did. Why doesn't he touch me, she had worried. She thought it might be her fault. Throughout most of their marriage she had been reluctant. Sex invariably resulted in pregnancy or the fear of it, almost as bad. Then she had gone on the pill and his interest seemed to wane. They went long periods without doing it. At first she didn't notice. Sex had never been a big deal to her. Then they weren't doing it at all! It began to bother her. Was he having an affair? She dismissed that thought long ago. She just couldn't conceive of Francis having an affair, besides he was home all the time, for lunch, supper and TV every night. No, it wasn't another woman, she'd concluded. It was

Francis. He wasn't interested. Now ironically she found that her own interest in sex was enkindled, sometimes it became inflamed. A couple of times since she returned from the hospital *she* had made the advances, had tried to fondle him, had even . . . He had turned his back on her, even worse, had gone off to sleep, or pretended to. Now, walking, she realized that it was the next morning that she had yelled at John. She was frustrated. Yes, she was sexually frustrated. I never thought *that* would be a problem too, she thought. Probably that's why she'd begun doing what she'd never done since adolescence, she was looking at men, with unveiled interest. Frank Sortino. She glanced at her husband. Had Francis noticed her interest? Probably. It was pretty obvious. What had she said, "A man who cares is rare today. I can admire such a man." I guess she had believed that all her life. But she never would have said it before, before now. She reddened a little as she thought about the words. Dear God, they were so-o-o obvious! Her redness momentarily turned into a flush. What could have gotten into her. It wasn't like her to brazenly . . . what? Proposition? No, not that, but, exhibit a heck of a lot of interest in a strange man. That much was true, why?

They were almost home now. Francis seemed tired. His pace had slowed and his head was still down. Sortino wasn't that handsome. But virile, yes. Yes, he was virile looking. That was it. He seemed so aggressive, so-o-o masculine, so much in control. Nobody pushed him around and he cared.

Kathleen was so engrossed she never heard the question. "What are we having for supper?" Francis repeated.

"What? Oh. Oh, I forgot. No, it is, it's ready. It'll be ready in about a half hour. Macaroni and cheese."

Francis nodded. He had left the school acutely embarrassed. Kathleen's comment about not being manly had only served to accentuate the embarrassment, the hurt. What made everything even worse was the fact that she didn't even seem to know how he felt. She seemed so insensitive to his feelings. He was embarrassed that he'd sat there like a dummy, with Kath as his ventriloquist. Christ! What's the matter with me?

And that crack a few minutes ago about not feeling "manly." Kathleen knew how to put the screws in. She'd probably say that she hadn't meant it, maybe she didn't, maybe she didn't, but like they say, "If you get hit in the balls on purpose or you get hit by accident—hurts just as much!" And right now he hurt. What in the heck is the matter with me? he wondered.

"Manly." No. I'm not manly. He glanced at his wife. She is pretty. He could tell the way Sortino looked at her that he thought she was real pretty. And Francis was very proud of his wife's looks. And built! Still well built.

This last thought evoked a muffled cry. Kathleen glanced at him inquisitively. He never noticed.

'Shit,' he was thinking. 'Shit! Shit! Shit!' He wanted her. Yes. Did he ever! He wanted her but when he got into bed with her, he felt like a eunuch must feel, unable, unwilling and not a little scared. What the hell is the matter with me? He'd gone to a doctor about it. Pills. He knew when he got them, hormone pills, they weren't going to do much. It wasn't his cock, it wasn't his balls. It was his head. It was him. He just couldn't hack it. He just couldn't get a hard-on. It couldn't seem to happen. Why? Why? Why?

That scene back there. It had shaken him, a lot. Especially that crap about "I can admire such a man, a man who cares." Was it crap? Did she mean it? What did she mean? Was it an open invitation, a proposition? If she ever did . . . what would he do? Kill her?

The thought was too fantastic even to kick around in his mind. They rounded the corner of their street.

What was apparent to him was that Sortino was an emotional guy. A strong, aggressive pol type, but a strong guy too. Very emotional. Kathleen was attracted to that. She was emotional too. He wasn't. He didn't show it. But there was something else that bothered, bewildered him, and a lot too. All his life he'd always felt put down by the "emotional types." They'd always seemed to be tuned into things, feelings, that he didn't even seem to know about. So? So what if this Sortino guy and Kathleen were tuned in to each other? Several times he'd got the feeling that things were happening, going on, that he felt out of. "I can admire such a man, a man who cares."

Only once had he felt "manly." Ha! Only once, when he'd made the crack about "John and the family being there!" Wherever the "there" was. "A man who cares, I can admire such a man." Sortino cares. That's what she had said, Sortino, and then he remembered! Remembered the worst of all. That was the part which had made him feel most humiliated. How'd it go? "I care Kath," and she had replied, "Oh Francis, what good is it if no one knows," No one being her. Sortino cares. "I can admire such a man."

And now he startled his wife. "Well goddamnit," Francis exclaimed fiercely and too loudly, "goddamnit, I care too!"

John arrived home before his parents. He had to go to the toilet, badly, but instead he went to the phone and dialed the very familiar number. One ring, two and . . .

"Dee there?"

"John?"

"Yeah." Fuckin' mother (his usual thought).

"Dee there?" he repeated.

"No."

Per usual the tone was glacial. Mrs. Henessey seemed happiest when she could say "no" to anything.

John's school days were usually bad. Today, however, had been worse than the usual bad. Maybe it was the iciness of her tone, maybe it was the simple fact that he had to pee real bad, whatever. His temper, never long fused, lit up.

"Mrs. Henessey?"

"Yes?"

The fuse hissed loudly.

"Do me a favor?"

"A favor?"

And his temper exploded.

"Yeah. Go take a flying shit for yourself."

He slammed the receiver back on to its cradle. Bitch! Bitch! Bitch! I need you, he thought savagely. Then he took the five or six steps to the toilet and relieved himself. For a long time now

John's mood had been dark. Right now it was black. Christ, what a bitch it all is. School, parents, life. Dee, he had so wanted to talk to her. Nothin' special. Just talk. She was the only one who listened. Listened good. Well, not all the time. But at least he could *talk* to her. Who else listened? Who else cared? And now that shitty mother of hers had cut him off from her. That bitch wouldn't tell Dee he had called. Even if she did, she'd never let Dee call him back. She didn't think it was right for a girl to phone a boy. It wasn't proper! What shit! And right now all he wanted to do was talk to her. He couldn't *talk* to anybody in this house.

His parents slammed in. That was unusual. They usually came in quietly.

"What did you say? Why did you yell that, Francis?" his mother asked.

"Nothin'. Never mind. It was nothing."

That's about right. Nothing. His father's favorite word, nothin'. Nothin' out of nothin'. Christ, we oughta' put that on his tombstone. Here lies "nothin', who heard nothin', saw nothin', did nothin'! Mr. Nothin'."

He went upstairs. Ma went downstaris. That too was about right. Everybody in this family went in different directions. A door slammed upstairs and a door slammed downstairs. About right. Everybody was in their own little cell, eating away at himself. Christ, what a family! What a house! Ain't life a bitch?

The phone rang. "Johnny?"

"Yeah."

"It's me."

"Hi, you." The extension clicked shut.

"What'd you say to my mother?"

"Nothin'."

"Johnny, don't tell me that. She's really rippin'. She's really mad, I mean, mad."

"I didn't say nothin'."

"I swear, Johnny Whiting, you use the word 'nothin' more than any twenty people I know. Everything is 'nothin', nothin', nothin'." Now, what did you say?"

"Dee, stop yellin', Christ, will you stop yellin'."

Quiet.

"O.K., I'm not yellin'. Now what did you say?"

"I told her to go take a flying shit for herself."

"What? You didn't!"

"Yeah, I did."

"No wonder she's goin' ape."

"Yeah," and he chuckled.

"You told Beverly Henessey to go take a flying shit for herself?"

Dee didn't chuckle back. She gulped, loudly, then she burst out laughing, then she just plain howled. John thought she was going to pee her pants.

He started laughing back. Who else made him laugh? No one. He loved Dee. She understood him. She knew how to laugh at this bitch of a life. He loved her. That was important 'cause in this miserable world there was so fuckin' little that you could love. He loved her, this classy little chick, this classy little chick with a face of a doll and a bod! And what a bod!

"See ya' tonight?" he asked matter-of-factly.

"Can't."

"Can't? Why not?"

"My mother's real pissed after what you said to her. I'm grounded. Her last words were, 'And you are not going out with that vulgar, crude animal tonight. Call him. Tell him. Those are my last words on the subject.' She meant it, Johnny. Honest."

Pause.

"Tonight's Friday night."

"I know."

"We always go out Friday nights."

"I know."

"Oh shit," he cried and slammed down the receiver for the second time within a half hour. Shit! Shit! Shit!

His mother's purse was on the chair next to the phone. He heard her in the kitchen. He'd hear him if he came down the stairs. He opened the purse noiselessly and adeptly slithered out a five dollar bill from the very modest wad.

Six hours later John was sitting on the curb in front of the

South End Dairy Bar, a popular hang-out for a large part of the high school population. The five dollars he had stolen from his mother had bought a bottle of Tokay wine, a pizza with mushrooms, peppers and Genoa salami and lastly, a Banana Boat Special. He had just vomited the Banana Boat Special and some of the pizza and he was still drunk.

"Hey, man!"

John looked up blearily and vaguely made out Danny Clark, a real pain in the ass.

"Hey, wow, man. You are really cocked off your ass, but I mean fuckin' drunk."

"Fuck-off, Clark."

"Ah, relax man. I'm not gonna bug."

John didn't answer. He felt too awful. Besides, Clark was a fag who tried to live in the world of the cool kids and graduate number one in a class of 579. A real ball-buster was Danny Clark.

John heaved again into the gutter. A lot of Genoa salami. Meanwhile Clark kept chattering away in an even more nauseating fashion.

"Man, are you sick. Christ, how much pizza did you eat. With salami yet. Christ man, you must be crazy."

He just kept hangin' on, like a blue-ass fly on a bad piece of meat. I need this bastard.

John gasped. "Will you please fuck-off now!"

"Oh, screw you, you sick bastard and I don't mean sick in the gut. This a public . . . "

Danny Clark never finished that sentence. Maybe it was the day he had had. Maybe it was the fact he'd not been able to see Dee. Maybe it was the wine or the Genoa salami. Or maybe it was the fact that Danny was a pain in the ass. No matter. John let out a horrendous shriek and simultaneously shot up off the curb. In what seemed one movement he kneed the unfortunate Clark in the groin, pummeled him to the ground and proceeded to choke him to death.

A large group of kids, mostly girls, began shrieking. And the police, ever ready to descend upon the South End Dairy Bar, arrived with the flashing light and its arresting siren.

Chris Donnelly cried, "Christ, John, stop. Don't ya' hear the piggies oinkin'?"

John, too mad, too uncaring, held Clark by the throat and was banging his head into the grassless lawn, between the sidewalk and the street.

The cruiser arrived manned by Joe Mazzola and Tony Acito. Mazzola was driving. Officer Acito is 5' 11" tall but he weighs 239 pounds. He's not all muscle, but Middletown's police regard him as their strongest cop. Besides this he has a temper controlled by no more than a hair-trigger. Nobody had phoned in this fight. Mazzola had been standing on the Park Knoll looking down on Maple Avenue. He had see the fight. And had yelled, "Let's go! Let's go!" Acito had only finished half of his pepper and tomato sandwich that his wife had packed. It was the only diet food he liked. He'd had to drop it. No food till tomorrow. Son-of-a-bitch! These son-of-a-bitching kids were a first-class pain in the "Eyetalian Culo", ass for short! And right now so was Mazzola. Acito, too big, but agile as a rabbit (especially when angry), leaped out of the cruiser before it had stopped. He picked up John, whose hands were steeled around Danny's neck, and thereby also lifted poor Danny off the ground. Danny's eyes literally bulged like those of the proverbial mackerel.

And it was in that lightning moment of Acito's onslaught combined with his own continuing nausea and spent force that John released Danny. The latter was whiter than a saucer of cream and the mewls that issued from his constricted throat were not unlike those of a terrified kitty. Acito pitched John into the back seat and tossed the mewling Danny next to him. He slammed shut the rear door, piled into the front seat and Mazzola, who loved the drama of it all, roared off to the station house.

They had driven less than two blocks when John knew he was going to have to vomit again.

"Better stop," he groaned.

"Why?" asked Acito

"Gonna throw."

"Christ, not here," screamed Mazzola. Mazzola had a very weak stomach.

"Stop," John croaked.

Mazzola made the most abrupt stop of his life, hurling both boys forward and John threw up onto Danny, the back floor and onto the back of Mazzola's seat.

Acito screamed, "Jesus Christ, kid!"

Mazzola gurgled an "Oh shit! No!"

Danny just mewled.

And John threw up the rest of the pizza and a little Tokay wine.

Mazzola emerged from the cruiser white-faced. He could smell the vomit crap on the back of his freshly laundered blue shirt. Fuckin' kid, he thought.

Acito yelled, "For Christ's sake get in here. Let's get to the station. Christ, I don't believe this!"

Mazzola held on to his stomach, with both hands.

"Tony, I can't stand this."

"For Christ's sake, Mazzola, get in here. Let's get this goddamned car to the station."

Mazzola, still holding his stomach, glanced into the back. Both boys were as white and still as two corpses. They lay sprawled out on the back seat. Gingerly he slid into the front seat, his chest hugging the wheel and thereby avoiding the vomitus still oozing down the back seat from the tiny pool collected still on his head rest.

"Christ, I don't believe this," repeated Acito.

John finally woke up at the police station, after repeated brisk prodding. He was no longer nauseated, but he was very, very tired and more than a little drunk still.

He heard one of the cops, Tony Acito, talking to the desk man.

"Picked them up in front of the South End Dairy Bar fighting. That one (he indicated John) was beating the crap out of that one. What do you wanna' do, Bill?"

John could see that Bill was annoyed. He was working on some paper. John, despite his fatigue and his inebriation, felt that they were all bothering this red-faced, bald-headed man.

"This one threw up in the cruiser. Smells."

The cop named Bill threw down his pencil.

"O.K. Have Mack clean up the cruiser."

"And Mazzola got some on the back of his shirt and he's gotta' go home to change. He doesn't have anymore in his locker."

"Is that all?"

"Guess so."

"O.K.," he said impatiently. "Again, have Mack clean up the cruiser. Take the old one for the rest of the night. Have Mazzola change at home and get back to your shift. Oh, before you leave put this one (Danny) in the back waiting room. I don't want them together. I don't want trouble here."

Acito nodded. "Anything else?"

"Nah. I'll take it from here, Chief wants to keep these things simple."

Acito led Danny to the back waiting room and left.

Sergeant Bill Perkins finished the report he was writing, ironically a six-month efficiency report on Officer Acito. He looked at the tall skinny kid who wavered while standing in front of him. Really crocked. Goddamned kids. More trouble from the kids today than anybody else. Not unkindly he asked, "What's your name, kid?"

"Whiting. John Whiting."

"Where d'you live?"

"Beaumont Street."

"What number?"

"59."

"Phone number?"

"924 – 5603."

The Sergeant dialed the number. He looked at the clock, almost 1 a.m. Mama and papa were gonna' be mad.

The phone hadn't finished its first ring when Kathleen heard it. Francis snored peacefully, per usual. Its continued shrill resonance pierced the quiet blackness of the wee morning hour. Kathleen rose and took the seven or eight steps over to the hallway phone table, awkwardly and confusedly.

"Lo," she said thickly.

The response was almost too cheerful, too distinct. "Mrs. Whiting."

"Ye-e-ss."

"This is Sergeant Perkins down at the police station."

Her heart felt as if it had stopped. It was John. Dear God, was he home? Where was he?

"Your son John is here, Mrs. Whiting, and we'd like you or Mr. Whiting to come down and pick him up."

"What's he done?" Kathleen asked fearfully.

"Ah, as I understand it, he got into a fight with another kid down at the South End Dairy Bar."

"A fight. A fight?"

"And he's really under the weather right now."

"Drunk?"

"Yeah."

"I'll be there in a minute, Sergeant." She dressed hurriedly, glancing at Francis as she did so. He never stirred, never even restled under the covers. She was too anxious to be resentful or maybe too sleepy. She hustled down the hall, down the steps grabbing at her purse with the car keys inside as she swept by the downstairs hall table.

Her heart was thumping as she pulled open the new all-glass door of the police station. She was met at the long reception desk by a fellow who was too young to be wearing the policeman blues.

"I'm Kathleen Whiting. Sergeant Perkins just called me. Could . . ."

"In there, Mrs. Whiting," he said, jerking his blond head to the right.

Kathleen walked hesitantly to the open door he indicated. Her son was half-sitting, half-lying in an ungraceful position on a modern blond bench. His head was back, resting on the wall, his eyes were closed and he was snoring, just like the husband she's left moments ago.

Never taking her eyes off him, she approached the baldheaded desk sergeant.

"That's my son," she whispered as if she were concerned about not waking him.

Perkins answered in a normal tone. "O.K., Mrs. Whiting, you can take him home."

"Do I have to sign anything or do anything?" she asked helplessly.

"No. Just take him home." Why was it always the mothers who came for the kids? he wondered.

Kathleen turned toward John. God, he was a mess. There was a bruise on his cheek. His trousers were soiled at the knees and he smelled of vomit. She wanted to cry for him, for her, for the whole mess. At the hospital she remembered telling the doctor that John hadn't gotten into any scrapes, yet. Well "yet" had arrived twice in a day-and-a-half. Lord!

"John, John," she called softly.

He didn't respond so she shook him hard. Yes, she was sad but she was getting mad too.

"Ma?" he asked dazedly.

"Come on, John," she said drily, "let's go, let's go home."

The sergeant, bent over his papers, never noticed their leaving.

Before she pulled into the driveway, Kathleen noticed that the porch light was lit. She was puzzled but only for a moment for, as she and John walked up the porch steps, she could see her husband framed in the doorway behind the screen door.

Francis had heard the phone ring. Instantly he had known it was about John, either the hospital or the police. Kathleen's response of "A fight. A fight?" and the word "Sergeant" had confirmed that it was the police on the other end.

She was gone no more than ten minutes. And during those ten minutes Francis had been pacing the living room floor waiting. Waiting, thinking and worrying. Damned kid! He flicked on the porch light and returned to his pacing.

Francis had never been close to his own father. They had almost never talked. In fact, it had happened so seldom that one conversation they did have stood out, vividly. His father's words, delivered with awful sureness, and not a little pomposity, came boomeranging back after more than three decades, "You will have the respect of the community. In the end, Francis, respect is what our lives are all about." Right now, he thought wryly, I got about as much respect in this community as a queer who got picked up by the police for propositioning a guy on Main Street! Francis remembered his father's words. Christ, he still remembered them. But he had not believed them much. And Francis had not believed them because he believed then and still did (Did he? Now?) that self-respect, what a man thinks about himself, what he makes of himself, for himself, that's what matters. His father, however, had believed absolutely in his own words. No doubt about that. His father had been so sure of himself. Christ!

Then came an awful thought. If he had believed and lived like his father, would John be in trouble today? But no! No! Father had lived for the respect of other people. Francis lived for his own self-respect. John, goddamnit, didn't live for nothing. He believed in nothing! The kid was nothing!

Anger, not a familiar emotion to Francis, began to well up. The conference with Dalton, his embarrassment because he didn't take part in it like he should have, damn, he was so quiet, for so long in that office, Kathleen's crack about manliness, his continued impotence (tonight he'd been scared she was going to make advances), and now this, this! The police and all because of that goddamned kid! Everybody in town would know, would know his kid was picked up. His mind went blank for a moment. So Francis Whiting Jr., you do care what others think!

Nah, but maybe, just maybe if I'd worried a little bit about other people's respect and a little bit less about my own . . . maybe it's not John. Just maybe it's me and how . . . Oh, shit John, you little bastard, he thought. Yes he was angry. Yes, he knew that now 'cause he . . .

The car pulled into the driveway and he opened the front door and waited behind the screen.

They entered, she first.

"Where ya' been," he asked in his usually controlled voice.

John sidled past both and headed for the stairway.

Francis barked, "Stop." Then he repeated, "Where have you been?" The words, which framed the question, came in one second intervals, and with all the authority and intimidation of a paternal despot.

Kathleen, a little scared herself, and not a little confused by the metamorphosis in her usually passive husband, stammered,

"We, we just came, came back."

"Back, back, from where? Will one of you answer, damn it."

What had gotten into him? He never swore. He was swearing all the time lately.

"From the police station."

"Police station, to pick up *that*?" He pointed threateningly to John.

"To pick up John."

It was then that he examined John. And the looks which swept across his face were such as Kathleen had never seen, not in the generation that she had known him. She was sickened, sickened because it was like a horror scene, resurrected from her childhood and adolescence. It was as if her father had been resurrected, and reincarnated into her husband, her quiet, quiet husband.

Francis gazed fixedly at his son. John was never comfortable when his father did that. And right now it was obvious to the three of them that John felt as bilious as he looked. Francis reared back, but just a little. He said finally, "You make my stomach turn." And without raising his voice he added, "You are no goddamn good boy."

John jerked back as if struck by the force of the words, the harshest and most demeaning that he'd ever heard his father utter, to anyone. He turned and staggered up to his room. After a moment his parents followed, wordlessly. Like a needle stuck in a scratched record, the same depressing thought kept spinning around in Kathleen's bewildered, tired mind. We're in trouble. We're in trouble. We're in trouble.

They entered the bedroom, he first. He slipped off his pants. Francis still had his pajamas on, both parts, and he slid into bed. Kathleen undressed hurriedly. He averted his eyes, per usual. However, out of the corner of his left eye he noticed that she slid off her panties. She did this as her nightie slipped down over her still lithe, young body. Christ, no, he thought miserably.

She eased gracefully under the covers. "Hold me, darling." It was more a plea, a painful-like request, than any command. He stretched a limp arm around her and she snuggled, too eagerly, up to him.

"Francis, I'm scared. What's happening? You lost your temper just now. You're acting awfully different."

He didn't answer. What to say? He never knew what to say.

She kissed him, lightly on the cheek and began to caress him. Nothing. He felt nothing.

After a few moments he said woodenly, "Kath, it's two o'clock and I gotta go to work in five hours. C'mon, I'm tired."

Without a word she released him. He turned on his side and silently expelled a breath.

"G'night," he mumbled, but he didn't sleep for a long time. Kathleen didn't either.

Discussion Questions

1. Is the school setting a place where John can grow emotionally? Why or why not?
2. Does John respect Sortino? Why or why not?
3. How does Sortino perceive John?
4. Why does John compare Sortino to his father?
5. Is Mr. Dalton a real person?
6. What kind of person is Mr. Dalton? How does he play his role of principal?
7. What does Mr. Dalton care about most?
8. Does he create a climate which is conducive to student health or sickness?
9. Are there may Dalton types in our schools?
10. What does Kathleen's reaction to Sortino mean?
11. Why can't Kathleen and Francis talk to each other?
12. Why is John so involved with Dee? Why does she provide so much meaning for his life?
13. Are Mazzola and Acito real?

FOCUS GUIDES

1. Consider Kathleen's image of herself, what she wants, what she needs out of life.
2. Reflect upon how she views her husband and how he views her.
3. Think about how Francis views himself.
4. Hypothesize why their marriage has soured so.
5. How much insight do they have into themselves and their marriage?

Chapter 2

TWO MONTHS EARLIER.

"Francis, I just can't go on like this. I just can't. I simply can't cope with all these problems." Kathleen was cutting a turnip with an oversized carving knife.

"What problems?"

"With you. Four children. I'm pregnant again. We have no money. We have nothing. Nothing at all."

"Well, whose fault is it that you're pregnant?"

"Well, goddamn it, Francis, I didn't do it alone!"

"Stop swearing, woman. Stop swearing now! For the past two months all you've been doing is using . . ."

"Son-of-a-bitching bastard, I'll swear if I want. I'll swear if I want to. [She bursts into tears at this point.] For the past two months I've been swearing. Ha! I wish that were all. For the past two months I go around here crying, crying, crying and I don't even know why. I think I'm going crazy. God help me. I think I'm losing my mind."

"Well, if you did a little work around here instead of wallowing in self-pity, maybe if you acted like a mother and a wife, maybe . . ."

"You lousy, insensitive, unloving bastard. I am through, through, through. . . ." She was screeching now and in the middle of her screech she hurled the knife directly at her husband. Kathleen then crashed through the half-opened screen door, sobbing. She leaped into the Dodge and thundered off at a maniacal-like speed.

These events occured on a hot June day, in the late afternoon. Kathleen Conley Whiting was in her fortieth year of life and she was in the throes of a psychiatric breakdown. She volunteered the following account.

"I drove out of the driveway, took a right and drove directly to the State Hospital. I didn't know if I was going crazy or not. I did know that I wanted to, I had to get away, away from that house, away from Francis, away from the kids. I thought those awful, demanding, constantly demanding kids. I was suffocating. I was trapped. Trapped. Trapped, like my mother. I couldn't let it happen to me. No. No. No, not like my mother!

"I don't remember the drive to the hospital. All I remember was taking a left on Elm Street, a man almost crashed into me and screamed, 'For Christ's sakes, lady, are you crazy, or something!' I laughed. Yes, I probably was crazy!

"I drove up to the main building. It had a sign Admissions. So I admitted myself. I remember there was a man about my age behind the desk, behind a sign that said Receptionist. I know I looked a sight. I was wearing a housedress that was split at the seams, in two places.

"He looked at me and yawned. He yawned! Then asked in a bored tone, 'yeah?'

"I'm here. I'm Kathy Whiting. I want to come into the hospital!

"He sat up and said, 'why?'

"I want to see a doctor. I guess I think I'm going crazy. I just threw a knife at my husband.

"Lady, my wife throws more . . .'

"At that point I screamed, goddamnit, I want to be admitted to the hospital!

"That did it. He shot up out of the chair and I remember thinking, Ole pa wasn't so crazy. Yelling gets results.

"O.K., lady, O.K. Calm down. I'll get the doctor right now. Just come with me. Relax, relax.'

"He led me down a corridor to a waiting room. I sat down and waited. It was a freshly painted room. It smelled it and there was a used paint can with a brush in the corner. I waited about five minutes or so and the door opened. A doctor, Filipino, Chinese or whatever came in. He spoke, but I could barely understand him. And that's when I started trembling and I couldn't stop it. I started thinking, Oh my God, Oh my God. I can't even be taken care of when I'm sick. I'm going crazy and they send me a doctor who can't speak English! That's the last thing I remember that night.

"I woke up the next day in a ward that was a throwback to the Middle Ages. It was a real snake pit. I don't know how long I was there. Three days, five days, maybe a week. I just don't know. All I can remember from that week is a very fat lady who kept urinating on the seat of a black leather chair that was ripped and she'd try to drink up her urine, try to drink it up with her cupped hands. The first time I saw her I almost vomited. The only reason I didn't was that I had nothing in my stomach. I was transferred from that ward to a so-called open ward and that was very comfortable. I came and went as I pleased there. My first day I met a Dr. Boudreau. He talked to me for a while and then he gave me a whole lot of tests."

TRANSCRIPT OF THE CLINICAL INTERVIEW

(Kathleen Whiting)

(Edited and Condensed)

B: Please come in, Mrs. Whiting. I'm Dr. Boudreau.

K: Hello.

B: I'd like to talk with you about why you're here. Let's see, you admitted yourself on, uh . . .

K: Last week, about ten days ago.

B: Yes. Yes. What happened?

K: I was having a fight with my husband. I threw a knife at him, a carving knife.

B: I see.

K: I think I might be going crazy.

B: Why do you think that?

K: I don't know. I'm crying all the time and I don't know why, I'm tired all the time. I get mad for no reason and I'm screaming at the kids, mostly for no reason at all. I've got so I hate myself, I hate my house, my husband, my kids, and I don't even know why. What's happened to me?

B: You're obviously depressed.

K: Yeah.

B: You don't see any reason for anything.

K: Right.

B: You're pregnant.

K: Yes and Doctor, God forgive me, but I don't want it. I didn't want it. I never wanted to be a mother. I never wanted to be married. Women get the short end in marriage. They always have and they always will, I guess.
[Pause]
I have nothing. I can't seem to do anything at home.

B: You told me that you cry a lot at home.

K: Yes, I do. I walk from room to room crying. The kids are all in school now. I don't have them to take my mind off my problems. And when they were small I could seem to do more too. Maybe it's because I was younger, more hopeful. Maybe I just had more energy. Now I walk from room to room. Sometimes I talk to myself. Kathy, snap out of it. Get a hold of yourself, I say. And I jump up with a burst of energy and start a project like cleaning the stove or re-frigerator. I get everything out. Look at the mess and start crying again. And Francis comes home, finds an even bigger mess and we fight. I'm a disappointment to him, I know.

B: Your husband is displeased with you because you're not an efficient housewife.

K: Yeah.

B: How do you feel about that?

K: Right now I could care less.
[Pause]
Isn't that awful? A wife who could care less about what her husband thinks.

B: I'm sure you have your reasons for feeling like that.
[Pause]

K: I just remembered something that happened, something that I said, that last time at home when I was fighting with Francis.

B: Yes?

K: I called him an insensitive, unloving bastard.

B: So?

K: That's what he is. That's what my father was too.

B: A few moments ago you said that, uh, women always get the short end in marriage.

K: Yes, they do. They do. Look at my mother. Look at me.

All her life my mother felt trapped.   I feel trapped too.

B: You feel trapped.

K: Yes.

B: You hate your life.

K: I do, yes, I do.

[Pause]

And mostly I do because it's very much a man's world. They come and go as they please. They come home, eat, drink, use you, leave and you're left with all the drudgery. My life is a drudgery! I have no money, no job, no dignity as a human being. I have nothing but problems.

B: You yourself never did anything in your own right.

K: Right.

B: Everything around you seems to be collapsing.

K: It collapsed, a long time ago. Our kids had people for parents who probably never should have been parents. Our kids are like me and Francis, they're not too much. They don't get along 'cause we couldn't get along. They're in trouble.

B: They're in trouble?

K: My kids are always in trouble.

B: You have four children and . . .

K: One on the way. Just what I needed. Anyway, my oldest, Thomas, quit school at sixteen, got a girl pregnant when he was seventeen, married her and was divorced six months ago. He isn't twenty years old and he's been married and divorced. Quite a record, eh? My next boy, Francis, Francis the third, we called him. I guess there was a time when my husband and I thought fancy, and were even optimistic. Heh, those days are over, that's for sure. Anyway, Francis, my son, has had four major auto accidents since he started driving. Last year he ended up in the hospital for over three months. We're still paying for that. Thirty-five dollars a month we have to pay for God knows how long. He quit school too, just like his brother. Neither has a trade, nor even a way to make a living. One's a dishwasher, the other's a night janitor. They've left home, the two of them. The best I can say for them is that they're close. They are that. They're living together in a rundown apartment. They take care of each other.

B: So you're proud of them in that.

K: I suppose, but it's the only good thing I can say about them. As men they're failures.

B: Why do you say that?

K: Thomas ended up divorced for God knows what reasons, but one of them and a big one was that he couldn't support his family. A month after he was married he lost his job. He had a fight with his boss. He's got a terrible temper, just like my father. But that's all he's got from my father. My father was a very good provider. We never wanted for anything. Thomas is more like his father than my father.

B: You mean that Mr. Whiting is not a . . .

K: No, he's not. He works every day but he doesn't always get paid. Some months we really have to scrimp and scrape. The only thing that man did was build our house. He's a carpenter but he didn't do that right either. He's never finished it. Can you imagine what it's like living in an un-finished house for twenty years? Rooms without doors, closets without doors. Thomas and Francis were brought up in a room with two unfinished walls. He didn't finish it because we didn't have enough money for the materials he wanted. Everything he does has to be done perfect. I just want it done. And when I yell he looks at me surprised, shrugs and walks away.

B: I see.

K: The boys became just like their father. Francis and the two other boys are like him. If I speak sharply they become moody and clam up. Once in a while they grunt, usually they just shrug their shoulders and walk away.

B: They're just uncommunicative.

K: To say the least. But they, especially Francis, I blame him, just won't help me, just won't do anything around the house to help me out, to make life more pleasant for me.

B: He's always been like this?

K: Always. Right after we first moved in we didn't have a

bedroom door. I was patient for a while. It bothered me but I put up with it. He did have a lot of things to finish in the house. But after many months I had had it. And finally I told him. No more would we do it until there was a door. He didn't seem to think I meant it until we had a real fight in bed.

B: And what did he do?

K: The very next day we had a bedroom door. But it's about the only thing I can point to that I got that I wanted. Isn't that sad? And even that was so I could give him what he wanted! But that's about the story of my life. I never got anything from my father, anything at all from my husband and nothing, but nothing from my kids.

B: Your children have also been a disappointment.

K: Yeah. Well, I know I sound terribly negative. My daughter Alice, she's twelve, so far has been O.K., I guess, but the boys.

B: You have another boy, uh, what's his name?

K: John. John Conley Whiting.

B: How old is he?

K: Almost sixteen. He's following in his father's and brother's footsteps. He's a very poor student. He hates school. Positively hates it. I've received more phone calls from the school about his truancy. I don't know what to do. He's like the rest of them—a problem. And besides, I think he's stealing money from my pocketbook.

B: What does your husband say?

K: Say? He doesn't say much of anything. I don't know, maybe he expects it. Francis is a very quiet man. Maybe he's just like me, bewildered. I don't know.

B: Do you talk about it?

K: No. We don't talk much. We never did.

B: Have you or did you seek help from anybody, about your kids, I mean?

K: For a while, a couple of times I saw the priest. He didn't help much.
       [Pause]
       I thought John might be different. And maybe I shouldn't

be so down on him now. He hasn't really done anything bad yet. He's been truant from school and maybe it isn't him who's stealing from me. But I thought for a long time that he'd be different than the rest. You know, we brought up the kids, all of them, Catholic, like we were supposed to. I wasn't that strong a Catholic myself but I did think the kids should know about God, and right and wrong. Anyway, John, of all my kids including Alice, took to the church. My mother gave him a lovely set of rosary beads when he made his first Communion. Every night he'd kneel down and say them. He used to go to Mass every morning right through junior high school. He never ate at night without saying grace before meals. The other kids, and even my husband, teased him about being a 'religious nut' as they put it, but it didn't seem to bother John. He went on his merry way doing his own thing.

B: And now?

K: He's changed a lot in the last couple of years. He almost never goes to church. He used to be a good student when he was going to church. Now he's barely passing, even flunking subjects. He's like the rest of my boys. He's gone to pot.

B: You mean he's not successful?

K: Yes. Maybe he's tried pot too. I don't know. I really don't know anything. And he's got a girlfriend.

B: Well, now, that's normal.

K: Maybe, but with my boys it seems to end up in a pregnancy. [Pause]
Just like for their father.

B: You were pregnant before you were married.

K: Yeah.
[Pause]
And that's another very long story. Do I have to go into that now?

B: Only if you want to.

K: I'd rather not now.

B: O.K. That's enough of talk for today, let's get to the testing.

K: Will I have to stay here long?

B: Only as long as you like. You admitted yourself. All you
     need do is put in a notice that you want to be discharged.
     You will be at the end of three days, after you put in your
     notice.
K: Oh. Do you think I should?
B: Let me go over all the tests and I'll let you know. Meanwhile,
     how do you feel about being here?
     [Pause]
K: I'm just so tired. It's so peaceful here, away from my family.
B: Have they visited you?
K: Only my husband. He won't let the kids come.
B: What does he say?
K: He's sort of confused about it all.
     [Pause]
B: I guess the knife missed him.
K: I guess so.
B: Do you want to go home?
K: I don't know. It's so peaceful here. Nobody bothers me.
B: Fine.   Let me go over the tests and we'll talk some more
     if you want.
K: O.K.
     The psycho-diagnostic report on Kathleen follows.

Kathleen (Conley) Whiting
40 years and 2 months old
98 Reed Street
City

Tests Administered: Wechsler Adult Intelligence Scale
                        Bender Gestalt Test
                        Apperception Tests (Local)
                        The Rorschach

Behavioral Observations:
    This is an auburn-haired, hazel-eyed woman who reports that
she is 5' 4" tall and weighs 125. Her small, pert nose and the upper
part of her pretty face are liberally sprinkled with freckles. The

freckles make her look younger, almost girlish. Throughout the interview she related to me in a deferential, but not reticent, way. Indeed, from the initial moments she was loquacious, cooperative and more than willing to participate. She is a bewildered woman and not a little depressed, but appears to have considerable strengths and very much wants help. In short, Kathleen is a warm, vibrant person, articulate and very fluent. In general she seemed to thoroughly enjoy the testing session and especially the attention which it afforded her.

Test Results:

Kathleen is of above average competence intellectually. Currently she functions with a verbal I.Q. of 110 and a performance or nonverbal I.Q. of 126. Scores such as these indicate that her mental competence is generally above average. Indeed, some of her competencies are within the superior range.

Within the verbal sphere we find that she functions in an average way only in the ability to reason arithmetically. In all the other verbal facets we find that she functions above the normal range. Thus her general fund of information and her general reasoning are at least bright-normal. Her general vocabulary development is of superior quality.

Kathleen's nonverbal competencies are even stronger. In no facet of this sphere does she fall below the superior range. Her perception of reality is very superior. She displays at least superior ability in both spatial relations and in the ability to understand and deal effectively with concrete interpersonal problems.

In short, Kathleen is very much intact intellectually, functioning well above the national average in both verbal and nonverbal intelligence.

In personality we find a woman who feels her past and present life is an emotional wasteland, barren of affection, attention and enhancement. As a child she felt ignored. As a woman she feels not only ingored but also used. As a child she felt desolate, now a woman, her sense of desolation continues but is compounded by bitterness.

Kathleen is an acutely unhappy woman. As noted, this is not a novel or unusual feeling for her. It was engendered in her primarily by an insensitive, unconcerned father and unfortunately not mitigated much by a mother who was emotionally inept. Her present unhappiness, then, is borne of a childhood and adolescence where she was emotionally starved, neglected and even exposed to cruelty.

She is a very suspicious person. Interestingly, however, her suspiciousness is compartmentalized. It is limited to men. Her deep-seated understanding about them is that they control. This control, she understands, can take only two forms. They can dominate absolutely with overt force or they can manipulate in a latent, covert way. The first type of masculine force she fears. The second generates strong feelings of resentment and hostility. She feels that all her life she was put down by them. She was never able to develop her best potentiality as a woman or as a person because first, as a child, she was constantly dominated into submission and prevented from development. Secondly, as an adult, she was manipulated, "outfoxed," into the passive-dependent, sterile roles of housewife and mother. Her father is responsible in the first case. Her husband in the second. She describes both as insensitive, unloving, uncaring.

Kathleen verbalizes fluently and fantasizes richly. Her verbalizations are registered as complaints, again mostly about men generally and her father and husband in particular. Not unsurprisingly, her fantasies are comprised almost exclusively of nurturant, loving paternalistic-type deities. In her private, uncomplicated daydreams, Kathleen is fondled, cuddled and tended. Thus, her response to one projective test card was, ". . . a tall, black-haired, brown-eyed man. He looks like a Greek God. He enfolds the child in his arms. He holds her like babies like to be held, crooning and stroking her hair and rocking her sort of . . ." Although her fantasies include these childlike yearnings, they include also the fairly strong libidinal strivings of a sexually interested woman. Thus, to a picture depicting a seminude woman in bed, with a man in the background, she wrote:

"The woman is a nymphomaniac, but a nice person too. She can't get enough love and unfortunately she's taken to obtaining it wherever she can. She picked up this fellow in a bar and he took her up to his apartment. She's older and taught him all about adult love. They had fun . . ."

It was in another picture where Mrs. Whiting's paternalistic and sexual love needs came together sharply. The picture shows a young woman and an older man in a kitchen. The typical description of this picture by clients revolves around household and familial-type activities. Kathleen's narrative is sharply different than most. "The man's very handsome. He could be her father, but he isn't. He's her lover. He keeps her. She's got a good deal! He pays all her living costs and treats her tenderly. He's very affectionate but he's also demanding, but in a very appropriate way and only in bed. She doesn't mind doing some of the things he wants her to do. In fact, she enjoys it all." Kathleen, then, attempts to compensate for the drab insufficiency of her real life by constructing exciting and rewarding fantasies. The probability of her acting out on these fantasies, however, is very small.

It is small because she incorporates in her personality a very strong conscience. She is imbued with a strong sense of morality, a very clear-cut, black and white understanding of right and wrong. Even more, her sense of morality was acquired via fear and punishment. She wants God to be loving, kind, understanding and giving. She understands Him to be vengeful, harsh, threatening, and demanding. She very much believes in retribution. Sinners are punished not only in an afterlife but in this life. As she sees it, there's enough punishment in her life. She doesn't need any more.

Kathleen's conscience, then, is an important dimension to her personality. It is so not only because it inhibits and thereby frustrates her need to act out, but equally important, it inundates her with a sense of guilt. And this sense of guilt over the years has contributed to the stultification of her self-esteem. Simply stated, Kathleen feels she's a "bad" person. From her church, from her father and from her mother she came to acquire many threads to self-understanding which her unconscious wove into a negative, demeaning fabric. Kathleen learned a long time ago that she had to be good to be loved. She feels today that she is not now nor has she ever been loved. Ergo, she's "bad." As a child, as an adolescent and as an adult she tried, she tried, she tried and inevitably she failed in being good. She recounted how as a child she went to confession every week and received lectures from her confessor to try harder even when her sins, she said, ". . . were less than venial." Her father's studied indifference of her needs altogether with her mother's cry of "through my fault, through my fault . . ." when she was beaten by her father, all of these, had the unfortunate effect of conditioning her to believe consciously and unconsciously that she, Kathleen Conley Whiting, was an unworthy person.

The effect today upon Kathleen of this all-pervasive sense of inadequacy is to make her feel overwhelmed, totally unable to cope with even the minimal demands of her maternal and house-wifely role. She feels emotionally unable to give to others, especially to those closest to her. Indeed, at this point, Kathleen functions far better with strangers than with family members. Why? Because family members impose emotional obligations that strangers do not. Family members make her feel guilty if she does not perform in her domestic roles. Strangers do not because with strangers she has no special role to fill. And so what we find in Kathleen is a neurotic-like perception of the relationship of emotional closeness to general performance. And all of this is permeated with guilt.

It appears to work like this. People close to her make her feel guilty if she does not perform. And perform is something she needs to do if she's ever going to get *any* love. We noted above that as a child she tried hard to perform and was always told, try harder. The communication to her was, "it's not enough, or, your performance is inadequate." Let us note something, Kathleen moved from her father's house into her husband's house. Her performance at work, even her schoolwork, all had to do with pleasing a man, a family. It was generally inadequate, making her feel guilty. This pattern to perform out of fear of failure or guilt, initially learned at home, became the pattern of interaction in her husband's house. In her whole life Kathleen never did very much because she wanted to, so much as she did because she felt she had to. Guilt was and is her prime motivator.

And today Kathleen is very tired. She is tired of feeling guilty. She is tired of having to perform and always to no avail. She is tired of the pressures of her family. She herself noted, "I'm just so tired."

Despite these problems, Kathleen's prognosis is at least fair. As noted, she is a person of notable intelligence. Interpersonally, especially with those outside her immediate family, she is fluent and vivacious. Physically she is indeed attractive and she is not unaware of this fact. Her strengths, then, are considerable.

Kathleen is a prime candidate for psychotherapy as she is both emotionally and intellectually receptive. However, it should be noted that her problems are directly related to her family, particularly her husband. An interview with her husband has been scheduled. Recommendations to include him in any planned therapeutic program will be deffered until after our meeting.

Albert Boudreau, Ph.D.
Staff Psychologist

TRANSCRIPT OF AN INTERVIEW WITH FRANCIS WHITING

(Edited and Condensed)

B: Come in. Come in, Mr. Whiting, I'm Dr. Boudreau.

F: How's my wife, Doctor?

B: Haven't you seen her today?

F: Yeah, I did.

B: How does she look to you?

F: She looks O.K. but that doesn't mean much. She always looks O.K., physically I mean. What I want to know is how's her head?

B: Well, uh, she's not at her best, I'm sure.

F: Yeah, I figured.

B: I suspect she's been depressed for a long time.

F: I guess so.
    [Pause]
    I'll bet she complained a lot about me.

B: She did but you're only one piece of the whole picture.

F: But a pretty big piece, I bet.
[Pause]
B: Your wife needs support, a lot of support.
F: Who doesn't?
[Pause]
B: Uh, you're not feeling very sympathetic to your wife and her problems.
[Pause]
F: Look, Doctor, we've all got our problems. Maybe Kathleen's got more than most but she doesn't do too much to help herself. That's for sure.
B: You feel she's brought this on herself.
F: A lot of it, yeah.
B: Would you explain, could you explain what you mean?
F: Geez, she doesn't do anything to help herself. She doesn't do anything around the house. The house in a wreck, a positive wreck.
B: She's a poor housekeeper.
F: And how!
B: You're disgusted with her about that.
F: Among other things.
B: What other things?
F: She never has a meal ready on time. I couldn't tell you the number of times she's ruined the supper. Yeah, there are other things I'm disgusted about.
[Pause]
Look. I'm not much of a talker and if you have to know, you oughta' know I don't like talking about her this way. She is my wife. Oh, I don't know.
B: I'm very much aware that you're embarrassed, Mr. Whiting. Uh, I'm not interested in gossiping if that's your concern. What is coming through to me is that you have a lot of anger built up in you over your wife. Now, if we are going to help her, and you for that matter, we need to know about it and go from there.
F: Yeah. I guess one of the problems with me and Kathleen is that I'm not much of a talker. Never have been. My

mother used to say I was the quiet type.

B: Uh, huh.

F: And I am. But you see, Kathleen isn't the quiet type. She's just the opposite. She's a screamer from way back. Boy, can that woman scream! If you want to know the truth, we never really had a fight about anything. I've sort of gone along with her, the messy house, the ruined suppers. She'd scream about her own burned casserole and I'd listen. Sometimes I think she'd want me to yell back, in fact she'd say so, but I'm just not the type. Maybe I should have. I don't know.

B: You never reacted too much to her.

F: If I did we'd have two fighting, two yelling. I always figured one yeller in a family's enough. We never had any in my own house.

B: I see.

F: No. I don't think you do. See, I'm not used to a woman like Kathleen. All the women in my family were, well, efficient. My wife, whatever she is or isn't, isn't efficient. She's a, I hate to say it, but sort of a slob.

B: You really don't think too much of her abilities.

F: No [sighing], I guess I don't.
     [Pause]
     She complains so much, about so many things. Like, I'd come home from work and before she even says hello, she starts in about the laundry, the kids, the work she's got to do and how I'm never around to help.

B: She figures you could help her.

F: Look, Doctor, I was brought up that a man works at his job and a woman works at home, that's her job. She don't get up at 7 a.m. and go out to work—I do. I don't figure it's my job to come in after a twelve-hour day and start to do housework. No way!

B: A man has his role and a woman hers.

F: Absolutely! My mother, whatever she was, ran a tight ship. The house I was brought up in was a very efficient place, let me tell you!

B: And Kathleen doesn't measure up that way.

F: No, she doesn't.

B: But there must have been qualities which attracted you, in the beginning.

F: Yeah, well, if you don't know, I'll tell you, we had to get married.

B: Even so, you've been married now . . .

F: Yeah, well, Kathleen used to be, uh, how do you say, well, affectionate.

B: Affectionate? Would you say she was loving, uh, warm?

F: Yeah. [Pause] At least she used to be.

B: Those qualities have begun to fade.

F: They've faded.

B: You don't feel she has them anymore.

F: Not to me.

B: I see.
    [Pause]

F: Kathleen's got . . . uh, I don't know. Maybe it's the kids, maybe it's me, maybe . . . She finds everything so hard to do. She finds everything, life, she finds life so hard.

B: Kathleen's been depressed for a long time.
    [Pause]

F: Look, I'm not a philosopher. I'm not educated. The way I figure, you do the best you can. I've tried and I've tried hard. I don't know how I'm at, where I'm at. I am where I am and I accept it. Right now I'm tired and I'm disgusted. I gotta go home after this and get supper for me and a twelve-year-old and John and I'm not used to getting a supper together. Kathleen is here, resting, and I gotta go home.

B: You don't want to go home.

F: No—Yes, what does it matter what I *want* to do? A man does what he has to and so does a woman.

B: And Kathleen is not living up to her responsibilities.

F: Christ. No!

B: And you are.

F: Yes. I live at home.
    [Pause]

B: And Kathleen, uh, copped out.

F: She copped out before she began.
      [Pause]
B: She's inadequate.
F: She's got her own problems. [Pause] We all got out prob-
      lems. [Pause] But just because we got them we don't have
      to, have to show them off to everybody around us.
B: Kathleen is too demonstrative.
F: Yeah, boy, is she ever! [Pause] She swears like a drunken
      sailor. [Pause] That's no way for a woman to act, a mother
      yet.
B: Perhaps she can't help it.
F: We all can help it. We don't have to . . . . Oh, I don't know.
      I know I sound like a prude, Doctor. I'm not. I've been
      around. I was in the navy in the war. I been around. I can't
      help it. I'm being honest with you. I figure a woman's a
      woman. A mother's a mother. She doesn't act like a sailor
      on liberty in a foreign port.
B: I'm not sure I understand.
F: She's got no self-control about her language or about much
      else. She don't care. If I have any real complaint about
      Kathleen, my wife, it's that she doesn't seem to care about
      anything.
B: And you resent that more than anything else about her.
F: Yes. I could put up with all the rest of it if only she could
      care about, about the house, about the kids, uh, that's it.
      That's the whole thing.
B: How about you, shouldn't she care about you?
F: Well, yeah, of course.
      [Pause]
      See, what I've learned over the years is that Kathleen, and
      I'm probably responsible, runs everything.
B: I'm not sure I know . . .
F: She runs everything. [Pause] It's hard to explain but with
      her yelling and crying she always tried to make me hop-to.
      I wasn't having any so she took it out on Thomas and my
      son Francis. Poor kids were always under my wife's thumb.
      When they were small I found them a lot of times in bed at

supper time 'cause they'd been bad. 'Bad' for Kathleen was not doing like she said to do. She'd send them to bed for the least thing. Then she'd want me to spank them when I got home. Who wants to play the ogre all the time.
[Pause]

B: So?

F: Well, that's not my way. I wasn't about to hit a kid who'd done something eight hours earlier. Besides, most of the time it wasn't much of anything at all. Maybe he'd yelled a little too loud or the two boys had had some kind of a fight.
[Pause]
Kathleen never should have been a mother. She never enjoyed her kids. They were always too much for her.
[Pause]
Never should have been a wife either for that matter.

B: You don't feel she loves you?

F: Nah. Maybe at first she did. She showed it more.

B: She used to be much more demonstrative than she is now.

F: She isn't at all now.

B: Are Kathleen's problems all Kathleen's fault?
[Pause]

F: No, course not. And I'm being unfair to her, very unfair. A lot of the fault for her being here is me, I'm sure.

B: What would you say you've done that brought about her admission here.

F: It's not what I've done, but what I haven't done.

B: O.K. What haven't you done?
[Pause]

F: Well, I'm not a very, uh, I think the word you used before describing my wife is demonstrative. Well, I'm not that, I'm not demonstrative.

B: You mean you don't show her or you can't show her that you love her.

F: Yeah.
[Pause]
I've always been like that. Like mother said, I was the

quiet type.
[Pause]

B: Mr. Whiting, did you ever love your wife?

F: I really don't know. I don't know the answer to that question.
[Pause]

B: I see.
[Pause]

F: See, showing love, being, uh, affectionate was never a big deal in my house. Nobody, my parents never showed how really mad, glad or sad they were. We weren't like that in my house.

B: I see.

F: I'm not either.
[Pause]
Frankly, I never thought it was too important.

B: You didn't?

F: No. See, I figured I made a commitment to Kathleen when I married, like her priest said to us at the reception, marriage is forever. I'm not a Catholic, but I believe it. That was my commitment. And believe me, I've put up with a lot these twenty years. A lot more than most would.
[Pause]
You want it simple and straight, Doctor, I honestly don't believe that Kathleen made the same commitment.

B: You don't.

F: No.

B: Why not?

F: She married me 'cause she felt she had to. I got her pregnant.

B: I see. But she's stayed married to you now for twenty years.

F: Yeah. [Pause] What else could she do?

B: You don't think she could have left you?

F: No. In this town?

B: So you figure she stayed with you all these years because she had no alternative.

F: Pretty much.

B: And you figure she never really loved you.

F: Yeah.
[Long pause]

Look, Doctor, I came here because you asked me to and because I need to get my wife home. We need her at home. She's not crazy, is she?

B: No, Mr. Whiting. Your wife will be able to go home. She's not psychotic.

F: She's not crazy. I know that.

B: No, she is not crazy but she does need help.
[Pause]

F: We all need help but why does she have to stay in the hospital?

B: Yes, yes. I'll need to talk to your wife again. She'll be coming home. It won't be long.

F: Fine. O.K.

Some notes on Francis Whiting.

Mr. Whiting is a sparse-haired, tall man (I'd judge about 6' 2"). He's broad-shouldered and has a developing paunch. His lined face and his stooped walk make him look about ten years older than his forty-two years.

Mr. Francis Whiting Jr. shows himself to be a confused, bewildered man who is interpersonally inept. His most acute deficiency appears to lie in the communication of feelings, especially love.

He has a somewhat simplistic view of the world and how to deal with it and becomes increasingly befuddled when he finds that life's problems are not remedied by simple solutions. He has little or no appreciation of his wife's problems. "We all got problems," he says. As he sees it, "She's not doing much to help herself." He implies that she could, she should lift herself up by her emotional bootstraps. He does not understand why she does not.

Mr. Whiting sees himself as "quiet," apparently uncommunicative, yet he communicated his thoughts and feelings surprisingly well. He is literally disgusted with his wife, with her lack of competencies as a housekeeper and as a cook. He is especially angered by what he perceives to be her "I-don't-care" attitude. Interestingly, he made the observation about her that she made about herself, namely, that she should never have been a wife and mother. He becomes especially dissatisfied with Kathleen when he compares her to his mother. Mother Whiting must have been a very efficient woman but one who had difficulty communicating her love.

And it is in the area of love, or, more precisely, in Francis Whiting's discomfort with it and all emotional display that we come to an important cause of the Whiting family problems. Francis Whiting is quite unable to show his love. His wife feels, and perhaps quite rightly, that he is an "insensitive, unloving bastard." But is he really? How does Francis Whiting understand love?

Love to him is commitment. He feels that he made a commitment, and indeed, that his wife did not. He feels he shows his love by living at home, by not "copping out." In his view, being affectionate, being demonstrative, is not loving, because he does not understand it. Worse still, ventilation of any emotion makes him uncomfortable. It was not part of the family scene growing up at home. Love to him does not involve demonstrative verbalizations, kissing or fondling. It does not involve expression; verbal, behavioral, or possibly even emotional. To Francis Whiting love has to do with commitment. And commitment to him means *putting up with*, putting up with inconvenience, nagging; it involves sacrifice and quite probably, constant worry. Francis does not appear to be a man who speaks idly. And what he said during the interview is that, "marriage is forever." Forever, he is willing to accept, may involve much unforeseen pain. No matter. To Francis pain is part of life. Indeed, superficially, he would seem to be a man with little or no ability to give of himself. Yet what he revealed in a very clear fashion during this interview is that he's a man of infinite tolerance, willing to put up with much interpersonal stress.

The problem here is not Francis, per se. The problem is Francis in conjunction with Kathleen. In his own way Francis is probably very self-sufficient. Kathleen is not. Kathleen is a person who needs not only to be supported but to be enhanced. She has a very deep-seated need to be loved. And the love which she can understand best, perhaps the only love which she can understand, is that love which is exhibited or at least communicated manifestly, or at the very least in a latent way.

Francis is quite unable to do this. Quite apparently this inability stems not from any hostility but simply from ineptness. At times he shows himself to be insensitive. For example, in the initial phases of the interview to the comment, "Your wife needs support, a lot of support," his response was, "Who doesn't?" This is an honest response. Everyone has problems. He has problems too. His understanding is that one copes with problems. One does not seek support for them. His insensitivity, then, if that's what it is, is an admission of his lack of emotional wherewithal to deal in a meaningful way with another person, even his wife.

The problem, of course, is what does he do now?

INTERVIEW WITH KATHLEEN WHITING

(Edited and Condensed)

B: Come in, Mrs. Whiting.

K: Hi. Well, when do you think I should leave?

B: Do you want to leave?

K: Not really. But I feel I should. They've been without me for almost three weeks now.

B: You feel you should get back now. Do you think you're well enough?

K: I don't know. I feel much better. It's really amazing what a little rest and a different environment can do.

B: Yes.

K: There were some things I thought I should fill you in on.

B: Fill me in.
    [Pause]

K: Well, just so you have the whole picture.

B: Yes.

K: Well, you know Francis and I had to get married.

B: Yes, you mentioned that the last time.

K: Yes, well we did, we had to.

B: I see.
    [Pause]

Did you want to?

K: Well, it didn't matter much one way or another. I had to. I was "with child" as the poets used to say.

B: I know, but did you want to?

K: I don't know, I don't know. [Pause]   What does it matter?

B: Well, uh, I was curious to know about the foundation which you and Francis built your marriage on.

K: I see. Well, it wasn't much of a foundation. I mean I didn't have much of a choice. I mean I was pregnant.

B: But, correct me if I'm wrong, but doesn't the church say, uh, doesn't the church discourage marriage because of illegitimate pregnancy?

K: Church had nothing to do with it.

B: Oh! What did?

K: [Chuckle] My father did.

B: Oh! Your father insisted you get married.

K: Yeah. [Pause]   Francis and I were dating. He was in the navy but he was home often. He was cute and I liked him. In fact my father liked him. Thought he was a real man 'cause he was in the service. My father was like that. Well, we were dating regularly and he'd given me a friendship ring. And the night he did I turned out to be a real friend for him. [Chuckle] [Pause]   I've often tried to figure out what happened that night. I was a virgin until then. Not that I was committed especially to that. Maybe I was, but I don't think so. I guess it was the ring, that damned ring.

B: Nobody'd ever given you anything.

K: Exactly. It was the first real present I ever got that was for nothing. [Pause]   Ha! For nothing! And I want you to know that even though I had the strictest father in town I wasn't exactly naive, I'd had many dates before that night and I'd even petted, a little. But that night was different.

B: How so?

K: I felt sort of relaxed yet daring. Francis was so unlike any boy I'd known. He was quiet. He was always so polite. He usually showed up at my house with candy or a flower or some little thing like that for me or my mother. Mother loved him.   She thought he was the greatest.   It was the friendship ring.   It was a pearl.   He gave it to me in the car. We were parked up on the lake front.   There weren't any houses there then.   Well, he slipped that ring on my finger and I felt like I was free.   Can you imagine.   I felt like I was free!

B: Free of what?

K: I don't really know.   Free of my home, my father . . . . I guess of my father.

B: You felt free to do as you pleased.

K: Yes.   Like I was an adult and there were no holds barred.

B: Hm.

K: Yeah.

B: How did you feel afterwards?   Do you remember?

K: Yeah.   Not as guilty as I thought I would.

B: Did it happen again?

K: Once.   After a party when I'd had too much to drink.

B: I see.

K: That was the only other time.   I guess I was scared about it.

B: You felt guilty.

K: I guess so.   The first time is what did it. Made me pregnant, I mean.

B: When did you find out?

K: Guess!

B: Missed your period.

K: Yes.

B: I bet you were scared.

K: Terrified.

B: Of you father.

K: Petrified.   I didn't know what to do.

B: When did you tell Francis?

K: I was almost three months pregnant.

B: Did you tell anyone?

K: No one.

B: That was a traumatic time.

K: A nightmare.   I don't remember it all too clearly.

B: It was the fear of your father?

K: What else?

B: What about your mother, did you . . .

K: No. I didn't want to worry her. What coud she do? She was even more scared of my father. [Pause] I guess I was more scared of his finding out, his reaction, than anything else. You have to remember that in those days that was the worst thing, the worst thing that could happen to a girl. And my father was so proud. [Pause] I was the proverbial apple of his eye. I was pretty. A couple of times he even told me I was.

B: You felt guilty about that, too, being pretty, being the apple of his eye, as you put it, and being pregnant.

K: And scared, mostly I was scared of his finding out.

B: How did he find out?

K: I told Francis, finally. We were walking home from a movie.

B: How'd he react?

K: He sort of grunted. He didn't act surprised. All he said was, "Are you sure?" I told him I was pretty sure. We walked home. It was around eleven. My father was sleeping and Francis woke him up.

B: What happened?

K: Father came down, sat in his big armchair, yawned and said, "O.K. What's up? This better be good. Must be to wake me up." His tone was gruff but then it always was when someone wanted anything from him. He knew we were nervous. Then Francis told him. He looked at me as Francis spoke the awful words, three words, "Kathleen is pregnant." He just looked at me. He didn't say a word. He got up and started walking up the stairs. Near the top, he called down in a toneless, frosty voice, "Kathleen, know this, there'll be no church wedding!" And we heard his bedroom door shut.

B: You weren't married in church.

K: Yes, I was, though.

B: Oh. What happened?

K: The next day he changed his mind and announced I'd be married in church, in a white gown. I didn't much want to but father was not one you argued with when he'd made up his mind. Anyway, I was. [Pause] That wasn't so bad, I was embarrassed. I was almost five months pregnant. I didn't show much, but I felt like I did which is just as bad. Maybe it's worse. [Pause] The worst was the reception. Father insisted on a big reception. Even though they all knew, people generally were very nice. The exceptions were my inlaws, especially my mother-in-law.

B: How did she treat you?

K: Coldly and correctly. After the Mass on the steps of the church when I leaned to kiss her, she pulled back but only so I could tell. She took the kiss, however, smiled sweetly and said ever so softly and so only I could hear, "You look nice. I do hope you'll be happy despite everything." My father-in-law shook my hand. Period. I didn't even want to kiss him. They came to the reception with my sister-in-law, Phyllis. Phyllis is just like my mother-in-law. The three of them sat there in a corner, unsmiling, like the three little prigs.

B: [Chuckle]

K: Everybody else was O.K. And I was even beginning to relax and enjoy myself when I noticed my father. He had started to get drunk and was table-hopping. I was standing only a few feet from him when he boomed out to a friend of his, "Well, Murph, congratulate me, here I am, father of a bride and an instant grandfather, all in one day. Pretty good, huh!" I could feel Mr. Murphy's eyes on me. He's dead now. He was a nice man. Then dear father came out with, "goddamnit, Murph, did ya' ever think she'd do that to me? Did ya' ever. My own sweet daughter getting knocked up like that. goddamnit, Murph. Ya' do the best ya' can and that's what they do to ya'." I was mortified. I grabbed Francis and we left. That was my wedding day.

FINAL INTERVIEW WITH KATHLEEN WHITING

(Edited and Condensed)

K: I haven't seen you in a while.

B: Almost a week, isn't it?

K: Five days.   You know, right after I left, uh, something happened, important.

B: Oh, what?   What happened?

K: I got back to my ward and I started hemorrhaging.

B: Oh.

K: Yeah.   I miscarried.   I've been in the medical unit for the past several days.   I could have left the second day but you know how it is here.   The doctors get a real medical problem, even a minor one, and they like to fuss over it.   Makes them feel important, like doctors.   Anyway, I had a "miss" and I'm not going to have a baby.

B: How do you feel about that?

K: [Chuckle]   For once God's will and mine are the same.   Let's just say I'm not devasted about not having a fifth child.

B: [Chuckle]

K: Yeah, and I put in my notice for discharge, you know, the pink slip, the three-day notice?

B: Yeah.

K: I just didn't want to leave, just go, without telling you, uh, at least goodbye.   You've really been good.   You've been kind.

B: So, so you're going to leave now, Mrs. Whiting.   Do you really think you're going to be able to cope with all the problems, I mean really, what's different now?

K: Well, for one thing, I'm not carrying a baby and I realize now that was the straw that broke the camel's back, or more accurately, that had a lot to do with my coming here.   Anyway, I can't stay here forever, my husband is just overwhelmed with house problems, he just can't do it.   I mean, whatever he is, he's not a housewife.   I can imagine the condition the house is in right now.   Staying here isn't going to solve any more of my problems.   I really feel I have to get back.

B: O.K., Mrs. Whiting, if there is anything I can do before you leave, let me know.   Or after, even if you want to give me a buzz, if not for anything else, just to talk, please feel free to do so.

Discussion Questions

1. Why did Kathleen "crack up"?
2. Do you think her description of the hospital is an accurate one?
3. How does Kathleen view herself, her husband, her children?
4. Summarize Kathleen's psycho-diagnostic report in your own words.
5. How does Francis view himself, Kathleen, and his children?
6. What do the interviews reveal about their marriage?
7. Do they understand the nature of their problems?
8. At this point do you think the Whitings can be helped?

Chapter 3

The roots of delinquency burrow deeply extending even to the grave and to those generations no longer alive.

FOCUS GUIDES

1. Try to decide whether John Conley is a patriarch in the best sense or just an egotistical, selfish man.
2. Consider if John's wife, Helen, deserves her life.
3. What emotional hang-ups did Kathleen acquire in her parent's home?
4. What price did Maureen Whiting and her family pay for her efficiency?
5. Note that Francis Whiting Senior was a cool, aloof and uncommunicative man who buried himself in his work. How did this hurt his family, especially his son?

John Conley died less than a year ago. He was seventy-nine and the very proud founder of the John Conley Enterprises Incorporated—Lumber and Building Materials. Opinions about John's character don't vary much. Most of the old-timers who knew him as "the boss" describe him as domineering, egotistical, and belittling. One sixty-four-year-old man stated it this way: "Whenever you went into John's office down at the yard, the first thing he'd do is get you off balance. He'd say something like, 'Well, whadaya want, another raise?' Then he'd remind you that time was money and you were wasting both. I don't know why but John always felt he had to cut you down before he could talk to you."

Why did people work for him? "There wasn't much choice. Never was too much work hereabouts during the 20s—and certainly none during the Depression. If John took you on you learned quick enough he hadn't done you any favors. Let me tell you, you worked for every nickel you got. Always putting you down, always. John Conley was a son-of-a-bitch."

His domineering ways are even now legendary. He intruded upon all phases of the business—purchasing, shipping, receiving, and even the small construction jobs that were contracted for

(He finalized all contracts.)   His meticulous supervision could better be described as harassment.   Indeed, company records show that between 1926 and 1942 no less than eighteen bookkeepers gave him their notices.   (This, mind you, during a time when work was very scarce.)   A former female office employee recalls John this way.   "Mr. Conley was a very difficult man to work for.   I worked for him longer than most, about eight years.   He came into the office every day and would lay out our work for us. Much as if we were children, school children.   What upset us so was the fact that he really did not understand accounting fundamentals and procedures.   But you could never argue with him. He terrified most people he dealt with, at least at the yard he did. I remember one young man who had just graduated from business school.   He was a nice young fellow.   Young and maybe a little too sure of his new knowledge but not a bad fellow really.   Anyway, he had been working for us for about a week or two.   It was right after a payday, I remember that.   They paid in cash in those days.   As you would expect, Mr. Conley went over all the pay envelopes.   And well, it seems that he had deducted some money from this young clerk's salary.   A dollar, I think.   The young man asked Mr. Conley about it—at 'lay-out time.'   (That's what Mr. Conley called his instruction period to us.)   I remember the scene vividly.   In a very deferential tone he asked, 'Sir, uh, could I ask you why I was docked a dollar.'   Mr. Conley responded with, 'You can ask, sonny, but I don't have to tell you.'   The young man pressed him.   'But I want to know, it is my pay.'   Mr. Conley responded again in that breezy way he had when he felt pretty good.   'O.K.   O.K.   You were late twice.'   'But I wasn't.   I wasn't.' Mr. Conley's face started to get red.   And I could see a real blow-up coming.   He became furious instantaneously.   It never took more than a split second.   And what made it worse for me was that he always used the filthiest language when he did so.   Even in these modern times I haven't heard such filth as Mr. Conley used when he lost his temper.   On that particular occasion he didn't fail to meet my worst expectations.   I think the young man's head snapped back when Mr. Conley roared his response. [She wrote rather than verbalized the response.]   'Why you fucking little son-of-a-bitch. Are you calling me a liar? Me? You little prick. Get your ass outa my chair, outa my office and outa my yard. You're fired. Fired. FIRED.' That young man left that office as if he were shot out of the proverbial cannon. It was winter and he left without his coat or hat. He never came back for either."

John Conley's strong penchant for profanity, while it cowed even the profane, also helped to earn him the reputation as a sort of "town character." Once his company, more accurately John, had contracted to do the painting on a local Catholic church. Even today this church has three angels on top of its soaring spires. It seems that none of his painters were willing to climb the shaky ladders to paint the angels. John came up to the group of painters who were standing with the pastor of the church. He was irked that his men were not working. As noted, John's constant frame of reference was "time is money." "What's the trouble?" he asked with his usual belligerence. It was the pastor who volunterred in a genial tone, "John, the boys are a little fearful of climbing up to paint the angels." "What!" he cried indignantly. "Gimme that brush. Gimme that brush. Don't you worry, Father, I'll paint those goddamned angels."

His daughter tells the story that John, who attended church and who appeared to be even a confessional Catholic, periodically had the pastor of their parish to dinner. John, in his usual fluent way, had been telling his stories liberally spiced with, for him anyway, mild profanities. It was after the before-dinner grace that the pastor gently reminded John that "we all need to try harder to keep our language clean." And it was then that John responded with his usual urbanity, "goddamn it, Father, I'm trying harder."

John never knew that he was viewed as some kind of a character. Had he known he would have been enraged, probably even hurt. For John was, among other things, an egotist. He was an impeccable dresser. A contemporary of his described him as one "who always looked like he had just stepped out of Abercrombie and Fitch or Brooks Brothers." After his death there were among his papers receipts from precisely those places.

He bathed every morning and each evening that he went out

and he went out very frequently. He was especially fond of after shave lotions. After his death his children found thirteen half-opened bottles of various bath perfumes and lotions, some of them imported. One of the foremen in the yard one morning good-naturedly observed, "Christ, John, you smell like you just stepped out of a French whorehouse." John flattened him. He was exquisitely sensitive to ridicule, especially about his dress or grooming habits.

And despite his belligerence, profanity, and transparent narcissism, John Conley was a very gregarious animal. He belonged to the Elks, the Lions and the Rotary Club. He held offices in each of these three and was a two-term president of the Elks. In addition, he was president four times of the Holy Name Council of his church and for thirty years a member in good standing of the Knights of Columbus, another church fraternal organization.

For approximately a decade, 1942 to 1952, John Conley Enterprises Inc.—Lumber and Building Materials prospered. During this period company books show assests in excess of $2,000,000.00. From 1948 through 1952 Conley Enterprises employed over a hundred employees. During this period and well into the 50s John Conley was perceived as a leading businessman of the community. He was asked to serve on the Boards of Directors of three of the six Middletown banks. John Conley "had arrived" socially and economically. At a Christmas party in 1952 he was in an expansive mood and did what he seldom permitted himself to do—he discussed his background. A long-time friend relates. "John was feeling pretty good. He'd had a lot to drink and I remember he put his arms around my shoulders and asked, 'Like your bonus, Murph?' 'Geez yeah, boss. Thanks.' 'More'n you expected, huh?' 'Yeah, boss, it was, thanks.' 'It's O.K. It's O.K. You deserve it, Murph. You deserve it.' John always had to make you feel grateful. That was his way. Anyway, that's when he told me about himself. I'd known John about thirty-five years. I had known him but I really hadn't known him. I'd gone to school with him and I knew that he came from the same kind of background as me. His parents were poor Irish immigrants, both of them. As a kid he was always a scrapper. He quit school around the ninth grade and worked with his father doing carpentry work. I never did learn where he got the money to start the business. He might have stole it for all I know. Knowing John he could have. Anyway, John bragged about himself that night. It was the only time I knew him to do that. He bragged, said things like 'Not bad for a poor Mick, huh, Murph? Not bad, huh.' I never knew him to use the word 'Mick.' I think he would have killed any guy who might have called him that. Not that he was ashamed of being Irish. He wasn't. But neither was he a professional Irishman like so many of the younger folks are today. He wasn't that either. Anyway, John said things like, 'Murph, you know I'm worth a million bucks. You know that. A million bucks. Just a poor Mick trying to make a buck and I made a million of them. I showed those bastards, I showed them all.' I never knew who he meant by 'those bastards.' I guess he meant people in general. Anyway I gotta hand it to him, he made it all right. At least up to that time. The troubles for John and the company started right after that. After his heart attack he had to slow down. He let his kids, Thomas and Bobby, take over. They just didn't have the know-how. They didn't have John's ability. And maybe it was John's fault. He never let anybody do too much on their own. He had to run things. He kept too much to himself about the company."

In the spring of 1953 John suffered a mild coronary. It scared him enough to obey doctor's orders about staying away from work. He did so for almost four months. Most of these four months were spent in Florida. His two elder boys Thomas and Robert attempted to manage the company. It was from this point in time that the company began to steadily decline in economic wherewithal. Records show that for the next 15 years company assets slowly but steadily declined until Thomas filed for bankruptcy in 1967. The employees numbered only six, two of them were Thomas and Robert. Assets totaled less than $32,000.00 while the liabilities figured at over $150,000.00. John Conley's pride and joy of over forty years was defunct.

As the family patriarch, John Conley showed a remarkable consistency in personality. His daughter Kathleen describes him as mean, cruel, and unkind. His other daughter Helen, the youngest child, remembers him as "petrifying and sort of distant." Christopher, the sole remaining son, says of him, "Dad never should have married. He never should have been a father. We were always so damned tense when he was around."

It was Kathleen who provided most of the family history. Family life in the Conley household was a series of constant anxieties. "Dad should never have been dad. He didn't love us or, if he did, he never knew the meaning of love. He never hugged any of his children, even us girls. When we were little he was either indifferent to us, or he punished us for some minor infraction. Punishment consisted usually of a bellow or of a short but very painful beating. We were always so nervous when he was around. It got worse as I got older. As I got older I learned that living with my father was an exercise in learning to live with pain and cruelty.

"I've never been able to understand why he married my mother, or why he would want to marry anyone. He didn't enjoy his family, not even a little bit. He was seldom home physically, but he was always home, too. Dad hung like a pall over our house. Even though he was out of the house, he was there. You might say he was like a kind of ever-present evil spirit.

"The house, all thirteen rooms, was dad's house. He bought it five years after he was married and he furnished it, right to the drapes and bedspreads. Mother and us kids felt like tenants, tenants who were at the mercy of a fickle landlord.

"There were five children in our family. Thomas, Robert, Christopher, me and Helen, the baby. I guess none of us children ever wanted for anything, but as a child growing up I never knew that we were financially well-off. I never saw any money. It was never visible. I was in the seventh grade before I learned that dad gave mother a weekly allotment. Knowing dad, I'm sure that she had to live within it. He controlled everything. And if he didn't buy he would decide if we could keep it. Every spring and fall mother would take us kids shopping for clothes. She would let us buy pretty much what we liked and then the bills were sent to dad. If he didn't like what was bought, it would be returned. His taste was O.K. but it was, especially for Helen and me, uh, well, conservative. I remember during World War II the peasant blouses were popular. I wanted one, badly. I was still in high school and they were the rage. My father wouldn't let me buy one. He felt they were immodest because 'a woman's midsection should always be covered,' he said. I always thought he was a prude about sex. Sex! It was never mentioned but what I've realized since is that it was ever present.

"There was no TV growing up. Movies were our passion. When I was in school I had a crush on Tyrone Power and Robert Taylor. All my friends read the movie magazines. I'd save my school lunch money to buy them and then would sneak them into the house. I had to sneak them because my father had forbidden me to read them. He said they were filthy trash and 'proper young ladies,' that was his standard phrase for both me and Helen growing up, 'proper young ladies' just didn't read such trash.

"Dad was always poking around the house. He made life miserable for all of us. Nothing was sacred to him. None of us had any privacy. He came into my room checking around. Once he had found a magazine on my bedside table. At the time I didn't know that I wasn't supposed to read them. He ripped it up and threw it into the trash. 'Miss Kathleen,' he bellowed, he always called me that when angry and since he was almost always angry, he generally addressed me like that. 'Miss Kathleen, I forbid you to read any more of this trash. Do you hear me? Proper young ladies do not read this. And since you are my daughter and this is my room in my house, you will not read this anymore. Not now. Not ever. Do you hear me?'

"It was hard not to hear dad since on a ten decibel level he always spoke at nine and three-quarters. I heard. But I continued to buy them, fearfully, and to sneak them into my room. I hid them in a bureau drawer under my underwear. I read them at night when he was out and afterwards gave them to friends. I never dared collect them.

"Dad was very up-tight about sex. I began to realize it for the first time when one evening after supper I came down in my slip. Dad was reading the paper, looked up and became instantly furious.

He bellowed out, 'You goddamned pig. Get upstairs and put on some clothes!' Then he launched into his tirade about 'proper young ladies.' What I marveled at in later years was that he never saw any inconsistency, nor did anyone else in the family for that matter, between his uttering comments like 'goddamned pig,' 'dirty slut,' 'filthy witch-bitch' (a pet phrase of his) and his unusual concern that his two daughters be brought up as 'proper young ladies.'

"His concern that Helen and I be 'proper' was very consistent with the reputation which he felt that our family should have in the community. What people 'thought' about us was of consuming importance to dad. 'What would people think,' is another phrase that I heard too regularly. None of us ever saw any inconsistencies. If we did we certainly didn't voice them. I remember once we all went to a church picnic. Dad per usual drank a little too much, too fast, an indication I think that he was basically very uncomfortable with people. Anyway, he started arguing with one of the lawyers in town. The lawyer had been gibing dad about the price of building materials. Well, dad started growling, then bellowing about how all lawyers were 'shysters'. It was all very embarrassing, even for me and I was about eleven. When he committed these faux pas or acted crudely, which was often, mother might utter a too gentle, 'Oh Johnny, please, hush now!' Sometimes he would calm down but not before he'd growled loudly something like, 'He can go take a flying shit for himself,' or simply, 'Screw him, that lousy bastard.' Mother accepted these embarrassments both at home and in public with resignation and sometimes even with a smile. We kids accepted it all. What else could we do? But we didn't smile.

"But if there's anything that hurt us kids at home and probably all our lives, it was his treatment of mother. He was cruel to her. He was worse than that. He didn't just put her down, demean her in front of us and sometimes in front of friends and relatives. He did worse, be beat her physically, especially when he had drunk too much. He was a monster.

"There were many embarrassing occasions. One that stands out too well happened when I was nine. It was Thanksgiving Day.

We were all gathered around the table and there were relatives, my grandmother, mother's mother was there and mom's cousin too. He was unemployed. It was during the Depression. Anyway, mother, who was a pretty fair cook, had not plucked the turkey well enough. You know in those days you had to pluck your own. Anyway, dad liked the drumstick and the drumsticks still had some of the feather shafts imbedded in them. Well, he started out slowly. I do think that in his own way he tried to control himself. But he started complaining. No one said anything until my grandmother observed that everything else was just perfect and it was, too. 'Well goddamn it. Everything should be. I like the drumstick and only the drumstick and that's not perfect. I can't eat it. And I bought it with my money. And if that isn't edible then as far as I'm concerned nothing is right. Nothing.' Then he yelled while looking at my grandmother. 'And further-more, if you had taught your daughter to do things right I wouldn't have this trouble. I'd be enjoying my Thanksgiving dinner.' We were all silent. No one dared say anything. 'You screwed up again, Helen. Screwed up. I don't know why I put up with you.' Well, mother never said much to defend herself and didn't then. And then she did what she seldom did. She broke down. She looked up with tears in her eyes and said only, 'Lord, John, I've been working so long, I'm so tired. How could you and on Thanksgiving Day.' She left the table and ran upstairs. We were all mortified. But it got worse. Dad then got up and stormed upstairs roaring, 'goddamn it, woman, you get your ass down here. Proper people eat together. A proper lady does not behave this way.' And then we could hear him slap her. It was just aw-ful. I wanted to die for mother, for me, from the embarrassment. Imagine being only nine and being so embarrassed you remember it thirty-one years later. No one said anything. No one did any-thing. We didn't even look at each other. We all wanted to die. In a few moments mother came downstairs. I stole a glance at her. Her head was high. Dad believed we should always walk with our heads high at the worst of times. Her eyes were red and the left side of her face was red from where he had slapped her. I wanted to die or at least cry but I did not dare.

"And then I remember getting mad. So mad that I wanted to get up and scream and use all the filthy rotten words I'd heard him use since I'd been born. I wanted to scream at him and even hit him because he had succeeded in ruining another Thanksgiving, another holiday. Succeeded! Yes, succeeded. I swear my father *tried* to ruin our 'happy holidays.' How else can any of us explain never having a happy one?

"And I also think he enjoyed torturing and degrading my mother. If not, why did he always do it? Anyway, we finished our meal in silence. Even good old dad didn't talk. It was one Thanksgiving I'll never forget. There never were any Thanksgivings that were too much but that one was the worst.

"Dad's cruel and abusive treatment of my mother, if anything, got worse as the years went on. He didn't beat her, uh, regularly or anything like that, but when he did he really hurt her. The last time he touched her was five years ago, just before a stroke put him in a wheelchair. He hit her again and again, then he started choking her until she was unconscious. She was unconscious for almost two days. My brother Thomas was home, thank God, and he called the doctor. My father wouldn't let him call the family physician. For once in his life at least he seemed ashamed of what he had done.

"As a teenager I wondered often why mother put up with it. At first I marveled at it. I thought she was a saint. Then I lost respect for her. For a long time I thought she was a nothing. I've mellowed my opinion about her since she died.

"What changed my mind about her was several very old letters which I found in my maternal grandmother's personal effects after she died. They were letters which mother had sent her after my grandmother had moved to Florida, to be with her sister."

Excerpts from these letters follow:

Letter 1   May 13, 1933
Dear Mother,

. . . The past several years have been a hell-on-earth for me.

John is constantly belittling me.   The church tells me that I should see Christ in my husband. Mother, he's a positive demon. I never told you before but he beats me!

What can I do? Where can I go? I have no money. I have nothing. The priest tells me I can not leave him. He tells me that if I were to leave him I would be living in sin. I can't leave him. I want to but I can not. I have no place to go and I have five children now. I couldn't leave them to the likes of him.

. . . How childish it is to say but how true! Life can be so very unfair! . . .

Pray for me, mother.

Letter 2   December 19, 1938
Dear Mother,

I don't know which way to turn. You saw how impossible he can be. You saw at Thanksgiving dinner. He seems to enjoy humiliating people and me especially.

I've been to the parish priest. He tells me to pray. He tells me that by continuing to live with John my place in heaven is assured. . . . It has to be. This life is hell or at least purgatory. . . .

Oh, mother, what should I do?

Letter 3   April 7, 1947
Mother dearest,

I have to stay with him. What will happen to the children? I'm bound to live with him. I wouldn't know how to go about getting a separation. I raised the question with the new curate. Every time I do so he hushes me up. I think he thinks I'm just some kind of neurotic wife. . . . He's a young priest. . . . . God forgive me, but he's too young to know about life.

He came to the house last week for dinner. John was at his very best. He didn't even pick on me once and he uttered only one "goddamn" the entire evening. I know the priest thinks I'm a spoiled, ungrateful woman. He kept telling John what a good provider he was. John loved him.

After he left John was very nice to me but pointed out that I was a lucky woman. I had so much! God forgive me, mother, but I do believe I've come to hate my husband. I have been so unhappy for so long! Truly, truly, how much pain we can endure and for so long. . . .

Letter 4   September 19, 1948

Dear Mother,

. . . I have so many awful thoughts! Suppose mother church isn't the only road to salvation! Did I absolutely have to live with John all these years? Did I really have to endure all this pain, all these years! . . .

"My mother, I've come to believe, was trapped. She was trapped by her own sense of morality and conscience. She didn't feel she could leave us. She probably did love us. In fact, whatever love we got we got from mother. But she was so harried by my father, all her household duties and her constant unhappiness and worry that she was unable to be very affectionate. Ours was not a loving household.

"Looking back, I guess she was also a very weak woman. Maybe she was weak when she married dad. And he kept her weak. He never helped her to become strong, that's for sure! He liked her weak. It probably made him feel stronger to have someone to lord it over—everybody around him.

"Mother didn't feel she could leave us but I think, too, it was an excuse. We kids provided her with the excuse not to do anything, not to move out. But I may be being unfair. I think sometimes, suppose she had left us during the Depression and we'd been brought up by dad alone! I shudder to think about that!

"Mother may well have been a saint, she made it through a lifetime of hell. But what's also true is that she wasn't much of a person. She never showed me what it means to be a strong, competent mother and wife. She never showed me that. She didn't show me what a really competent woman is. She did not do that. And for that I blame her.

"Sometimes I think she was a masochist. She had to enjoy at least a little bit, always being demeaned, being hit and slapped.

How else could she have put up with it for half-a-century? The priests and nuns would say she had faith, I suppose.

"And a lot of it I blame on the Catholic church. I'll tell you the nuns and priests sure do know how to instill a conscience and the guilt! We grew up with that. *Mea culpa, mea culpa, mea maxima culpa.* Through my fault, through my fault, through my most grievous fault! Mother used to cry that out sometimes when dad hit her or was really mean to her. Imagine that! What kind of respect could I develop for her?

"That's probably why I married a man who wasn't brought up a Catholic. I was rebelling, I guess. We went the whole church route, Communion, Confirmation, Mass every Sunday and holiday. My mother was very religious. She fasted during Lent and even when she didn't have to. She was always visiting the priest. We had priests in for dinner, often. And my father was very much a churchgoer. What good did the church do us? We were more Catholic than most families and I swear my mother was holier than the church in putting up with my father. What good did it all do her? The priests, the church didn't help her or us. They kept telling her that she'd get to heaven, she was sure of it, if she'd accept her life here on earth. She was living in hell and so were her children. What did the church care about it? God forgive me for saying all this but that's the truth about how I feel."

Francis and Maureen (Casey) Whiting died within four months of each other. He was seventy-four, she seventy-one. The Whitings and Conleys were lifetime acquaintances, but not especially friendly with each other. Francis was born, reared, and lived all of his life in Middletown. His wife Maureen was born in Ireland but immigrated to this country and Middletown with her parents when she was four years old. She too has spent her entire life in this same community. Both were reared in the Protestant faith.

Francis was an only child and growing up lived in a very substantial home in a very respectable section of town. The house is still standing. He graduated from high school and attended a two-year business school located in the nearby city. He graduated from business school and obtained a job in a local bank at $15 per week for a forty-five-hour week. The year was 1922. He stayed with this job for exactly one year and left to work as a free-lance accountant for various small businesses in the community. He was to do this during all of his vocational life. And apparently he was able to earn a decent living almost from the start as less than two years later he married Maureen Casey, literally the girl next door. Both sets of parents were delighted with the marriage.

The couple moved into a small apartment in the center of town and within three years the enterprising Francis had saved enough for a down-payment on a relatively new ten-room home within walking distance of Main Street. They lived all of their wedded lives in this house.

Francis, an only child himself, sired four children, Francis Jr., Mary, Phyllis, and Martha. And what kind of a father was he? The consensus among those who knew him (associates and his children) is that he was a very hard-working man, a good provider. He worked late on many evenings in his home office. He was a quiet man and one who rarely intruded upon the family scene. He almost never argued with anyone and seldom even raised his voice.

In 1928 he hired a young clerk, Allen Benton, on a part-time basis. Mr. Benton recalls that, "Francis Whiting, nobody ever called him Frank, was a little bit of a stuffed shirt. He was a very serious man. I don't recall that he smiled much. I remember on occasion being asked to dinner. Incidentally, this was always one or two days in advance, never on the spur of the moment. He was the only man I ever knew who always ate in a suit jacket—at home! He never ate in his shirt sleeves, even in the summer! Meals at the Whiting home were very serious affairs. Can you imagine a serious meal with four kids all under ten years old? I used to leave that house, uh, I don't know, relieved, I guess.

"Mr. Whiting as an accountant was the ideal accountant. I swear the man never made an error. He was a very hard-working guy. He worked nights at a time that white-collar people didn't. But only certain nights: Tuesdays, Wednesdays, and Thursdays. Monday night was Rotary night. He's got to be the only fellow who received an award for not missing a meeting for ten years straight.

He was that kind of person, dependable to a fault, you might say he was like a machine."

A former mayor of the city remembers Francis Whiting very well. "Francis Whiting was my accountant for about forty years. A very competent, dependable fellow. I ran a good sized operation down on Franklin Avenue, car dealership, and Mr. Whiting kept my books. He came in regularly, did his work and left. He was a very able man, never made a mistake. My only criticism about him was that he was, uh, sort of detached, aloof. Not that he was aloof in his work. He wasn't. Like I say, he was a crackerjack accountant. He gave the impression of not being interested in people. He'd come in, say goodmorning, do his work and say goodby. Never once in forty years did he stop to chat. Just zipped in and zipped out. Maybe it's 'cause I'm an old politician but I never thought it was quite right to be like that. I never could understand Francis Whiting. I never could understand him. He was kind of a strange fellow. Competent but strange."

A college teacher who lived next doot to him for forty-five years remembers him as a "taciturn sort of fellow, very much his own man. I never really knew him. He was hardly the gregarious sort. He made out my income tax for me. I would go to his office once a year at income tax time, sit down next to his desk and he'd make it out. He was very efficient and very concerned about my keeping proper records and receipts. He was a very meticulous sort of fellow. He charged me by the hour for the service and kept track of the time to the minute. He had a scrupulous sense of conscience, of fairness. As I think about it I find it really strange that I lived next door to him for such a long time and never really got to know him. That's not so strange today, I know, to live next door to someone for a long time and never get to know him. But you must remember that in those days people knew their neighbors and knew them pretty well."

Perhaps the one who had the keenest insight into Francis and Maureen Whiting was their daughter and third child, Phyllis. Phyllis is a registered nurse who went on for a bachelor's degree in psychology. Presently she is employed as a head nurse in a psychiatric hospital She describes her father in a rather detached,

clinical way. "Father was a conservative, aloof sort of man who
was very much imbued with the Protestant work ethic. In fact
he imbued and very much identified with all of the Pilgrim puri-
tanical values. He was always mouthing values like, 'An idle mind
is the devil's work-shop,' and 'waste not, want not.' He didn't
talk much. He never, well almost never, displayed anger or any
other emotion. I don't remember his ever kissing me, my brother
or any of my sisters. Maybe he did when we were very small, but
I doubt it. He was a dependable fellow and certainly a man of
his word. I doubt that he ever told a lie. If he said he was going
to do something, you could count on it's being done. He was a
man we kids always held in awe. As I think of it, it's funny, we,
or at least I, didn't think of him as a father. He was not the kind
of father that I read about in story books as a child. I have since
learned about what a father is supposed to be. I held him in awe
because he was very quiet, quiet, but not mousey, if you know
what I mean. He was a man who radiated a quiet confidence.
And he was staid. Father wore spats and old-fashioned shirt
collars, you know the kind that were separate from the shirt,
until World War II, when they stopped making them. He always
wore a suit, even at dinner. I don't think I ever saw him eat without one.

"Father was devoid of emotion. He never cracked a joke,
seldom did he smile. He was a humorless man. He was unable
to show affection. I told you before he never kissed any of us
children. I think he thought it was effeminate to show one's
feelings. Perhaps he felt his masculinity was in jeopardy to do so.
But he was the same about displaying anger as he was about displaying love. The most I ever saw him emote was after Roosevelt
was reelected in 1936. Hearing the news of his victory over the
radio, I watched surprised, I do think mother was shocked, as he
clenched his right hand and hit his left plam hard and cried out,
'damn.' I think that's the most I ever saw him show for feeling.
Apparently he hated Roosevelt's government, but he never said
much about it.

"He was a stern man, too. There was an aura about father.
He commanded a lot of respect, I know that, both at home

and in the community. You might interpret my description of him as if he were a 'funny character' type. He was not that. No one, I don't think, saw him as a character. He was sure of himself but not egotistical. He was sure of himself but, uh, uncommunicative and not the sort of person which you could snuggle up to or even sidle up to. You kept you distance. I suppose that's why he was never elected to any office in Rotary even though he seldom failed to attend a meeting. He just wasn't one that you would think to nominate."

Maureen Casey Whiting was a very pretty girl. The many photographs of her as a young and mature woman depict a slender, brown-eyed brunette with regular features. Apparently she kept her figure throughout most of her life. She attended local schools and graduated from high school. Maureen saved every one of her school report cards. They show her to be a satisfactory but undistinguished student. Upon graduation she went to work in the local hospital as a clerical bookkeeper. She quit her job a few weeks before her marriage to Francis Whiting.

Maureen had her four children over the course of fifteen years. Francis Whiting, as noted, was a good provider. He provided her with domestic help, both a part-time cleaning woman (at first one and later on two days per week) and a girl who came afternoons to help with the children.

Maureen was a very efficient mother. She lived on a schedule. Breakfast was served every day at 7:30. Lunch for children and father (Francis always came home for lunch) was on the table at 12:30 and supper time was at 6:00 sharp. Her mornings were filled with the usual housewifely chores which she did thoroughly and well. The Whiting house was always picked up and sparkled cleanly. Her children were maintained in the same way and on their way out to school in the morning were strongly encouraged to remain that way. All of them learned to do so. From all accounts, Maureen Whiting ran a tight ship.

Unlike her husband, she was very active socially. She belonged to several church groups, a garden club, a sewing club, a hospital service group, and a local historical society. In all of these she was a vibrant, active member, held some office in all of them and was elected president of some.

Despite her very busy social schedule and involvements, Maureen has been described as aloof rather than approachable, as distant rather than warm. A woman who had known Maureen during most of her adolescent and adult life offers some interesting comments. "Maureen was a very pretty woman. She dressed well, perhaps not in *haute couture* but well. She was one of those women who wore clothes well. She was physically attractive and knew it. You might say that she was a trifle vain, but only a trifle. Her hair was always done up in the latest fashion. When we were adolescents and even into our early 20s the style was to have your hair piled up. When that was the style she never had a hair out of place. Then bobbed hair came in and she always had a little bit, but just a little bit of her hair appropriately awry.

"Maureen was an American version, but a pretty American version, of England's Queen Victoria who I understand was homely. Maureen could best be described as a woman who did everything appropriately. She never wore too much jewelry, nor too much makeup. But she never went out without either. At the annual tea she put on for the garden club, there were always just the right number of cakes and breads. Not skimpy, not lavish, appropriate. And that's how she was all of her life with people. She wasn't exactly cold, but she was hardly the effusive type either. She was, uh, socially correct. And I think it was this very strong concern of hers, to always be correct or very appropriate, that kept people at a distance. Maureen was not a person whose shoulder you'd cry on.

"You see, everything about Maureen had a purpose. She was a very efficient person and she didn't do anything for nothing. Even her charm, and she could be charming, was turned on only for special occasions, like at the annual garden club tea. She wasn't charming, for example, if you were to just drop in on her. Newcomers to town learned quickly enough that you just didn't drop in on Maureen Whiting. I wasn't a newcomer but once I did that. I don't remember why I did so. She treated me correctly enough, but, uh, coldly. At least I knew I had done the wrong thing. I left her house feeling like I had committed some kind of social sin. She did the same thing to others. I suppose it was because I'd caught her unaware. She was efficient. I guess she had her day planned to the minute and my visit was not included in her schedule. The young people today would say that she was totally 'programmed.' And programmed people are important to have around, too. They get things done. And that was the reason, the major reason, she was elected to so many offices. Everyone knew if Maureen was elected that things would be done and appropriately too. All I'm trying to say here is that you should understand that her elections to office or her popularity was not due to any personal qualities of warmth of personality, but to her efficiency and her, uh, social correctness. She must have been aware of this herself. I don't know how she felt about it. It isn't the kind of thing she would discuss with someone, probably not even with her husband, who was an awfully proper person in his own right.

"She was the pillar of the Congregational Church. She taught Sunday school, even when she had very young children. She coordinated a couple of church bazaars every year. She was the only woman asked to serve on the committee to build the church hall. The men of the church felt they should have a woman on the committee because they planned to include kitchen facilities. Well, Maureen, in typical fashion, offered polite responses to questions about the kitchen layout but ended up designing the kitchen and most of the other facilities of the hall, too. And she did it without offending anyone too. For a woman of her generation she was aggressive but as in everything else, appropriately so."

Maureen at home and Maureen in public were pretty consistent personalities. Phyllis had much to say about her mother. Her view and description are understandably biased and, in that, perhaps she reflects something of her emotional identification with her mother, Maureen. "Like most people, mother was a very complex person. I know what most people said and still say about her, that she was efficient, detached, aggressive but very much a woman, and so on, and so on. But Maureen Whiting was more than all of those things. You see, she was the most important person in my life and in the lives of my brother and sisters. Why?

Because it was she who ran the house. It was she who took care of us, who disciplined us. Even though he had an office in the house and ate lunch with us regularly, father was seldom home. What I mean is he never involved himself in the family. His office might just as well have been in another state. Although he was present at meals, he did not participate in them. When he spoke, he did so only in pronouncements. It wasn't that we didn't respect father, we did. It was that mother was the vital force in the house. She was the queen of the castle and he may well have been the king, but he was *in absentia*, so it didn't matter that he was the king.

"So it was mother who ruled the house. Mother had her rules and her regulations. And she expected that they would be obeyed to the letter. They were. In fact, it never occurred to any of us not to obey them. Mother was not the kind of person whom one disobeyed. Mother was stern, very stern, but very fair. She had an exquisite sense of justice. Mother mediated all the disputes among us kids. Her judgments were always accepted as final, and what I realize now is that they were because they were eminently fair.

"Mother was not just the source of discipline in our home, she was also the only source of love. I already pointed out to you that father was a very unemotional man, not a hugger. Well, for that matter mother wasn't much of a hugger either. Stroking, fondling, hugging were not part of the family scene. But you should know that demonstrative love wasn't totally nonexistent in the house. Mother's helpers often expressed their love that way. They were Polish, Irish, Italian ethnic types who were far more emotional than either of my parents. So we children were exposed to it but it wasn't part of the parental-child relationship. We children came to understand that love was expressed through hard work (both my parents were very hard working), meeting one's familial obligations and duties, being fair with each other and most importantly, never demeaning each other. Mother never tolerated infractions in any of those areas.

"More than anything else what I learned from my mother was that one can meet the obligations which life imposes. And what's more, one can do this with propriety or, as they say today, 'with a flair!' What I learned from my mother, who was very feminine, is that love can be expressed in different ways. Mother was very feminine but she wasn't nurturant in the traditional, demonstrative way. I don't remember any of us running up to her crying to obtain solace for a hurt. We must have done so when we were very small but I suppose we learned early not to fall and get hurt. I never thought about it but while most other children had minor accidents, minor accidents were not part of our family scene either. Minor accidents precipitated emotional displays and as I'm sure you've learned by now, emotional displays were not considered good form. It's hard to explain all this because you see none of it was ever explained to us but it was indeed communicated. We all learned it and very well. And I know too that our family, our home sounds like it was a cold, mechanistic place. If it was we never knew it. We accepted it. It worked and it worked very well. You see, there were never any passionate arguments or fights or anything even remotely like that. You see, our parents' concern in bringing us up was not to make us happy. They brought us up to make ourselves happy. I've learned over the years that people love in their own special way. Our parents loved us by teaching us that love involves industry, responsibility, inconvenience, hard work, courtesy, and consideration. And if our home was cold and devoid of unnecessary emotion, it was also very serene, and I might add, a nice place to live.

"At least it was for my sisters and me. You should get another view of our home from Francis. It would be only fair to do so. You see, I have the greatest respect for mother. I'm not sure that Francis does. But to be truthful, I don't know how he feels. Francis is pretty much a close-mouthed person, he always has been.

"As I indicated to you before, our home gave a lot to me and to my sisters. And we got it all from my mother. I don't know how Francis feels about it."

Francis Whiting Jr. is a tall, broad shouldered man with thinning sandy hair and a thickening waist. As were the other interviews, he was asked to either tape or write down his observations. Phyllis' observation that her brother was "close-mouthed" seemed confirmed by the fact that he chose to write down his thoughts rather than tape them. When he turned in his effort, almost a month after he was asked to do so, he observed, "I'm not much of a talker. I preferred writing it all down. That way I can check what I say, think about it all better. Kathleen, my wife, changed some of the words to make it read better. But it's like I want it." Francis Jr. is a self-employed carpenter and house builder.

"As I understand it, I'm supposed to write down what I thought about my parents. I prefer to write it. I think I'd be too embarrassed saying it. I think that's because of how I was brought up. I was brought up different than most kids. That's why I'm a loner today. I don't shine up to people too easily. Frankly, I find it hard talking to them.

"I remember when I was about ten years old overhearing two women who'd come to my house for one of those teas mother was always having. One of them described my mother as Queen Victoria and my father as her consort, whatever that is, Albert. The other lady, new to town, laughed hard. I didn't know what the description meant. But I never forgot the conversation. I remembered it for years. Funny, huh? I also remember as a junior in high school listening to my history teacher describe Queen Victoria. I'll never forget his words, 'pompous, prim, proper, and prudish.' Those words fit mother. They fit father too. They fit them both to a 'T.'

"I was a disappointment to my parents. I know they wanted me to go to college and a place like Amherst or Harvard too. I didn't like school, not one whit. I wanted to go to vocational school to learn to become a carpenter. When I raised the question with my parents, first my mother, then my father, I got the same reaction from both, first bewilderment, then a cold, matter-of-fact 'no.' I dared to raise the question again, with my father alone. It was the only time I ever tried talking to him. He was reading the paper in the living room. I remember he was in his shirt sleeves, and that was unusual 'cause if he didn't have his suit jacket on he always wore his 'Chesterfield' or smoking jacket. Anyway, he was reading and I asked about the transfer. He put the paper down, took off his glasses and started polishing them with a small cloth he kept in his watch pocket. I knew right then that he was going to say no. And I also knew that he was polishing his glasses 'cause he wanted to be careful of the words he used. Father was as thrifty with his words as he was with his money. (A fellow I know said this about me. I guess I'm like my father in how I use money and words.) Anyway, he finally put on his glasses (never talked without them on), looked me straight in the eyes and said as kindly as he could, 'Francis, please know this. There is no future in carpentry. Carpenters have always earned poorly. I see nothing to suggest that they will do better in the future. We are presently in the midst of an economic depression. Even the college graduates have a very difficult time finding work. Those of lesser education find none. Education is the vehicle to a better life. You should think about an education, about becoming a professional person. You will have the respect of the community. In the end, Francis, respect is what out lives are all about.' It was the longest speech that I ever heard father make, to me or anybody else. Usually he spoke in no more than four or five word sentences at one time.

"One thing I want to make clear, father really believed in his way of life. At least he lived it like he believed it. He was no hypocrite. My problem growing up was that I didn't believe in much of what mother and father did. I liked working with my hands. I knew that. At fifteen I was already a pretty fair carpenter. I worked part-time afternoons and Saturdays with a carpenter (father was proud of that). And I hated school and books and studying. (He wasn't proud of that.) I didn't understand about the respect that father spoke of. A man should do what he's fit for. Maybe I never understood my father. I couldn't talk to him. I know he never understood me. He couldn't talk to me. See, I think first a man has to respect himself. I couldn't respect myself in school. Books never helped me to respect myself. I wasn't good with books. I've always been good with wood. When I finish a house I feel ten feet tall. Books made me feel real small.

"I wish that I'd been able to tell my father what I just wrote,

'I'm good with wood.' But if I had he wouldn't have understood. With him what you liked wasn't as important as what was the right thing to do. Problem was that what was right always was what *HE* thought was right. If you saw 'right' another way, he'd give you one of his looks—either pity or surprise, and even though he'd been awfully polite, you'd always feel like you were wrong. Mother was even better at this than father. I've figured out that that was because a person always felt very inadequate in front of my parents. My parents were very sure of themselves. Most of us aren't. Most of us are just people who aren't too sure of ourselves. Father never seemed to understand that. Neither did my mother.

"Of the four kids I'm probably the one who turned out to be the biggest disappointment. Phyllis once wrote a paper when she was in college about our family. It was supposed to be about my mother but it turned out to be about the whole family. The way she put it, I was the rebel of the family. Maybe I was. I didn't live up to the standards of my parents. I wasn't a good student, I wanted a trade. Phyllis and the other two graduated from college, I didn't. She thinks I brought the family down.

"I don't know if she's right or not. She's like mother, all hung up on what others might think or not think. I could care less. A man has got to do what he thinks is right for himself. Period. My parents didn't give me that notion. I learned that myself.

"As a matter of fact, my parents really didn't give me much at all. That's probably why I was always very shy as a kid. I never had many friends. I was very lonely. I took that part-time job because I didn't have anything else to do.

"I remember once my mother describing me to a friend of hers as being very quiet. What else could I be? She and father spoke only the 'truth.' When they were through with their pronouncements there wasn't much left to say. So I learned not to ever say too much. I leaned to be by myself. I learned to like wood.

"My mother was very active in the church but she wasn't especially religious. We went to church often as a family but we didn't go every single Sunday in the winter, fall and spring. We didn't go at all in July and August. I don't think I ever saw my parents pray in the house. My mother did teach Sunday school for about three years. During that period that she did we all had to go over our Sunday morning lessons on Saturday with her. All of us kids had to sit at the dining room table and study and answer the questions she asked about our lessons. I know now that mother didn't make us go through this because she wanted us to be religious. She did it because she didn't want other people to think that the children of a Sunday school teacher didn't know their lessons. It wasn't for us that she spent an hour and a half every Saturday morning with us, it was to keep up her image of the efficient wife and mother. It was for herself that she did it.

"So religion was part of the scene at home. But religion in my house was, how to put it, permitted and it was because in a real way it supported my mother's and father's notions about how to live. Nobody ever talked about God at home but they did talk abut honesty and the 'nobility of work' and thrift and courtesy. These were the important virtues. There were others which I don't remember now. Anyway, they were held up to us kids like they all came from God or at least the Congregational Church. You might say that my parents seemed to have their own religion and they let the church support them in their beliefs.

"My sisters would say that my parents gave me my love of work and my sense of honesty. That's a lot of crap! I learned to love work, but if I do and I'm not so sure I do anymore, it's because I had to escape the house and my family and how they made me feel. And I went to work to escape the boredom and the loneliness. Any maybe a little because I had the feeling that my father was proud to have a kid who worked. My mother didn't seem to care one way or another, if anything she was a little embarrassed because my work was, as she put it, 'manual.'

"The girls looked up to mother. Phyllis especially is very much like her, sort of cold and a know-it-all. Yes, mother was a know-it-all, but a kind of refined know-it-all. People respected mother, I know that, but not because of the kind of person she was so much as the fact she lived what she believed. She was honest,

I'll say that for her.

"I never liked my mother because she never let me. Mother never showed me love, she never showed anybody love for that matter. She never kissed us kids. I know that's one of my troubles today, showing my feelings, talking about them. Showing your feelings is a big thing today (I learned that from TV). That's my problem. I can't show how I feel about things, about people. If it's true that we learn to be what and who we are, then I blame my mother and father. Our home didn't school us in showing our emotions.

"And how do I feel about them today? I guess I'm indifferent toward my father. I don't know how I feel about him. I know how I feel about my mother. I don't like her, even her memory. I feel I was neglected by her. Even though my father never showed me much, I guess I don't feel it was his job to do that. He was the provider for the family. It was mother's job to take care of me. And she did but only on the surface, where it really doesn't count. Mother never really cared about the 'underneath' of people, even her kids, at least this kid.

"So I didn't get too much from my mother, I think the girls did though. They're like her. But what's interesting is that none of them have married. They're all smart, educated and pretty but they're not married. And I think it's because they're like me, they never learned how to show their feelings. They're cold fish. A man doesn't want a wife who's a cold fish."

The Conleys and The Whitings

Comparison and Contrast

The Conleys and Whitings were very different families. The Conley family was very much a patriarchal unit. Although physically absent much of the time John Conley's presence was constantly felt, indeed, he "hung like a pall over the house" much of the time. His brand via personality and decorative taste was imprinted on the house and its contents, "right to the drapes and bedspreads." He even dictated the kinds of clothes which the Conley women were to wear and the material which they could read.

His values and his neuroses intruded on every aspect of family life. Thus, he was vitally concerned that his family be viewed as proper and respectable (especially in the women's department) yet he himself was unable to interact with refinement, either within or outside the family. For example, his language both at home and at work was vile. His public faux pas became legendary. The observers' consensus seems to be that John Conley was a despot and not a benevolent one.

The Whiting family, on the other hand, seemed to be very much a matriarchy. This, despite the fact that Mr. Whiting "was a man the kids held in awe," and "a man who radiated a quiet confidence." If John Conley controlled his family via bullying, beating, and bellowing, Maureen Whiting ruled her house with a quiet, almost serene-like efficiency. Her life was scheduled, perhaps even programmed. The children were expected to conform to her husband's and her own schedule, values, and expectations. On the surface (which seemed to be the maternal concern) at least, they did. It was Maureen's vital, purposeful, appropriate aggressiveness which permeated and would seem to have dominated and molded the personalities of her girls. Her son today would seem to be the person he is in large measure because of the type of person she was and/or wasn't. He remembers her with distaste but the girls apparently identified with her. He remembers her as a "refined know-it-all." Phyllis remembers her as "the most important person in my life. . . . the queen of the castle." Perhaps the most communicative description of Maureen Whiting lies in the two independent observations of her as "Queen Victoria" . . . "it was mother who ruled the house . . . she had an exquisite sense of justice . . . mediated all the disputes . . . her judgments were always accepted as final . . . they were eminently fair." For Phyllis and her sisters she was an effective "Queen Victoria." Francis, however, never liked her "and deplores his inability to emote today, attributes it to his mother's unwillingness or inability to deal with the emotional (underneath part) aspects of his personality."

To continue, the Conley household was an emotionally charged household. The beatings, the hollering, the strict demands and expectations of John Conley together with the famous Conley "instant temper" kept the whole family in a constant state of anxiety.

The Whiting household was different in that on the surface at least, the house ran in an efficient, serene and very appropriate way. Phyllis observed for us that "there were never any passionate arguments or fights or anything even remotely like that . . . our home . . . was also very serene . . . and . . . a nice place to live."

A very important difference between the two households was the role and impact of the mother. Mrs. Conley, we learned, was passive-dependent in her relations to her husband, if not ineffectual in her own right. Mrs. Whiting, on the other hand, was very much her own person and thoroughly competent.

Despite these significant differences between the two families there were at the same time important similarities. Communication between parents and between parents and children was virtually nil. In neither family did people seem to talk to each other. John Conley issued edicts fully expecting to be obeyed. And he was. Often he "blew up" for the least provocation. The best that can be said for him and the family milieu is that everyone knew how he felt all the time. Seldom did anyone know how anyone else felt. Except for John Conley no one else had an opportunity to express thoughts, feelings or emotions, especially if they were negative ones. Any frustrations which Helen or the children might feel were ignored, were not considered worthy of attention. The Conley home then was very much father-centered. Familial interaction was virtually nonexistent since the only emotional needs to be met were those of John. The climate created by John's despotism served to block emotional expression and communication.

The Whiting household was generally peaceful. Phyllis tells us that there were relatively no arguments among the children. Maureen never permitted them, "emotional displays were not considered good form." From what we know about Maureen and Francis it would be hard to conceive of any kind of heated arguments between the parents (especially in the presence or within the hearing of the children). The parents apparently had a very similar understanding about the rearing of children. Children for them were not so much human beings to be loved as they were little people to be appropriately conditioned in the right values. Their lack of concern, even indifference for how their children may have felt about anything sprang not from callousness nor cruelty but from their Victorian-like convictions about emotions and communication in general. Emotional display, especially such feelings as anger, love, sadness, gladness or despair, interfered with one's social decorum. And social decorum was of paramount importance because if one lost his social decorum, he lost the respect of others. In the Whiting house Maureen (and Francis to a lesser extent as he was "in absentia") was the personification of social decorum. According to Francis Jr. there were two emotions which were used by the Whiting parents, these were pity and surprise. The pity and surprise were displayed with a latent but definite condescension and always with exquisite manners and self-control. The effect upon the children was unmistakable, "You'd always feel like you were wrong." It is doubtful if this interpersonal method of the Whiting parents was calculated, or premeditated. It doesn't matter. The climate effected was the same as that achieved in the Conley household, it served to bar emotional expression and communication among family members.

Both families had fathers who were strong personalities in their own right. But there the similarities ended. Thus it was that while Francis scarcely participated within the family, John ruled with an iron hand. Francis complemented and generally supported his wife's behavior. John, on the other hand, at best ignored Helen, often demeaned her and at times even beat her. Both fathers verbalized a strong concern with propriety but while one lived it, the other behaved both at home and publicly in a crude and vulgar fashion.

An individual's personality is in considerable measure a function of what he learns at home. The parental personalities are critical determinants for whatever values, attitudes, ideas and ideals the individual will incorporate into his personality. What then did Francis Whiting Jr. learn from his home, from his parents? And, what did Kathleen Conley learn from her home?

Francis learned that fathers are strong and that they control. The paternal will may be rightfully exercised at any time but should always be exercised with courtesy and self-control. He was made to understand, too, that emotional displays are crass and inappropriate and have little or no place in the paternal method of relating.

One of his most important learnings was that women control more than men, especially within the home. Indeed, at home, women are far more influential than men. A basic aspect of the maternal role, he concluded, is to rear the children. He learned that women are emotionally detached, not warm but cold. He learned that women are difficult to get close to.

He learned too, that a most important, if not the most important, value is to make a good impression. Both his parents cherished the respect of other people. It seemed to be their raison d'étre.

It should be noted, however, that self-respect seems to have acquired a higher priority in his value system than what others thought. Thus, his own words are, ". . . first a man has to respect himself."

Unquestionably he learned about the "nobility of work." And he found work enhancing. Indeed, the more he worked, the more he felt enhanced. He escaped boredom, loneliness, and gained the *respect* of his father. Moreover, from the earliest years he learned that a man works. It is his basic role in the same way that it is a woman's basic role to rear the children.

Even at this early point in the design of the Whiting family profile we can see that Francis Whiting entered marriage ill equipped emotionally to deal with the obligations imposed by the roles of husband and father. We have learned enough to know that the values, ideas and ideals which were held out to him as being important, desirable and rewarding were not those which are conducive to the creation of a warm, nurturant, and loving home.

It might be well to point out what Francis did *not* learn at home. Indeed, he himself points out that there was much with which he did not identify, there was much which he rejected, "I was the rebel of the family. Maybe, I was . . ." He did not learn how to relate effectively to others, men or women. Indeed, his own words in this regard are, ". . . I'm a loner today. I don't shine up to people too easily. Frankly, I find it hard talking to them." And he holds his parents responsible for this. ". . . my parents really didn't give me much at all."

Francis felt unloved at home. It is for this reason that he may well have never learned to give or receive love with a feeling of reward. "I never liked my mother because she never let me. Mother never showed me love. . . . She never kissed us. I know that's one of my troubles, showing my feelings." He indicates again and again that his father was comparable to his mother as far as being demonstrably affectionate, and thus as far as teaching him about love.

Quite probably, Francis today is a person with low feelings of self-worth. We find that this is true of the individual reared without love and who feels that he has failed to meet parental expectation of success. And Francis is apparently quite sensitive about his inability to meet his parents' standards. He alluded to this when he wrote that "Of the four kids I'm probably the one who turned out to be the biggest disappointment . . . I didn't live up to the standards of my family . . . I wasn't a good student . . . I brought the family down."

Quite probably, Francis learned that religion is very much associated with propriety. He learned that it should be part of the family scene but only in a casual way. As he came to understand it, the prime value of religion is to support you in how you want to be, how you want to act, how you want to live. It should not so much interfere in your life as it should enhance it. Some of his thoughts in this regard are, ". . . my parents had their own religion and they let the church support them in their beliefs."

And what did Kathleen Conley learn and not learn at home? Unquestionably the learning which was impressed upon her most strongly was that a man in his role of father is a very strong person. He is dominant, aggressive, and very controlling. Fathers walk all over mothers, perhaps men walk all over women. Certainly they walk all over children. Via her father, too, she learned that a man is capable of much crudity and vulgarity, both in his social realtions and in familial ones. Swearing, for example, she learned is very much a part of the masculine scene.

One of her most painful learnings, and again via her father, is that a man can be positively cruel and unkind. He could be a "monster." A man, she found out at home, can and does beat up a woman—and worse—a woman takes it, and passively. As a consequence of all these learnings she acquired another one, namely that a man engenders inordinate amounts of anxiety. In this regard she wrote, "We were always so nervous when he was around. . . . He made life miserable for all of us."

The mother and woman image presented to her was very different. A woman, especially in her role as a wife and mother, is weak, dependent, and generally passive. Indeed, in these roles she tends to function incompetently because a woman at home functions as a man's servant. She is dependent upon him because she has no economic wherewithal to escape or to even remedy the situation. A woman, she learned, may "trap" herself because she is not assertive. Perhaps she learned that a woman is not assertive by nature.

Kathleen learned, too, that a man is the provider for the family. A woman apparently puts up with him or has to because he does provide the daily bread. He works and works hard. He's out most of the time but the home is *his* home. A woman is only his tenant. She has privileges but these privileges a man can take away at will.

Kathleen came to understand also that the feelings and frustrations which a woman or children have are unimportant. A man does not care about them.

What others think about you and your family was also a value held out to her and constantly. To be a "proper young lady" was very important. Kathleen indicates, or at least implies strongly, that it was a value which engendered frustration, even hostility. It is not unlikely that for Kathleen propriety came to be associated with emotional pain.

Religion, too, came to be associated with pain. Why? Because the church seemed to support rather than ameliorate the unholy status quo at home. Home was a place of constant and unmitigated anxiety and Kathleen growing up kept hearing how her mother should accept her lot. At no point did a priest try to intervene or even try to ameliorate the domestic climate.

As is true with Francis, then, we can safely assume at this point that Kathleen was not exposed to an emotional climate which would teach her how to be a successful parent. What is undoubtedly true is that much hostility and frustration were instilled into her. For example, two fundamental and negative learnings were acquired, namely, "Life can be cruel and love is not obtained at home." Thus, she speaks much about the cruelty at home, "Dad's cruel and abusive treatment of my mother . . . He was cruel to my mother . . . living with my father was an exercise in learning to live with pain and cruelty." On the topic of love at home (and it is most interesting to note that in her long discussion she alludes to it but briefly), "She probably did love us. In fact, whatever love we got we got from mother. But she was so harried by my father, all her household duties and her constant unhappiness and worry that she was unable to be very affectionate. Ours was not a loving household."

Discussion Questions

1. Explain how John Conley perceived himself and his role in the family.
2. To what extent was Helen, John's wife, responsible for her problems?
3. How would you rate family life among the Conleys?
4. Summarize what Kathleen Whiting learned and did not learn at home about herself, and about men.
5. Would you have predicted that she would become illegitimately pregnant? Why? Why not?
6. How would you rate Maureen Whiting as a mother, as a wife?
7. Was Maureen's husband a successful husband and father? Why or why not?
8. How would you rate life among the Whitings?
9. Summarize what Francis learned and did not learn about himself, and about women.
10. Would you have predicted that he would father an illegitimate child? Why? Why not?

Chapter 4

FOCUS GUIDES

1. The social worker writes that Mr. Whiting is a "boring, introverted man with many personal problems." Consider what the effects would be on a boy growing up in such a family.
2. Reflect upon John's perception of the world: "phony, crooked, and nobody gives a crap." Why would such a perception of the world lead to problems?
3. Think about John's indentity confusion. Does his relationship with Dee ameliorate it or compound it?
4. Consider if John's problems are very different or more serious than most kids his age.

Michael Fontina, twenty-six and the newest member of the Middletown Police Force, looked at his watch. The luminous dial shone brightly, 10:30 p.m. Another half-hour and he could take his coffee "and." Connie would be waiting at the diner for him, a brief but very pleasant break from this "drag" duty.

He coasted the cruiser down the steep but short incline and parked there. He was behind Middletown's newest and biggest shopping plaza. He got out, flashed the light on a door, checked it and ambled casually around the building, flashlight out.

As he rounded the first corner he saw a car and then, a second. They were parked close together. Too close. Mike edged noiselessly up to the second car and watched the kid screw out a tape deck. Mike felt like he was at ringside! The kid never heard him.

Mike flashed on the light and said almost softly, "What the hell do you think you're doing, kid? Get out slow and easy." The boy looked up and then backed out of the car, feet first. Mike grabbed him, leaned him hard up against the car and searched him with lightning speed. Christ, the kid didn't even have a wallet on him! "What were you doing?," he repeated. This time harshly.

"Nuthin'."

"Nothing! For Christ's sake, kid, is this your car?"

"No, that one is," he mumbled jerking his head.

The kid had left the dismantled tape deck on the front seat. "O.K., pick up the tape deck and let's go. You're under arrest."

Officer: Michael Fontina, Badge No. 42   Today's Date

Arrested Subject: John Whiting, Age 16

Approximately 10:30 P.M. this date, I encountered John Whiting forcibly breaking and entering the motor vehicle of William Norling, Mass. Registration A–12349.   This vehicle was legally parked within the parking lot of Princess Department Store. One other store in the same complex was open for business.

I personally observed subject using a screwdriver with which he removed a cassette radio from its original place, and some tapes from a container.   I ordered John Whiting out of the car, searched him and placed him under arrest for larceny over $100.00

Subject was driven forthwith to Police Headquarters where I advised him of his rights and booked him.* He was charged with aforementioned crime.   I then notified Chief Probation Officer that John is a juvenile. The Chief Probation Officer ordered me to release the boy in the parents' custody to await arraignment. I did so.

Michael J. Fontina
Arresting Officer

*See attached enclosure.

Arrest Book Entry

Address: 59 Beaumont Street
             Middletown
Date of Birth: 3 September 19
Place of Birth: Middletown
Social Security No.: 049-22-1011
Mother's Name: Kathleen Conley Whiting

Father's Name: Francis Whiting Jr.
Parental Residences: Same

Alleged Offense: Larceny over $100 (Cassette Radio)
Arresting Officer: Michael J. Fontina
Date of Arraigment: 2 June

Disposition: Probation—6 months
Addenda: Mandatory one week conference with Probation
         Officer. Parents have promised to enter into Family
         Therapy.

REPORT OF SOCIAL WORKER

John Whiting lives about three miles from the center of town.
The house is situated on an acre and is approximately twenty
years old and of a colonial type architecture. It's big, rambling
and was built by Mr. Whiting himself. He's a self-employed
carpenter. There is a long, gravel driveway leading up to it,
trees, flowers, and shrubbery abound. Nothing is too well maintained, however.

Mrs. Whiting is a pretty, auburn-haired woman who looks
much younger than her forty years. Mr. Whiting is only a few
years older than she but looks to be in his middle fifties at least.
Both appear to be unhappy, even desolate. I should note here
that it was Mrs. Whiting who responded to my questions in one
or two word answers. He was polite but noncommunicative.
He was not unfriendly, however.

They are very concerned about John. Mrs. Whiting reported
that to the best of her knowledge the trouble started only recently. It seems that in the past month they have had to see
school authorities about John. He was involved in selling marijuana in the school. I checked on this with the assistant principal,
Mr. Sortino, and found that it was indeed true. Mr. Sortino caught
him at it. Also in the past week Mrs. Whiting has had to go down
to the police station to pick up John. He had been involved in a
fight in front of the South End Dairy Bar. He was very drunk

according to Sgt. Perkins who was on duty that night. Officers
Acito and Mazzola, who stopped the fight, reported that John
was choking the other person (also a teen-ager) and might well
have killed the fellow if they had not intervened.

Mrs. Whiting reports that she and her husband have been
married for twenty years. They have two older boys, Thomas
and Francis III, neither of whom are living at home any longer.
They are rooming together on Green Street here in town. Both
boys, she indicated, were also problems growing up but not to
the extent that John is presently. Neither had ever been involved
in any law breaking. There is also a younger sibling, Alice, who
is twelve years old.

If nothing else, Mrs. Whiting is genuinely and sincerely concerned about all this turmoil with John. Mr. Whiting gave me this
same impression. She feels that, "Everything is closing in on
me." Three months ago she was admitted to the State Psychiatric
Hospital. She states that it was for nervous exhaustion and
depression. I was unable to obtain the hospital records to confirm
this diagnosis. At any rate she was in the hospital for approximately
three weeks. She states she enjoyed her stay as it got her away
from (her words) "family pressures and demands." These pressures have now all returned via John's delinquencies. Several
times during the interview she murmured, "We're in trouble in
this family," or "We're a family in trouble," or words to that
effect. At this point I would be inclined to agree.

Later on in the conversation she indicated that her depression
and consequent stay in the hospital was a function of an unwanted
pregnancy. She miscarried while in the hospital. She explained
this miscarriage to herself then and does now as "God's will."
She believes this because it is the only miscarriage which she has
ever experienced. Another baby, she honestly believes, especially
at this time, would have (her words) "sent me over the edge."

I asked her what were the "family pressures and demands"
which had brought on her "nervous exhaustion and depression."
Her response was vague. "Mostly it was the pregnancy, the worry
of it." One more time I inquired about "family pressures" to
which she had first alluded. "I don't know honestly. It's probably

all tied up with being bored, with being a bored housewife.'' I believe her, that is I believe that she didn't know, that it may well be tied up with being bored. I believe in retrospect that Mrs. Whiting did not want to use her husband as a scapegoat, but that she very much had him on her mind when she talked about being bored. There is little question that Mr. Whiting is a very quiet man. I could understand a woman feeling bored when with him.

My best judgment on the basis of this interview is that Mr. Whiting is a detached introverted man who does not involve himself very much in the family. According to Mrs. Whiting, and he did not object, it was she who brought up the children, she who disciplined, she who rewarded them. It seems to be a lone parent family with two parents. What seems to compound the problem further is the fact that Mrs. Whiting is very much an emotionally dependent person. Her husband, however, does not seem to be one upon whom she can lean. He has too many problems of his own. I do not know what these problems are specifically, but they do indeed interfere with his ability to be a nurturant, demonstratively-loving husband. Mrs. Whiting's present desolate condition is a dramatic testimony to this. Also, Mr. Whiting's obviously unhappy state may well be an indirect function of his feelings of ineptitude as a husband.

According to Mrs. Whiting, her pregnancy with John was perfectly normal. She did not gain a disproportionate amount of weight (22 lbs.), she suffered no morning sickness or any difficulty of any kind. She delivered John as a full term baby. He weighed 8 lbs. 3 ounces.

As a child John followed almost a sterotyped developmental progression. He crept at nine months, and walked at just under a year. He was able to feed himself before he was two. He was trained fully before he was three-and-a-half.

According to Mrs. Whiting, John was a very easy child to rear. He was a passive, introverted child who accepted maternal requests easily and gracefully. Virtually no paternal demands were ever made.

An interesting aspect of John's childhood was his uncommon

and abiding interest in religion, specifically the Roman Catholic faith, its doctrines and teachings. According to Mrs. Whiting, John took to his C.C.D. (Confraternity of Christian Doctrine) classes in a positively zealous fashion. He led his first Communion class in knowledge of prayers and doctrine. He was rewarded for his efforts and at the first Communion class served the Mass. The pastor of the church, a Father Carrig, reports that John Whiting learned the Mass prayers and routine faster than any boy he'd ever known. Father Carrig is now sixty-two.

John's devotion to religion did not end with his first Communion (age seven) nor with his Confirmation (age twelve). In between those years he served Mass as an Acolyte of the church (altar boy) on the average of four times per week. And if John did not serve the Mass, he attended it, seven o'clock, virtually every day.

Mrs. Whiting was heartened by this behavior. She's a Catholic. Mr. Whiting, who is a nonchurch-going Protestant, apparently was indifferent, at least he admittedly never took notice of John's zealous involvement in religious life. Mrs. Whiting was heartened by John's spirituality. She observed him often kneeling by his bed saying his rosary. The latter was a gift from his maternal grandmother on the occasion of his first Communion. John hung them on his bedpost and according to his mother fingered them to sleep every night. She reports that until he was fourteen or so, he often spoke to her about becoming a priest.

John's inordinate interest in the church, its teaching and its practices, continued unabated into the ninth grade, his last year of junior high school. Sometime during that year his daily attendance at Mass began to wane. It never perked up. Presently he does not attend church at all.

Until the age of fourteen John's life was fairly typical. He had a goodly number of friends, was a better-than-average student in school, played in Little League and even the Babe Ruth League. In the winter he sledded and ice skated. His teachers (third, fifth and one seventh grade) remember him as a quiet, serious boy who laughed uproariously when another boy did or said something even marginally funny. They report that while he was not a leader he was well liked by his peers.

Perhaps the most significant fact about John's life for the past couple of years is that he's been heavily involved with a girl, Diane Henessey. He calls her "Dee." They have been going together since the middle of tenth grade. His mother says that he spends virtually all of his free time with her. They are, according to her, "inseparable." Mrs. Whiting does not know Mrs. Henessey but has the distinct impression, on the basis of a short phone conversation, that John is *persona non grata* in the Henessey home. She herself likes "Dee" and sees her frequently as John brings her home four or five times per week. This pleases her, but it worries her a little too. Perhaps they are spending too much time together. I asked pointedly if it concerned sex. She blushed a little (Mr. Whiting did too) but admitted she'd not brought it up to John. She did not know how to approach the topic. This is a point which might be explored by Dr. Morissey, the psychologist.

Ethel Johnson, MSW
Consulting Case Worker

DIAGNOSTIC INTERVIEW WITH JOHN WHITING

CLINICAL INTERVIEW WITH JOHN WHITING

(Edited and Condensed)

M: Hi! John Whiting?

J: Yeah.

M: Hi! I'm Dr. Morrissey. Judge O'Brien asked me to see you, so we could talk, and so I could test you and . . .

J: You a shrink?

M: [Chuckle]   Yes, I guess so.   I'm a clinical psychologist.

J: Huh, [kind of grunt].

M: I'm supposed to learn about you and write a report.

J: What for?

M: Well, so the Judge can be more intelligent about how he deals with your case.
     [Pause, with no comment from John]

As I understand it, you were caught, uh, stealing a cassette radio.

[No comment from John]

Is that correct?

J: [long pause] Guess so.

M: [softly]   Uh, how do you explain what you did, John?

J: I don't.

M: You just did it.

J: Yeah.

(At this point I was unsure of where I was going. John was one of the more reticent boys I'd seen to date. I was probing blindly, hoping I'd get a response which would provide me with some meaningful data. I didn't want to ask the absurd, "Why did you do it!" I felt he didn't know why and at this point had he known I doubted he'd share the reason. Up to this point his responses had been characterized by a marked surliness.   With my next question his surliness began to dissipate.)

M: Uh, John, do you have a girl?

J: Yeah.

M: How long have you known her?

J: Couple years.

M: What's she like?

J: She's a girl.

M: Oh, come now. [chuckle] You can do better th . . .

J: She's sort of, uh, blond and long hair and [sheepishly] pretty.

M: You've never described her to anyone before.

J: No.

M: How does she feel about all this?

J: She's not happy.

M: [laugh] I suppose she's not. What's her name?

J: Dee.

M: For Diane?

J: Yeah.

M: You've been going with her for a year or so.

J: Yeah. She's real.

M: What do you mean by that?

J: Dee's for real.

M: Everybody else is phony?

J: Yeah and crooked and doesn't give a crap.

M: I see. The world is full of dishonest, uncaring people.

J: Yeah, right. It's a rip-off world.

M: And you're ripping off the cassette was just part of the bigger scene.

J: Right on. That's a good way to put it.

M: You feel any, uh, guilt over it now?

J: Nah. Guy got his radio back.

M: Suppose he hadn't?

J: Well, he can afford it, new car.

M: I see. [pause]   You really believe that or are you putting me on?

J: [chuckle]   Maybe a little. But it is a rip-off world. I believe that. [pause] I learned that when I was only a kid. I used to watch TV every Saturday morning. One of the cartoon shows advertised that if you sent in fifty cents and two cereal box tops you'd get a secret message recorder and a ring to keep the secrets in. I was a kid and a sucker. I believed it.

M: You sent in the money and the box tops.

J: Yeah, and I waited and I waited and I waited. You know, to an eight-year-old or whatever I was, a week's a helluva long time. I must've been nine before I got the stuff.

M: And?

J: And it was crap. The secret recorder was a piece of paper with writing I couldn't understand and the ring was made out of plastic to fit the finger of a grown-up. Rip-off. Lookin' back that's when I started to see it. [pause] Even though I wouldn't admit it. See, [chuckle, but not too convincing] I used to be very religious.

M: Oh, tell me about that.

J: Tell what?

(John liked to tease. There was now a kind of constant mocking quality in his tone. It wasn't exactly belligerent or even unfriendly, however, as it was complemented by a

little ironic smile which played around his mouth and oc-
casionally showed in his eyes.)

M: About being religious. You're a Catholic.

J: I was.

M: You're not now?

J: I don't know what I am. Who knows?
[pause] Who knows.
(I could have pursued this comment on his identity or lack
of it. I chose not to. I was more interested in his thoughts
regarding the church and thereby about his conscience,
amorality, etc.: Was he a full-blown socio-path? At this
point I didn't know.)

M: You were very religious, you said that I think.

J: Yeah, I was an altar boy. I used to serve Mass damn near
every day. [pause] You know I wanted to be a priest once.
In fact for a long time I wanted to be a priest. [pause] My
mother used to like that. I think she was proud of me for
that, for wanting to be a priest, I mean.

M: I gather you're not too keen on the church now.

J: Nah, 'nother rip-off.

M: The church is too? Why do you say that?

J: You know what turned me off?

M: Tell me.

J: The whole money thing. Always askin' for money. Christ!

M: You resented that.

J: Well, maybe not just askin' but like the priest would be
elevating the Host and . . . you a Catholic?

M: Yes.

J: O.K. So you know what I'm talking about anyways, he'd
be at the most important part of the Mass, raising the Host
and these bastards would come down the aisle with baskets—
BASKETS—to collect money.

M: So?

J: So I thought it was a shitty thing to do.

M: Why?

J: I'd learned that a church was the House of God.

M: So?

J: So I'd be on the altar ringing the bell or hitting the chimes and it was supposed to be still, I mean like deathly quiet and all you'd hear was money jingling. Christ, the House of God! Maybe but if it was, it ain't no more.

M: No?

J: No. The bastards turned it into a den of thieves.

M: [chuckle]   When you want to, you can be very expressive.

J: Yeah.

M: So-o-o, it's a rip-off world and nobody cares. Screw 'em all.

J: Yeah.

M: John, who do you care about?

J: Dee.

M: Just Dee?

J: Dee, period.   Nobody else ever gave me anything to care about.

M: How about you? You care about you?

J: Whaddya' mean?

M: Just what I said. Do you care about you?

J: You mean am I in love with myself?

M: No, just, do you care about you?
     (This was the one time in the interview that John seemed genuinely perplexed. It was no put on. He seemed totally befuddled by the question. His response reflected his bewilderment.)

J: I dunno. I don't. I guess so.
     [pause]

M: Dee makes you feel good about yourself.

J: Yeah, she does.

M: How was it before Dee?

J: I dunno. I was very religious. I had the church.

M: Dee replaced it.

J: Dee's my real thing.

M: She's honest, sincere and makes you feel important.

J: Yeah, all'a that and more.

M: More?

J: Never mind.

M: She makes you feel, uh, manly.

J: Yeah. [pause] Let's leave it at that.

(There's little question in my mind that John is having relations with Dee. John had been staring at my chest during
a good portion of the interview. At first I had been a mite
embarrassed, then I think annoyed, until I began to realize
that John was quite unaware of it. He did this automatically
with women, even those of very common appearance like
me.*)

M: You think about sex a lot, John?

J: [He reddened and laughed] I guess so. What's a lot?

M: It's on your mind, a lot.

J: All the time. That's normal, ain't it?

M: I suppose.   [The projective tests proved interesting here.]
      Let's get to the tests now, shall we?

J: O.K.

Name: John Whiting   Date: Today's Date

Age: 16 years 3 months   Examiner: Helen Morrissey

                      Referral Source: Christopher M. O'Brien
                                     Justice District Court

Tests Administered: Wechsler Adult Intelligence Scale
                    The Rorschach
                    Clinical Interview (see attached enclosure)

Behavioral Observations:

   When John presented himself for the testing session he appeared
in blue denim jeans and a long-sleeved red plaid shirt. Both articles
needed laundering. The red bandana handkerchief which he wore
around his brow contrasted sharply with his long, dark-blond
hair. The only expensive item of attire was his shoes, thick soled,

---

*Most people, men and women, would consider Dr. Morrissey, 38 years old
and unmarried, a very ordinary looking woman. She's 5′ 5″ tall and weighs
140 lbs. Her figure could fairly be described below par. She herself volunteered, "My measurements are not my forte. I learned a long time ago that
I'd probably never make it to Atlantic City and the Miss America Pageant."

kid-skin half boots.   Altogether then John's studied intent was
to present the rather formidable picture of the "cool," uninterested,
mildly bored adolescent.   Ironically, the "altogether" effect was
of a ridiculous scarecrow—straw-colored hair, style of clothes,
hanging too loosely on too slender a frame.   Mostly, however,
the scarecrow impression was the result of the starry glazed look
which he wore.   I'm convinced now that this was a "put-on."

Initially, at least, John's whole demeanor might best be described as surly.   As the testing session proceeded, however, his
manner softened considerably, so that before we terminated he
was participating cooperatively.   In fact, periodically during the
clinical interview he was warmly responsive.   The last test I administered was the WAIS which he appeared to enjoy, especially
the nonverbal part.

Test Results: Intellectual Aspects

At this time John functions in the upper 5 percentile of the
national population (Full Scale I.Q. 125).   His verbal competencies
(I.Q. 121) are below his nonverbal competencies (I.Q. 126) but
not significantly so.

John's most salient verbal abilities lie in reasoning and in
vocabulary development.   In both of these he displays very superior
ability.   His general fund of knowledge, however, and his ability
to deal with theoretical social problems is only average.

Within the nonverbal sphere we find that he functions especially
well in spatial relations.   Indeed, in this aspect of intelligence he
displays the ability of those in the upper 1 percentile of the
national population.   His perceptual accuracy and his ability to
understand and deal effectively with concrete interpersonal
problems are at least in the superior ranges.

In short, intellectually John is very much intact.   He has the
mental ability to perform in a very successful way in the normal
classroom.

Personality Assessment:

What we find in John's personality is a fascinating panorama
of conflicting impulses:

1. He harbors very deep hostility but desperately seeks love.
2. He is scared yet belligerent, i.e., his constant impulse is "to hell with them, it, or whoever."
3. He lacks normal inner controls but can also serenely accept an abnormal amount of abuse.
4. His delinquent behavior clashes sharply with his strong belief in retribution.

The problem which underlies these conflicts has to do with sexual identification, more particularly with, "what does it mean to be a male, to be a man." John wants desperately to know. And currently, emotionally he does not know. And this emotional bewilderment explains in part at least his inordinate preoccupation with sex.

Let me return to his first conflict, hate vs. love. John is an angry boy. He hates both the classical father figure (with all the authority figures associated, i.e., parents, police, teachers, principal, etc.) and the mother figure with its complementary nurturant types such as aunts, girlfriends, nurses and of course "mother." His hate stems from the fact that he feels he has been emotionally shortchanged. In his view his insecurity and acute need for love are the direct result of parental rejection. In his opinion, both emotional and cognitive, he's never been wanted. His self-hate, of which there is so much, comes from the fact that he feels so worthless. He feels that this self-hate comes from his parents, mother and father. He is able to verbalize this. John has learned to hate from them. Not that they hated him. Simply, he feels that they never loved him. The effect upon John was that he learned to hate himself. His emotional understanding is this, "I am so unworthy that even my parents don't love me." And as is true of all of us, all his life in his own way he has been seeking to find, to earn some measure of self-respect, some measure of self-worth. Ms. Johnson in her report discusses "John's zealous involvement in religious life." This involvement may be directly attributed to his acute need for the love which he did not feel he received at home. To be religious was a way to feel worthy in his own eyes ("maybe mother and father don't love me but God loves me") and in the eyes of others, priests and nuns. He even obtained fringe benefits from his mother who complimented him upon his religiosity. John may be understood in part, then, as a young man with an insatiable, all-consuming need for love. He is attempting to make up for many years of deprivation. His current love affair is a manifestation of this attempt. (see transcript enclosure)

John is also a very frightened boy. His fright is best discernible in a kind of free floating anxiety that he binds, sometimes unsuccessfully. He perceives a hostile, threatening world, full of uncaring, unloving people. Such a perception feeds his fright and worse, precipitates his belligerent stance with others, especially strangers and most especially, father figures. Very probably, John is a very scared boy when he verbalizes or feels, "screw him, it or the world in general."

As far as inner controls are concerned, John sometimes functions like a seven or eight-year-old child. Very often he wants what he wants when he wants it. He is quite unable to defer any goal, quite unable to work and persevere for a long term objective. He may well flash into a temper if contradicted or nagged by an adult or peer. His very violent temper, a function of the love-hate conflict and the awful fear-anxiety with which he loves, is very near the surface and explodes unpredictably. At the same time his constant and acute need for love and the fear force he lives with inhibits him from standing up for his rights. Or, to put it another way, the ever-present little boy in John makes him absorb a remarkable amount of abuse from selected adults and peers.

John lives with a Jekyll-and-Hyde type of conscience. His history indicates that for the past several months anyway, the Mr. Hyde in him has been very much on display. Despite this there is a constant and transcending moral aspect in his conscience makeup (this is fed by his anxiety, too). John is rationally and emotionally convinced that he will need to make reparations for any and all moral violations. In short, John can and does break his own moral code and of late has done so regularly. He does so, however, at considerable price in guilt and anxiety. The theologian would classify John as an immoral person, never an amoral one.

John is a very unique delinquent, then, in that he harbors few if any psychopathic strivings. Unlike the psychopath, John very much believes and fears a judgment day.

Most boys of John's age have a strong interest in sex. John has a preoccupation with it. It seems to be a prime topic of thought with him. Sex permeates almost all of his fantasies. These latter involve both women with amazonian breats and men with monstrous penises. John seeks to identify with both and to date has unequivocally identified with neither. These percepts, which he made on the Rorschach, reflect not only his own lack of security in his maleness but reinforce the observation made above that he is sorely lacking in love, nurturance, and succorance.

Some comments should be made regarding his emotional strength. And John, despite his many problems, indeed possesses strength. First of all he is of superior intelligence and given the motivation, he can solve most intellectual problems easily. Physically he will be very attractive (right now he's too skinny), blond, blue-eyed, and tall. His conflicts, which fuel his anxiety, contain the seeds for the amelioration of his many ills. Thus he seeks love desperately (as we all need to from time to time), he can and does bind much anxiety and he possesses a conscience. He seeks to be a man and to understand its meaning. In this search (and hopefully discovery) lies the potential for a healthy individual.

SUMMARY AND RECOMMENDATIONS:

This is a slender, sixteen-year-old boy who functions with superior intelligence (I.Q. 125). His personality is beset with conflicts: love-hate, fear-belligerence, control lack-abuse absorption, and antisocial impulses versus fear of retribution. These conflicts are symptomatic of a more basic problem, namely, confused sexual identity. His current preoccupation with sex may be understood as a function of the last problem. His strengths, if developed, can mitigate most of these problems. These strengths include intelligence, physical attributes, search for love, ability to bind anxiety, and his conscience. His search for maleness is another positive indicator for a potential for health. Finally, he's still only sixteen, he's trying in his own way to get out of his problems. He has not yet settled into them. He can learn to change. Change does not yet hold the dread for him which it does for the older person.

My first recommendation is family therapy. Ms. Johnson's report indicates clearly that most of John's difficulties find their source within his family. If family therapy is not possible, individual therapy should be begun at once.

Everything considered, I think the prognosis is good—provided treatment is started soon.

Helen Morrissey, Ph.D.
Consulting Clinical Psychologist

Christopher M. O'Brien is viewed by most county residents as a liberal and enlightened judge. Since his appointment three years ago he has channeled most of his energy into improving the staff of the juvenile division of his court. To this end he has labored and politicked successfully, increasing the number of probation officers from three to eight. He has also retained the services of a clinical psychologist and a social worker on a part-time basis.

This morning he had just finished hearing the case of John Whiting who had been caught in the act of stealing a cassette radio. After a hearing, he likes to move the juvenile cases to his chambers to explain his decision not only to the offender but to his parents. He found that the kids talked more, explained more meaningfully, and even listened better if they were sitting in his office. A few of his colleagues on the bench disagreed with this procedure, feeling it detracted from the dignity of the courtroom. Chris O'Brien shrugged this off. The juvenile system, he believed, was designed and set up to help kids find themselves, not to impress them with innane ceremony.

Judge O'Brien had read the reports by the social worker and the psychologist. They substantiated his basic belief that this case involved not just a boy, but a whole family. He was convinced that it was not just John who was in trouble, it was his parents, his family, too.

He looked at the boy and smiled. He understood the psychologists description even better. Yes, John presented a stereotyped image of studied adolescent "coolness," both in dress and demeanor. But Judge O'Brien knew too, because he had read the psychologist's report, that beneath that thick veneer of "coolness" beat the heart of a scared boy. Right now John had a blank expression on his face, as if he were meditating, or more likely, "tuned out" his present situation.

The parents looked desolate. Mrs. Whiting fidgeted in her chair, obviously uncomfortable, more probably scared. Mr. Whiting sat with head and shoulders drooped, the picture of an acutely unhappy, even defeated man. Yes, sighed O'Brien, life can be cruel.

O'Brien began, "We've had our hearing in court, it was a necessary formality. I wanted us to sit down here now and talk about it together. John pleaded guilty. I'm bound now to put him on probation. The length and terms of that probation are up to me. As his parents, do you have any recommendations before I do so?"

"No," said Kathleen weakly.

"Mr. Whiting?"

"I guess not, you honor."

"My staff has recommended that the Whiting family enter into family therapy," he said briskly.

Kathleen responded wearily, "We've had that recommendation. We've already agreed to it. We're waiting on an opening at Children's Aid and Family Service."

"Oh, that I didn't know. Splendid. You see," said O'Brien, "I'm convinced that it's not just a boy who's delinquent, to a considerable degree it's his family too. The family's delinquency is not always seen, at least easily, but the delinquency in some form is there. Mother, father fighting. Older brothers beating on the court offender. Extremely harsh punishment. Maybe never any punishment. I have learned that a boy growing up in an environment that beats him down, somehow, some way, when he's small, is a boy society will have to contend with, usually during adolescence. A lot of them, probably most of them, never come to court. For whatever happy reason, they straighten out enough so that they get along, maybe become very successful people. But a lot of them on their way through a very hectic adolescence stop at this court. I believe it's a critical juncture in their lives. From here they can go the right way, they can go the wrong way. I mean to see to it that most of the boys who come here take the right way. At least, I'm going to give it my damnedest."

O'Brien turned to John. "So, I'm going to impose a three months probation. You've agreed to attend the sessions, the therapy sessions with you family, is that right?"

"Yeah, I have," nodded John. Much of the glazed expression had left his eyes, noted the judge, with not a little satisfaction.

"Fine, you will be released into the custody of your parents," he announced. "At the end of three months I will receive a letter from the psychiatrist, psychologist or whoever is conducting the therapy. If I learn that there is substantial progress, the probation will be terminated. However, I . . ."

Kathleen interrupted, "But, your honor, we've been told that there is a waiting list and that we will have to wait a while yet."

"I will see to it that the Whiting family begins very soon," answered O'Brien crisply. The firmness, the authority in his tone conveyed the distinct impression to Kathleen that whoever the therapist was, he would be waiting for them at the door ready with instant therapy.

"John, do you have anything you want to say?"

"Uh, no. Uh, well, yeah. What did you mean when you said a kid who's beat down when he's real small ends up here. You mean like, you think I'm here now 'cause I wasn't treated right, is that right?"

"Ye-s-s, but don't get me wrong, John. I hold *you*, you John Whiting, accountable for what you did, or at least what you attempted to do. That's why I am imposing a three months probation, to be reviewed at the end of three months. You are responsible for that attempted larceny, not your parents. But they are responsible to some extent for what you are, whatever it is you've become. That's why I want them to go into therapy too. Do you see?"

"Yeah," he answered dimly. This was another one of those rare times that John was genuinely perplexed.

"Fine. Mr. and Mrs. Whiting, this court will be in touch with you."

Discussion Questions

1. What were the most important findings in the social worker's report?
2. According to the psychologist, John's preoccupation with sex is due to his confusion, his uncertainty about who he is. Do you agree with this? Why or why not?
3. Why should John be confused about who he is?
4. To what extent is his father responsible, his mother?
5. Some would take the position that John himself is responsible for what he is like. Do you agree?

Chapter 5

1. From Donnelly's account we learn that while growing up John apparently had a lot of respect from his peers. Consider why he lost touch with them.
2. In reading over Dee's diary, what do you see about her that would attract John?
3. Researchers claim that most adolescent girls who become illigitimately pregnant do so to prove to their mothers that they too, are women. Illigitimate pregnancy they tell us is often an act of defiance. Consider if this is true here.
4. The same researchers find that the father in such a case is irresponsible and needs to prove his sexual identity. Is this true about John?
5. Reflect upon the impact which Thomas and Francis III made upon John's view of himself.
6. Consider the Alice-John relationship. What are its strong points? What are its weak points?

CHRISTOPHER DONNELLY'S VIEW OF JOHN WHITING

Christopher Donnelly, John's long-time friend, wrote these observations about John.

I think John Whiting's a real good kid. I've known him practically all my life. I grew up with him. You see, my family moved to Middletown when I was three years old. When we moved here, we moved two houses away and we've stayed there. So have they. I guess one of the reasons John and I were always close was that he and I are the same age almost. My birthday's in August and his is in September.

We started in kindergarten together. We had the same teacher in the afternoons, Miss Mullen, and the same teacher in the morning, Miss Goodacre. Outside of that I don't remember too much about John and me in kindergarten. We were both there together, that's all.

First grade we were in the same room with Miss Hart. I remember one time a whole bunch of us got caught playing in the mud, must've been the spring time, well she was ripping cause we all got covered with this mud and we had to go home right after. She lined us all up and started screaming. We were all scared. At least I know I was. At one point she stopped for breath and John spoke up, I can still remember his words. What was he six or seven? "Miss Hart, we were just playing. It's not your fault. It's our fault. We'll tell our mothers like that. Don't worry about it." That ended the screaming. Looking back it was John and only John who figured out why she was screaming and who had the guts to tell her. None of the rest of us did, that's for sure.

You got to understand John. He was always a little bit different than the rest of us. Not that he was weird or anything, 'cause he wasn't that. He was different in that he was kind of a leader. He never took any shit (pardon the French) from anybody, not when he was six and not when he's sixteen.

And he was kind. You want to know the truth? John Whiting was the kindest kid I ever knew. We used to go fishing a lot when we were kids, like nine, ten maybe, up to thirteen. We used to go fishing all day and then we'd spend the night looking for crawlers to go fishing the next day. Anyway, John and me would get up early and go and there'd always be one or maybe two little kids who didn't know anything about fishing, like baiting the hook or watching out for tangles in the line, stuff like that. Anyways, John would be so patient with them, helping them. Christ you'd think he was their father or their brother. He didn't even know them most of the time. Lots of times I'd see he'd have a bite and he'd be fixing this little kid's line. I would'a told the kid to go screw off, not John!

And he never got mad! I mean like some kid at recess or after school might wise-ass him, you know a little kid, like we'd be in the fifth grade say and a third-grader or something would try to screw him. He'd just smile and shake him off. Even if the whole thing was unfair. Let me explain better.

John was a great marbles player. He always won. I mean he won so much nobody really wanted to play him. He was real good. At least with all the kids in his class. Anyways once this wise little kid, say he was eight or nine and we were like ten or eleven, started playing him. Pretty soon there were a lot of marbles in the pot. And John flipped the "Biggie" in the hole and won, like always. Well this little bastard started screaming, 'Whiting didn't stay behind the line,' that it was unfair or something. John, who was kneeling, smiled up at him, I can still see him, and he agreed. I mean he agreed with the kid and gave him the whole pot! I couldn't get over it. He was like that! He should have been ripping mad but he wasn't. He just smiled.

And he had unbelievable guts. I mean he had balls like you wouldn't believe. The only time I ever saw him fight was once when we were about ten or eleven, I guess it was ten 'cause we were in the fifth grade. A whole bunch of kids, maybe fifteen or twenty, were standing in front of the Bond Hotel on Main Street waiting for these baseball players to come out. It was when Middletown was in the semipro league. Anyway this Clinton player came out and threw a baseball into the bunch of us. We all jumped for it but this little kid, maybe seven or eight, real small, he got it and this big Jr. High School kid took it away from him in the scramble. Well the little kid started crying and the big kid started to walk away. That's when John stepped in. And he said real quiet like, "Give him his ball." The older kid just kept walkin' away. John wasn't too big yet and he was just as skinny. But he said it again, "Give him his ball!" The boy turned around and looked down at John. He said, "You little shit, you gonna' make me?" John looked at him real serious like he still does when he's mad and then I guess it was the first time I ever saw him do it but he licked his lower lip and he said, "I don't wanna' make ya', honest, but it's not fair. You're being dishonest." I swear to God that's what he said, "You're being dishonest." Well this big kid started laughing and he laughed and laughed. All the kids were laughing except me and John. John waited till everyone stopped laughing, then he said, "Give him his ball you prick." And just as he said it he bent over and head first plowed into the kid's stomach. Then he jumped on him and started choking the kid.

All us kids loved it but some old guy broke it up. John took the ball and gave it to the kid. And you know what he said?

"It's your ball kid, you deserve it." That's what I call balls, not baseballs either.

One of the things you ought to know too, is that John was one of the smartest kids in my class, every year right up to high school he always seemed to understand so quick. But John was different there too. He was the only smart kid I ever knew who never acted like he was. And what was really different about him was that nobody else acted like he was super-smart. 'Cause you know, supersmart kids either got shit on or they were just ignored. Kids acted like they didn't exist. It wasn't like that with John. The only word I can think of which fit him was "respect." Kids, even little kids, respected John. I've asked myself a lot why, why did they, did we respect John like we did? And I got no answer. No answer. John Whiting was the kind a' guy you respected. There's no deep explanation. That's how it was.

Maybe part of the respect we had for him had to do with the fact that he was such a daredevil. He used to do dangerous things, wild things. We used to call them crazy. I guess 'cause we were too afraid to do them ourselves. Like once he set up a rope and tied it to this old oak tree up at the reservoir where we used to go swimming. And he'd swing on it and go sailing sixty, seventy feet into the air and then dive into the water. What you gotta' know to appreciate this is that the water wasn't that deep. But there were a lot of rocks and boulders. He did that. We used to all sit there and watch him, too chicken to follow. He didn't rank on us for being chicken, though. He wasn't that kind of a guy. He wouldn't do that.

Probably the craziest thing he ever did though, was when he blew up one of the toilets in the high school with a homemade bomb. John made the bomb himself. I know, I watched him make it. He had all the chemical liquids and powders, wire and all kinds of crap. He made it in his garage. At first I wasn't scared 'cause I figured he'd use it in the forest. I asked him if he was going to blow up anything. He looked at me with that funny smile and he said he didn't know. I believed him. I asked him how it worked. I only asked him 'cause I knew he was proud of how good it was made. He showed me and I really didn't understand too much about it. I do remember though that it was complicated. It even had a timing device on it. Anyway, two days later we were all in English class. I'll never forget it, tenth grade English, Miss Scully. She was kind of flaky. The Boys' Room was right across the hall. She was reading from the book *So Big*. It's funny but I remember exactly. She had just read, "She literally took the reins in her hands," and she asked me Christopher, what does the author mean "literally took the reins in her hands?" and right then, Wow! Explosion. We all jumped. Miss Scully let out a little shriek. Everybody jumped and ran to the door. The corridor was full of kids and teachers yelling and hollering. And then right in the middle of the disaster there's Mr. Dalton just as white (he always gets white when he's nervous) as a bucket of new snow. He kept screaming "order here, now, order" like a judge in the movies. Water was coming out from under the Boys' Room door. The door was locked. So Dalton started screaming, "Who locked this door? Who locked this door?" Nobody told him. Meanwhile his feet were gettin' wet 'cause the water was coming out from under. Sortino was there and he opened the door. It's a swinging door, see, so when he undid the lock the force of the water swung it open. Christ, there must've been a foot of water, with toilet paper yet, come rushing out. Dalton got soaked to his ass. He was jumping and hopping around like somebody had just shoved a hot poker up his ass, screaming, "who did this, who did this." He grabbed one kid after another and yelled, "Did you do this?" I mean Jesus. It was a real genuine disaster. Nobody ever found out who did it.

It was right after that scene that John and I parted company, if you know what I mean. We didn't see much of each other. I didn't talk to him about the explosion. There are certain things even if you're friends that you don't ask about. I didn't ask. We just didn't see much of each other. Oh, we'd meet in school and we ate with each other in the cafeteria, but it was never the same like it was. He sort of went his way and I went my way. It was funny. He became sort of distant from the kids. And another thing too, like you know the respect that everybody had for him, that began to change too. Not that anybody ever tried to put him down. Nobody would ever do that. He was part of the scene, but he wasn't. I guess the fair thing is to say that nobody paid attention to him. And for a long time now he's been flunking in school, I know. He used to be so smart.

Anyway, right after that blow-up in the john he started to go with Dee Henessey. Now there is a chick. Built! I mean built and it would be Whiting who'd get her. All the guys were real jealous of him, jealous in a nice way if you know what I mean, anyway we all wished we had her. I'm sure he's makin' it with her.

And since he's started going with her nobody I guess has seen too much of him. I know he's gotten into a lot of trouble with his dealing (Christ, I almost did myself, just buying from him). And I know he's gotten into trouble with the fuzz about other things. I was there when he almost killed Danny Clark! I hear he's on probation for trying to rip off a cassette. I really don't know what's happened to him. I'm sorry about all of it. Anyway, as a kid, especially when we were small and like they say "innocent," he was the greatest. The best kid I ever knew was John Whiting.

EXCERPTS FROM THE DIARY OF DIANE HENESSEY

Monday, December 15

Dear Diary

I'm so *pissed* on mother. What a stinking *bitch*. All she ever does is nag, nag, nag, nag. What a stinking *nag*. And it's always about little things. Like tonight, I came to dinner wearing my nice, worn farmer jeans and the bitch acted like I walked in nude or something. She carried on for about ten minutes abut a lousy pair of jeans that I happen to love. Daddy just sat there taking it all in. I couldn't believe it! For Christ's sake. How the hell can he put up with her! Ugh!

Well, I just had to get *that* out! Now, I'll tell you about my weekend . . . and, what a fantastic time it was! I met this guy named John, John Whiting, at Sue's party Saturday night. He was so *funny*! God I couldn't stop laughing and not just because I was drunk. I mean I had a few beers, a good buzz, but he would've been funny, anyways. He's so understanding, too. I mean he listened to all my hang-ups about mother and everything and he didn't yawn once! I guess he gets hassled a lot by his own parents too. Why can't they leave us alone? Anyways, we went outside and smoked a few bongs and got really wrecked. Then he drove me home. It was really great. He's just the neatest guy I've met in a long, long time. He's in my gym class (we're starting coed sports this semester). I can't wait. It ought to be a blast.

I ate so much today, I feel like a balloon. Oh, well. I haven't had much of an appetite lately so I guess it's O.K. Well, I gotta' go. See ya' around.

Good ole' Dee

Friday, December 19

Dear Diary,

It's Friday! Not only is it Friday, but it's the last day of school for two whole weeks!! I'm so happy!

Well, dear diary, remember John? Well, I'm seeing a lot of him now. He meets me at my locker in between classes and everything. I guess we're "going" now. I thought I wouldn't let myself get involved again after the problems I had with Paul. But it's different with John. He isn't on any sports or anything and doesn't try to impress me like Paul used to. John is just John and I really like him for being so honestly himself. He doesn't take any crap from anybody; not because he's tough; just because kids don't *want* to give him any 'cause he's just too nice of a guy. I really do like him. I've never felt so comfortable around any guy like I do when I'm with John.

Everybody I know likes him and thinks it's really great that we got together. Everybody, that is, except Karen. She's really worried about my rep. I guess she's heard that John deals and figures he's some tough kind of hood or something, but he's *not*. He's really *not*. He just likes to do people favors and please them any way he can. Besides, when he's around me, he hardly talks about it at all. Once, I did tell him I was kinda' worried about them getting caught and he just smiled like he does and said not to worry 'cause he's really careful who he deals with. I mean, nobody he sells to would narc on him. Anyways, Karen doesn't know him that well.   She's kinda' square.   Everybody thinks so.

Well, me and John are going out tonight.   I know I'll have a good time.   In a way, he's like my best friend too.   It isn't all physical at all.   He doesn't press me and that's another thing I like about him.   Gotta' go.   Just heard the doorbell.

Good ole' Dee

Friday, January 3

Dear Diary,

I had such a *fantastic* vacation you wouldn't *believe.*   It was just great.   I went out with John every single night and we just had the *best* time.   He gave me this really beautiful spoon bracelet for Xmas.   He had my name engraved on it and everything.   He had LOVE, JOHN, engraved on the back.   He's so sweet.   I feel so awful, too, 'cause I didn't give him anything.   But when his birthday comes up I'll get him something then.

Let's see, last Saturday night me and John and a bunch of his friends just drove around and ended up at the Drive-In.   I felt kinda' weird at first 'cause I was the only girl but they all treated me really nice.   All his friends are funny.   At the Drive-In we smoked and had a great time.   Late Sunday night we watched an old movie on TV.   Neither of us had seen it, "Serpico," and we both loved it.   That's the kinda' movie that John loves.   He told me he'd never be a cop and that movie just proved to him what pigs they all were.   I had to agree.   At least that movie sure made it look that way.

Tuesday night was New Year's Eve and we went to a New Year's Party—my very first one!—and I had a blast except for one thing, well, I got into trouble.   I drank almost a pint of gin and then smoked two, maybe it was even three bongs, just with John. I was *soooo* gone!   When I walked (sort of staggered, I guess) into the house at 3:30 P.M., guess who was waiting up for me? Right!   The *Bitch* herself!   She yelled at me till the sun came up.   All I could do was sit there.   Twice I got up and went to the bathroom and threw up.   Each time I came out, she yelled even more.   She told me that it served me right, that I had "fallen into a bad crowd" and that "John is a no-good-for-nothing bum." That got me so pissed that I started crying. I was so tired that all I wanted to do was sleep but she kept right on yelling. She said that she wouldn't be surprised if I got pregnant and she started calling me "disgustingly loose" and then she got so worked up she called me a "whore"! Dearest diary, I never thought I'd ever hear her use that word. I wasn't sure she even knew it! Would you believe it, after that she went into her whining act about "what will the neighbors say?" and everything. Honest, I don't think she'd really care if I lost my virginity so long as the neighbors didn't find out! I finally got pissed and started agreeing with her about everything just to shut her up. Daddy came downstairs at one point and just sat there giving me his silent look of disgust. They finally let me go and I walked upstairs—to bed-bed. Was I ever *t-i-r-e-d*!

Good ole' Dee

Monday, January 6

Dear Diary,

I woke up this morning. What were the first words I heard? Again and again and again the *Bitch* was complaining to Daddy, "What am I going to do with that girl?" And Daddy just kept grunting her to death. It's the only thing that calms her down. I'm not talking to mother and I'm still seeing John. There's nothing she can do about it. I'll be damned if she's gonna ruin *my* life. I mean, John's the only one that understands and she's not going to take him away from me. No way! No way at all!

Good ole' Dee

Wednesday, January 15

Dear Diary,

Yesterday me and John went to school but didn't go to gym. They didn't miss us though 'cause they couldn't keep track of everybody; it was such a hectic day. We went to McDonald's for breakfast instead and then John lit up a joint. I didn't want to smoke 'cause I had a test in French the very next period. But then I said "what the hell." I mean, I didn't want to take it in the first place but mother saw the guidance counselor and she advised that I take it. I'm getting an "F" in it anyways, so what's one more test? I ended up doing O.K. on it tho'. It was pretty easy.

John's been talking about quitting school but I talked him out of it. I mean, it's gotten to the point where I'd miss him at my locker if he wasn't there. Besides, all those kids at the high school kind of depend on him for their dope.

Well, I've gotta' go. John's coming over to do "homework." It's the only thing that mother would allow so we say that and go into the den and close the door and listen to records and well, everything. See ya' later.

Good ole' Dee

Friday, January 31

Dear Diary,

I wish I'd never been born! What an absolutely rotten day! Everything went wrong. First off, and most important, me and John got suspended today for skipping school yesterday. *Shit*!! What a complete and total bummer! They called home and mother was eating her lunch. What a scene!! She apologized to Sortino for about twenty minutes and discussed me in his office privately for another twenty while I waited outside on the bench going crazy. Shit, what a bummer! I think I'm still a little bit shocked. So's everybody else. I'd skipped a class before and got caught but Sortino never did anything 'cause he always thought I was a "nice girl." But he's never liked John and he's always been down on his back 'cause of his brothers' reputations when they were in school. Sortino sees John the same way. He never even gave him a chance. So now I think John's kinda' relieved that he finally fulfilled everybody's expectations. I am now "marked" in Sortino's mind and once you're "marked" forget it. Needless to say, I'm grounded indefinitely and mother's forbidden me to see John. *That* right now is the least of my worries. We'll manage somehow. But mother's not gonna' forget this too soon . . . Shit! Why did this have to happen to me? John and I were like in our own world. We were so happy! Why, dear diary, why can't they just *leave us alone*! *ALONE*! Gotta go now.

Good ole' Dee

Tuesday, February 11

Dear Diary,

How can I tell you? I've been going with John for almost two months now. Yes, dear diary, it happened. How can I tell you? I guess the simplest way is to tell you I'm no longer a virgin. Nobody was home at John's house yesterday and we went there like we've done a lot lately. Only yesterday it was different. He didn't press me either. I can't and I won't blame him. I don't know how it happened. It just, well, happened. I can't say that physically it was too pleasant. It wasn't. But I just felt mentally so close to him, so content with him, that I really *love* him. Yes, I do, I love him. Why should I feel guilty? I mean it's *not* like I'm a *whore*. 'Cause, dear diary, I'm *not*.

No, the only regrets I have now is that John and I are suspended for skipping school again, yesterday. Another big scene with mother and Sortino. I feel like a branded calf, no, I feel worse. I feel *sooo* down! I feel like a branded calf ready for slaughter. Oh, this is terrible. It's nothing to joke about. God knows, dear diary, I don't think any of all this is funny. Gotta' go—I don't want to but gotta'.

Good ole' Dee

Wednesday, February 26

Dear Diary,

. . . If I wasn't feeling so miserable, I'd say it was worth it, dear diary. How can I tell you again? I guess having sex sounds too impersonal and making love sounds too professional. Anyways, John and I have done it four times since the first time. It's not that I'm keeping score . . . I just figure you should know . . . gotta' go.

Good ole' Dee

Saturday, March 15

Dear Diary,

First off, I woke up this morning feeling just awful. My stomach was so upset that I thought I was going to throw up when mother set down my plate of scrambled eggs and when I walked upstairs to brush my teeth I felt so dizzy that I had to lie down for a minute. I hope to God it's the flu. Dear God, if it's what's been on my mind for two weeks now?! I didn't get my period but I never get it regularly. God, let it be the flu!

O, dear diary, I feel so miserable about everything. I wish I'd never been born.

Good ole' Dee

Thursday, April 3

Dear Diary,

I'm pregnant. I told John today. Actually, I knew about it almost a week ago but I just had to make sure so I went to this doctor that Jane told me about and he confirmed it. It's not even a question of what to do. I know that I have to get an abortion. I know that. No way would mother survive the news. So I have to keep her from knowing. There's this place about twenty miles away that will do it for $110.00. Jane is lending me half . . . . She's been great through it all. . . . I know that I'd never been able to do it alone. John's putting up the other half. I think he's almost as scared as I am about it but at least, well, when I'm with him he's just reassuring. He's gotten a lot more serious about us now. Truly, Diary, John *is* good and sweet and kind and *responsible*. He's *not, not, not* what everyone says about him. He is responsible, he's a man.

This whole thing has made me realize a lot about everything! *God*, I feel like I've aged twenty years in the past twenty days and I'm not even sixteen yet!

That doctor who confirmed it was a real bastard. He just kept giving me dirty looks and condemning stares. If I hated my job as much as he does I'd quit. What a bastard! Gotta go now.

Good ole' Dee

Wednesday, April 9

Dear Diary,

Yesterday I went to the abortion center for a conference. They told me what would happen, no pain, etc. But I'm a little scared. No, I'm terrified! It's hard to imagine how I was before this happened. I know I'll never really be the same person after it's over. It's funny, though, John and I never even thought of keeping the baby, getting married. Why? And somehow I can't feel compassion for it. None of this, "It's a part of me and John" bit you see in the movies. Oh, no, I hate it and I wish to God it never happened. Shit!

Good ole' Dee

P.S. Tomorrow's the day. Ugh. Relief? No! Scared? Yes!

Friday, April 11

Dear Diary,

Well, it's over. It's all over. All I can feel is relief.

They were right, there was no pain. They just shot something up my cervix and sucked it out. Physically, there was no pain. But all the same, it was *hell*. Pure *hell*. I mean, all the time they were sucking it out it suddenly hit me that *that* was life being sucked through that rubber tube. If it had lived, it would have been a human being. *A HUMAN BEING*. Oh God. Dear diary, I can't stop thinking about it. No matter what angle you approach it from, THAT WAS A HUMAN BEING and I killed it. God!

I spoke to John and he feels it too. Tried not to show it too much but he feels it. I know. For that I love him. If I didn't have him to share this with I'd die. Thank God, Thank God for John Whiting. We talked about it all yesterday and today. He's been with me every minute he could. We decided to go on the pill. No way would I like to go through that again. *No way*.

John's glad it's over for me but I don't think even he knows how much guilt I still feel. I'll be guilty all the rest of my life.

Shitty ole' Dee

DIAGNOSTIC INTERVIEW WITH THOMAS AND FRANCIS III

Thomas and Francis Whiting III are nineteen and eighteen years old respectively. Both quit school when they were sixteen. They moved out of the parental home almost two years ago and are presently living together in a cold water flat in the only deteri-orated section of Middletown.   Both young men have worked at a variety of unskilled, marginal type jobs.   Recently they both contracted to work for a national landscape firm in a nearby state.

Thomas and Francis refused to meet with their family in therapy.   Thomas, especially, feels embittered toward his parents and particularly his father.   "Dad's a nothing" is a phrase he used again and again over the phone in reference to him.

They consented to appear for a diagnostic interview to relate their feeling about the family and to present their views about the father, mother, John and Alice.   The interview comments which follow were taped and then edited for readability and basic syntax. Some of the material was derived also from notes made during the interview.

The psychologist who conduced this interview was the same one who led the family sessions which follow.

P: Come in, fellas, I'm Joe Mansfield, the one who you talked to on the phone. I appreciate you're coming.

T: Yeah, well, Frank and I are here but we wanna' make clear it's only for this one time. We're goin' to Maine in about ten days and we're gonna' be gone for two, maybe three months.

P: I understand that, Tom, but before I begin meeting with your folks and your brother and sister I thought it would be real helpful to talk to the two of you. You're not living at home, right?

T: Right.

P: Uh, mind telling me why?

T: Why?

P: Yeah, why don't you want to live at home?

T: 'Cause it's not a home.

F: Yeah.

T: It's not a place I wanna' be.

F: Me neither.

P: You don't feel any warmth or . . .

T: It was never a warm place, our home. My father's a nut about fireplaces, we always had a fire going in the fall, winter

Note: P = psychologist; T = Thomas; F = Francis

and spring. So the house was always good and comfortable like that. But it was always cold. Nobody talked to nobody. Nobody gave a shit about nothing.

P: Sort of impersonal.

T: Right on! Impersonal, that's the word. Sometimes I wondered if my father knew I even was alive. Honest-to-God! Why would I want to live there?

P: So you don't have any special feelings of loyalty to the old homestead.

T: Loyalty! Ha! I got as much loyalty to that place as an orphan does to an orphanage.

F: Right on!

P: You feel that way. too, huh, Frank?

F: Yup!

P: I see, and where are you living now?

T: On Green Street.

P: Together?

T: Yeah, together.

P: How is it living together? You must get along pretty well, to do that. You both always got along pretty well?

T: Yeah. I guess.
[Frank chuckled at this point.]

P: Yeah, Frank?

F: I was just thinkin' I get along better with him than he does with me.

T: That's 'cause I have to act like his father, look out for him. He still acts like a little kid once in a while.

P: You act like his father?

T: Yeah.

P: He act like your father, Frank?

F: Yeah. He's a real pain in the ass sometimes, I'll tell ya'. He worries enough for the both of us. So I let him worry.

T: Yeah, I do. That's true. That's how I'm different from my old man. He never worried about nothing. Like I told you on the phone Dad's a nothing.

F: Right.

P: Well, if he's a nothing, where did you learn how to be a father?

T: Who knows? I never thought about it. See, our old man never took much interest in too much that we did. I don't think he even minded when we got into trouble or if he did he never showed it, that's for sure.

P: What trouble?

T: Hey man, we both had our share, lemme tell ya'.

P: Such as?

Tom looked at Frank and they both smirked knowingly.

T: Well, we both left school right after we were sixteen. We didn't get along in school. Ma was rip-shit about that.

P: Your father didn't say anything.

T: Nah. And I was married and divorced in the past couple of years. Hey, I ain't twenty and I've had my share of problems, lemme tell ya'.

F: Me too.

P: You too, huh?

F: Yeah. I had a few accidents.

P: Car accidents?

F: Yeah, four of 'em.

T: Last one he had was bad. Put him in the hospital for three months.

F: Yeah, my old man's payin'. What's he paying, Tom?

T: Thirty-five big ones every month. Christ, he'll be payin' forever, I guess.

F: Yeah, forever.

T: Probably the only thing he ever did for Frank was to pay his hospital bill.

F: I think I oughta' pay him back. I probably will someday.

T: Oh, bullshit!

F: Yeah, well, I'm gonna' try.

T: Yeah, I'll bet. You couldn't save a dime a week from your dishwashin' job.

F: Well, you're not doing much better.

(These last exchanges were good natured. It was quite apparent that the boys got along very well. Tom was the leader of the two, he did most of the talking, apparently he also made the decisions for the two of them.)

P: How do you handle the finances?

T: When he works he gives me all but ten bucks a week. I pay the rent, and food, and stuff. Frank don't make much. Whaddaya makin' now?

F: Fifty-five a week.

T: Yeah. But this Maine job, man, we oughta' do pretty good on that.

P: Just what is it you're gonna be doing?

T: Tree work.

P: Have you had any experience, either of you?

T: Nah. But a guy in the office is a friend. They're short-handed and they can't seem to find a . . . Who the hell knows? Anyway, we got the job. Seven-fifty an hour plus fifteen dollars a day living expenses.

F: Looks like a good deal.

T: And we'll see a little country.

F: Yeah.

P: It does. It sounds good.

T: Yeah.

P: Yeah, well what can you tell me, both of you, about your family?

T: Whaddya' wanna know?

P: Well, they're going to be coming in to see me. They figure that there are problems there. You know, about John.

T: Yeah. Poor kid never had a chance. Hey, we didn't either, but we weren't never in court except once for speeding.

P: Let's start with John. What can you tell me about him?

T: He's about four years younger than me. I really never had that much to do with him. I remember as a kid at night him and me and Frank here used to sleep in the same room. He used to kneel down by his bed at night every night, he never missed, and he used to say the Rosary. He wanted the light on to say it. Real pain in the ass. 'Cause we'd wanna sleep. But we put up with it, we put up with it, except when he got this thing about saying prayers for everybody. Christ, he trotted out ma and dad and our grandparents that we never knew and half of Middletown. That's when I blew my stack and told him to pray in the dark.

P: You sort of ran the room.

T: Yeah.

P: What did you think of him. I mean, as a person?

T: Ah, he was always a little kid. I remember him just as a little kid. I guess he was O.K. He was smart in school, I remember that. And I remember he was quiet around the house. But then our house was a pretty quiet place except when ma got going. She was always mad. Always bitching about something.

P: What do you remember about him, Frank?

F: I remember he was crazy, honest.

P: How do you mean?

F: Yeah. Like once I was about maybe ten and he was about seven or eight and I stole some cherries from in front of Mario's grocery store. We were about a block from the store when I whipped them out of my pocket. Christ, he went ape! He started crying about bringing them back 'cause it was a sin. He put up such a stink! He cried until I gave him all the cherries, about a handful, and he brought them back. Christ, what an honest kid!

T: Yeah. John was always different. A little bit weird. He never swore. He used to say a prayer for me every time I swore. I used to think it was funny. Like I'd swear on purpose just so he'd pray, like when he was small. Once I was real pissed and I said "Jesus Christ" about a hundred times on purpose just to get a reaction. Geez, I had him saying so many Hail Mary's the kid spent the rest of the day prayin'. But John wasn't what anyone would call a bad kid when he was small.

F: Nah, he was O.K. He was just a little kid. Probably better than most.

T: Yeah, and I gotta be honest, he was never *really* a pain in the ass about his praying either. As I think about it and after he learned to pray in the dark, he'd go off in the corner or up to his room and do it. He didn't bother anybody.

F: Yeah.

P: So when did he develop these problems like selling pot, fighting and ripping off cassettes?

T: Search me.

P: What was it like with your parents, when you were growing up?

T: Dad was quiet. Ma was noisy.

P: Uh, your father didn't, uh, get involved in the family. Is that what you mean?

T: He was around a lot, like he'd be home for supper and just about every night. He was there but that's all. Like he never said much. If we had a problem we went to our mother. We just never would have thought to go to Dad. Like he never hit us. He never told us what to do or not to do.

P: Did he ever take you anywhere or do things with you?

T: Christ no!

F: No, Tom, I remember once he took me and John and Alice, she was about four or five, John was what, about nine maybe and I was eleven, I guess. Anyway, he took us slidin' to the park where there's some hills.

T: Yeah, so what'd he do?

F: He sat in the car and we slid down the hill. We slid down about three or four times. Then John kept buggin' me about going back. I guess he figured Dad would be bored waitin', I don't know.

P: The whole thing wasn't much fun.

F: Nah. It was, uh, embarrassin'. Me and John didn't enjoy it, anyway. Maybe Alice did. She was so small she didn't know what was going on. We drove back in the wagon. Real quiet.

T: Yeah. It's a funny thing, I never thought about it, but I guess what bugged me always most about my father I was always kind of embarrassed around him. I never knew what to say around him, or to him. Now ain't that weird? To be embarrassed around your own father. I mean Christ's sakes! [There were a few moments of silence here.]

P: I was interested to hear you say that it was John who pushed you and Alice into returning to the car. I mean, he's younger than you. Did he worry about things like that?

F: Yeah, yeah he did.

T: He always, as a kid anyway, acted much older than his age. I guess he worried a lot. Maybe it was his religion. Who knows.

P: How did your father react to him?

T: Christ, he didn't even notice him. He didn't notice any of us.

P: How about your mother?

T: What about her?

P: What was she like when you were kids growing up?

T: Nervous.

F: She did a lot of yellin'.

T: Yeah, I remember she was always after us about everything.

P: Did she show you kids a lotta' love, you know, was she a hugger, kiss you, that sort of thing?

T: No. No, I don't remember much of that. Not with me. You, Frank?

F: Nah.

T: I think she did with Alice though. I used to see her hold Alice a lot.

F: Yeah. I think I was in the first grade when Alice was born. I used to come home from school. She was holdin' her and singin' to her. She used to sing her to sleep at night.

T: Yeah. I remember that. Yeah, she used to sing "I'll Take You Home Again Kathleen," only she used to change it to Alice—Alicia for Kathleen.

F: I used to like hearing her do that.

P: Why?

F: I don't know, we weren't used to hearing that. It was kinda' cool hearing that at night, her singin' to Alice, I mean.

P: How did she treat you guys?

T: I don't know. I guess the best I can say for her is maybe she did do the best she could, but it wasn't much. Wasn't much at all. Ma had a lot of problems. I guess she used to yell about pickin' up our room and makin' our beds, stuff like that.

P: She took care of all your physical needs, is that what you mean? But as far as being a loving, uh, caring kind of person, uh, there wasn't too much of that. Is that right?

T: Right.

F: Yeah, right.

[At this point Mansfield had made a notation: There's an awful lot of the "Little Sir Echo" in Francis Whiting III.]

P: She seemed bent on training you guys to be and do the right things and she seemed and was very good about getting meals for you, etc. But it all seemed to end there. Is that right?

T: Yeah.   But there's something maybe you'd like to know. Has to do with John. Mom had a whole thing about how we should keep our room clean and picked up. Well, I was lousy at it. I didn't care and Frank cared less.

F: Yeah, that's right, and John used to do it. He used to make all three beds.

T: Yeah, and you know what was sort of weird? He never told her he was doing it. He just used to do it.

F: Yeah, he was that kind of kid.

P: I see.

P: What about Alice?

T: What about her?

P: What can you tell me about her, I mean, what's she like?

T: I don't know that I can tell you an awful lot about her. I never had too much to do with her.

F: Me neither.

P: Uh, Frank, you said something about her, uh, that your mother used to hold her a lot and lullaby her to sleep at night.

F: Yeah, that's true. I think ma liked her a lot, liked havin' a little girl.

T: Yeah, I think Alice was spoiled a lot. She used to cry a lot. She was spoiled. She had her own way too much as a kid. And if she didn't get it, she'd cry a lot.

F: Yeah, when she was born everything turned around her.

T: That's right. I forgot that. When Alice was first born for a long time we didn't get our supper regular. We used to have what ma called "a pick-up meal." Sandwiches and stuff like that.

P: You mean you feel that your mother gave most of her attention to Alice at the expense of the rest of the family.

T: Yeah. Alice used to get her bottle and right when we'd be eating. I don't know why it had to be like that.

P: You resented that. She fed Alice during your supper hour.

T: I think all of us did. Even Dad. He used to like a warm supper. For a long time there, none of us got it. I think he was real pissed about that.

F: I didn't know that. He never said much.

T: He never said much about nothing. I think he was pissed, though.

P: So when Alice was born she really upset the family schedule?

T: Yeah, you can say that.

P: You think you all resented that.

T: Yeah, except ma. It gave her an excuse not to get supper and do the other things.

P: Other things?

T: Yeah. I remember havin' to go around scroungin' for clean clothes to wear in the morning when I'd get up. Like I'd ask for a clean shirt or somethin' and she'd yell at me, tellin' me to keep my clothes clean. And it was all 'cause she didn't wash them. I mean for Christ's sake, she'd yell at me 'cause she didn't do her work! It was like she was yellin' at me 'cause I was alive and she didn't like that, that I was alive.

P: You figure your mother resented your being alive?

T: Yeah. She gave the excuse Alice took up her time. All her time. I think she overdid it.

P: Alice was a very demanding baby.

T: Maybe. I don't know nothin' about babies. I think it was that Alice gave Ma the excuse to not pay attention to the rest of us.

F: Yeah, she spent all her time with Alice.

P: So I guess you all felt somewhat resentful toward Alice.

T: Yeah, probably, and ma too, I guess.

P: So how would you say you both treated Alice, Frank?

F: I never bothered her.

T: We didn't do nothin' mean to her. I mean we didn't hurt her or hit her or anything.

F: Yeah. I guess we just didn't notice her.

T: Yeah, we ignored her.
P: I see.
      [Pause]
T: Hey, look, we gotta' go. We been here a long time. I guess
      we told you pretty much what we know.
P: Yes. Yes. And it's been helpful. Thanks. And good luck
      to both of you on your new job.
T: Yeah.
F: Yeah, thanks.

FROM JOSEPH MANSFIELD'S NOTES

What was clear from this interview was that both young men
were very much alienated from the nuclear family. Clearly they
viewed themselves at best as uninterested, distant relatives who
no longer had any ties.

Their childhood was unaffectionate, unnurturant. Home met
their physical needs in the same way that a dormitory and a
cafeteria would. It provided a place to sleep and a place to eat.
Their home very obviously did not meet any emotional needs
such as security, love or self-esteem. Seemingly both parents
perceived their parental roles as material contributors only.
Francis dutifully provided money. And, until Alice was born
anyway, Kathleen faithfully performed the necessary household
chores. In short, neither Tom nor Frank remembers his home as
a source of love, or support. Quite understandably, then, few if
any ties of loyalty were ever established. Tom's words in this
regard were poignant: "I got as much loyalty to that place as an
orphan does to an orphanage." Home, then, was a place from
which to escape. Presumably, Tom's illegitimate paternity and
short-lived marriage were a function of their need to escape. He
was probably seeking the love and nurturance which he never
received at home.

What is most interesting, unique even, here is the warm relationship existing between the two. Tom does apparently function in a quasi-paternal role with his brother. There is a fraternal
relationship here too, however. Thus, Tom looks out for his

brother, supports him economically, yet berates him amicably too. One gets the impression that they "scrap" a lot at home. Interesting too, Tom does seek to learn the paternal role. He resents acutely his own father's neglect and what Tom perceives to be incompetence in that role.

There are few positive comments about Kathleen. Both hold her in little esteem. The best either said about her was, ". . . maybe she did do the best she could, but it wasn't much. Wasn't much at all. Ma had a lot of problems." They view Kathleen, then, as a neurotic mother who maybe tried but didn't succeed much in the maternal role.

The description of Francis is short and succinct. "Dad's a nothing." Tom said it and Frank agreed. The comments about sledding in the park indicate in a pretty clear fashion that Francis couldn't relate to his children very well when they were small. John's behavior in that incident suggests, if nothing else, that as a very young child he was exquisitely sensitive to his father's feelings and behavior.

John is viewed as pretty much a good kid, albeit a little eccentric. He prayed too much and too often, never swore and he was, as Frank put it, "crazy honest" and "he was O.K." They have little information or opinions to offer about the past couple of years (apparently when John's problems became manifest).

There's little doubt that Alice's advent into the family engendered much resentment and further alienation among the male members of the family. The supper hour was disrupted. Laundry was not done, etc. According to Tom and Frank, Kathleen devoted a disproportionate amount of her time to Alice. Frank observed, and not a little bitterly, that, "when she was born everything turned around her." Certainly this is an area which merits exploration with the nuclear family.

ALICE'S DIARY

Alice is twelve years old. She has her mother's auburn hair, hazel eyes, and freckles. Alice could be fairly characterized physically as a budding Kathleen. The following excerpts from her diary provide another view of the Whiting family.

Monday

Dear Diary,

Today was a rainy day but mom gave me a ride to school. Probably not because she wanted, cause she never wants to do anything, but so I wouldn't catch cold. (She's a real nut about my health.) School was dreary, as usual, and I'm about to kill my science teacher. He gave us a surprise quiz on things I never even heard of. At first I thought it was one of those tests to find out how much you know. In my case it's more like how much I don't know. Then at the end he told us this was going in his grade book. I swear, some kids would have punched him but they didn't 'cause he could kill them just by sitting on them.

After school mom was right out front waiting for me. She decided that she would go grocery shopping and was that all right with me? I wanted to say "no" but I knew that it would sound like sass so I said all right. It wasn't that bad but it wasted time. When we got home mom made me unload and carry in the groceries because quote "She didn't feel well." I've noticed a lot lately she never feels well when there's work to be done. I bet she didn't feel well! She just didn't want to do a little work. Watch, she'll probably decide at supper that she's got a headache or a fever or an ache or something and tell me to throw some frozen dinners into the oven.

I was right, she just yelled up to do just that! See! The dinners are in and I just asked her if there was anything else I could do. I guess she didn't hear the sarcasm because she said "yes," could I get her an aspirin because she had a terrible headache. Then, would you believe it? She asked me if I wouldn't mind getting her a glass of water. So like the perfect obedient child, I said "no" and I brought it.

Only Dad and I were home for dinner, the queen didn't feel up to it. It was a terrible meal eaten in near complete silence. During it I asked Dad how his day was. He just grunted. So terribly talkative! After supper I had to do the dishes. Yeah! again! Dad ran off to the dining room, I know so he wouldn't be bothered by either the dishes or me!

At about 7:30 her majesty decided she was hungry and came

down to eat. She really got mad when she heard John wasn't home and asked if I knew where he was. He was with Dee somewhere but I wouldn't tell her. She suspected I knew and started yelling at me to tell her. Then I really clammed up and she finally realized that I wasn't going to tell. He wasn't supposed to go out cause it's a school night. Now that I think of it, I should have told just to get him in trouble. I hate him and I know he hates me. He's always saying that mom babies me and that I just adore it. I don't.

Good night

Tuesday

Dear Diary,

Today I found out that there will be a dance on Friday night. It's for "chorus" and it's from 7:30 to 10:30. It's gunna' be fun! I'll go with Ann and Sue. In math, Mr. Smith gave us tons of homework on percents and I don't understand it at all. I guess I'll save it for study and hope that Sue will help me. At breakfast mom asked my brother where he was last night and he said, "around." She didn't like that but he got up and left for school. I just know that at supper she's gunna' make a big deal about where he went. I hope he comes home 'cause he's gunna get it! Mom has finally gotten her behind out of a chair to make supper and I just bet she's gunna' make me set the table. Watch, she just put forth her order! Bye!

Later.

At supper mom asked John where he was last night, again. He grinned that shitty grin of his and said that he'd been to the moon and hadn't she seen his spaceship blast-off? Then she really got pissed at him. (I would've too!) She said that she wasn't going to put up with his sass and if he didn't tell her he was grounded for the night. There was silence while he thought up a good excuse and mom took that time to ask me where he had been. I told her that I didn't know. Then she got mad at me and said that I was sticking up for him because I hate her. (Lie!) At that point he gave me his "thanks" look which I answered with a grin. He then told her he'd been at Al Amenta's house to do geometry homework. Like I told you before, Diary, he was out with Dee partying. But mom was fool enough to believe him and then she asked him if he had any wild ideas about going out tonight, a school night? He got really mad at her and said that it was none of her business. Mom got madder than she usually does and screamed that it was too her business because she was his mother and he was her son. And then John smiled his shitty smile again, looked right into her eyes and said very dramatically, "I never would have known." Well, mom was floored and she turned to Dad and she said, "Well, aren't you going to ask him where he's going tonight? Dear God, Francis, be a man. You know he's you're son too." Dad said, "Kathy dear, let him go, he'll be all right." "Don't dear me," was her response. "I think you should take a little more interest in family matters especially where it concerns the welfare of our last son. Look what happened to the other two!" My father just shook his head and said he thought it would be O.K. if John went out tonight provided he was home by 9:30 and if he had his homework all done. "Don't make a big deal out of nothing, Kathleen," he ended up saying. At this mom got up. She was crying and she screamed, "Nothing, nothing, the child is going out on another school night and he says nothing. Nothing, nothing, nothing. Oh, Francis. You are the nothing. Dear God, don't you see that?" I could have died for her. She cried those words all the way upstairs and her bedroom door slammed on the word "that." Sort of like a period at the end of a sentence. John shot out of the house, this time, like he really was a space-ship blasting off for the moon. Dad left for the dining room to do his meditating or whatever he does and I was stuck with the pile of dirty dishes, as usual. Oh, I do hate John so for sassing and fighting with my mother! She cares whether he kills himself or not. My father doesn't give a damn. He never says anything about what we do. He's always trying to avoid me. Maybe he just doesn't like the family I don't know. We never go anywhere, but anywhere, with him. He never wants to do anything. He's such a "blah." If I want to go anywhere it's always mom who takes me. Mom's still bawling. I'm really afraid of breakfast tomorrow.

Good night

Wednesday

Dear Diary,

Today was horrible! It started out with a big long speech issued by mom. She said she was sick and tired of doing all the work a-round the house. Ha! I'd like to remind her who did the dishes for the last two nights when she was sulking or whatever she was doing.

Boy, what a jerk! When she finally let us go she made me change into a dumb dress. I hate her! I felt like the real jerk in school. So many kids teased me! When I got home I screamed at my mother that the kids had teased me for wearing a dress. Do you know what she answered, Diary? She said that they (the kids) were all jealous of me because I looked so nice in it. I was so mad I could have hit her. She is so out of it!

Today I decided to make cookies. So I spent the afternoon making peanut butter crisscrosses.

My brother wasn't home for supper again and I could tell that even though my mom was talking as sweet as candy she couldn't wait to be alone with my father and have a fight. Dad just picked at his supper and didn't dare look up because mom would shoot him a mean look with her eyes. Finally I couldn't stand the suspense any longer so I asked mom where John was. She tried real hard not to yell and as a result her voice cracked. She said that she didn't know but why didn't I ask my father. When I turned to Dad he just shook his head. I was about to drop the subject when my mother exploded. "Is that shake supposed to mean you don't know? You know goddamned well he's not here but you could care less. He's *our* son. Why don't you accept a little of the responsibility of bringing him up?" "Kathleen, I do the best I can. I try," was the answer. "No you don't, Francis." I was so embarrassed. I excused myself and ran up to my room. Mom is right about Dad not giving a damn. Although I must admit at times she's too strict and old fashioned.

Good night

Thursday

Dear Diary,

School was such a drag today. After school I saw John hitchhiking to the center of town. He was smoking and not just cigarettes, either. When he saw me he started calling me a "straight priss." That got me sick and I told him that I hoped that he would be picked up by someone with a gun and that the person would shoot him. He started swearing at me so I cycled real fast before he could hit me. I hate him *so* much! He only smokes 'cause he thinks he looks cool. I think he looks like an asshole. I know he hates me 'cause he thinks I'm ma's pet and because I barely ever get into trouble. I ate supper alone and watched TV until now.

Good night

Friday

Dear Diary,

Today when I asked my mother for money for the dance she said I couldn't go. When I asked her why, she started rattling off the letters of the alphabet like she does, "Well, A, 10:30 is way past your bedtime. B, the kids get drunk at the dances. And C, I don't want you walking home alone in the dark." "But mom, there's a phone. I could call you." And after much persuading (I really can talk her into most anything) she gave in. I got my ticket and after school I invited Sue over for supper. My parents couldn't fight tonight. Yeh! The dance was fun but my mother came early and saw me dancing too close with Jim Elton. She got real pissed. Right in front of all my friends she started yelling at me. I don't think I can ever forgive her for this. Then she took me home. All the way home in the car all I could think about was how ashamed I felt. I hate her, she's beginning to make my life hell and hell is where I wish she'd go. NOW! And the worst thing of all, the worst thing, is that everybody tells me I look just like her and I act just like her. But, dear Diary, don't, don't let me be like her! I'm Alice, Alice, Alice. I'd just die if I became like her.

Good night

Dear Diary,

Mom was mad at me so I spent the day at Sue's. When I got home she said that I was banned from watching TV because of my behavior last night. Boy, now I know how my brother feels with her on his back all the time. I don't think I'll ever like or agree with her again.

She and dad are going to the annual dinner of the Carpenter's Union tonight. John's having a party. I'm sure it'll be a blast, if I know my brother.

Later.

I'm ready for bed. I smoked too much. I drank too much beer. I think I'm drunk and can barely write.

Good night

Discussion Questions

1. How does Donnelly's description of John help you to understand John better?
2. What needs did Dee Hennessey fill for John? What needs did John fill for Dee?
3. Did she seem a candidate for an illegitimate pregnancy?
4. Did John seem the type to father an illegitimate child?
5. Can you see any similarities between the Dee-John relationship and the Francis-Kathleen relationship?
6. What influence did Thomas and Francis III have on John's childhood? What do you think he learned from them?
7. Why are Thomas and his brother so "turned off" by their family?
8. Why are they so close?
9. Did Alice's existence contribute to John's problems? If so, how? If not, why not?
10. What did John learn from his sister? What did she learn from him?

Chapter 6

FOCUS GUIDES

1. Fantasies reflect the motives which a person harbors and often are the unconscious causes for much overt behavior. Accordingly, consider how the fantasies of each of the Whitings reveals their personal needs. Consider also how they conflict and complement each other.
2. As you read John's interview see if you can detect fear, confusion, and hostility.
3. Reflect upon Francis and Kathleen's ineptness as parents as you read their comments in therapy. Focus particularly on the strengths and weaknesses they imparted to their children.
4. More often than not sexual impotence in a man is a function of his self-image, particularly of his feelings about his general competence as a man. Focus then, upon what this reveals about Francis and his relationship with Kathleen. What would you conclude about what they feel about each other?
5. Conscience is a critical ingredient of human personality. Observe to what degree conscience functions in each of the Whitings and how it is manifested in them collectively.

THE INITIAL INTERVIEW

The Whiting family-four arrived for the first session on a Monday evening. I greeted them at the door of the family counseling center which is decorated like a comfortable but nondescript family living room; three easy chairs, two couches, a coffee table, etc.

"Please sit," I said, "make yourselves at home."

Kathleen walked over to the larger couch. Alice followed and sat next to her. Her husband hesitated a moment, then sat two chairs over from his wife, in a worn easy chair. John sat further away, in the chair most distant from his family. I've learned that how the family positions itself in the room is often symbolic of the intrafamilial relationships. My initial impression from the positions they took then, was that John and his father were loners within the family but that probably some kind of relationship

146

existed between Kathleen and Alice. We would see.

I offered them coffee, coke and brownies. Kathleen only accepted coffee. Alice took a coke and a brownie.

We exchanged amenities for a few moments and I made a banal comment about the weather. It was to that, that Francis nodded pleasantly. "Yeah, I haven't lost any days for the past two weeks."

"You're a carpenter, aren't you?"

"Yeah, self-employed."

"Are you working outdoors, right now?"

"Yeah, he's shingling a house over in Riverdale," Kathleen interjected.

"Oh, do you come home for lunch, Francis?"

"Not if I pack him one," she responded for him. "He prefers to come home."

"And what do you prefer?"

"Well, it's six-of-one and half-a-dozen of another. If I make it and he takes it, then I don't have to worry about lunch the next day, but the problem is that I have to remember to make it and I don't always. And if I don't, then I have to stop whatever I'm doing and make his lunch 'cause he's coming home, either way it's a bother."

"You resent making it."

"I guess I do, a little anyway."

"I see."

"Has it been a source of trouble between the two of you, Mr. Whiting, uh, Francis?"

"I don't . . ."

"Oh, it has sometimes," Kathleen interrupted.

"I see."

"How's work going, Francis? Has it been pretty good so far this year?"

"He never earns enough. He works hard but it's never enough." Again Kathleen answered for him.

"What do you think, Francis? I'm interested in what you think."

"It's been O.K., I mean like I haven't missed many days at all this year."

"You enjoy your work."

"Yeah, I do."

"I take it you're good at your work and you . . ."

"Well, he may enjoy it, but he always comes in so tired. He . . ."

"Mrs. Whiting, right now, anyway, I'm interested in what Mr. Whiting has to say."

Several times now Mrs. Whiting had interrupted her husband or had answered a question directed at him. It was becoming very clear, very rapidly, that it was she who was the dominant force in the family. I wondered how many times he had been subtly, even embarrassingly, put down in private conversations and in front of others.

"You come home tired sometimes."

"Yeah, sometimes."

"Often," Kathleen contradicted. "He's just not interested in doing much of anything. Comes in, eats and then retires to the dining room where he closes the door and watches the TV set that his sister Phyllis gave him two years ago. He doesn't want to do anything. And you have to admit, Francis, that you go to bed real early."

Francis just sat there looking at me, not responding. No question about it, Kathleen Whiting was in charge of this family, dominated it and was its spokesperson.

"Francis, how would you respond to Kathleen?"

"You can't respond to Kathleen. She's got her mind all made up. You can't talk cause she does all the talking. Every time I try to say something she talks louder and faster. I can't keep up with her."

"Don't tell me, Francis, tell her," I said.

"What do you mean, you can't talk to me. That's all I've ever wanted, you to talk to me. All I get from you are shrugs and mostly silences." Kathleen's voice had risen several decibels.

Francis shrugged, looked at me and said, "See?"

"Tell her, Francis, tell her how you feel, or is it true that you're silent and you just shrug at her?"

At this point Kathleen edged forward on the couch and was about to speak. I raised my hand and signaled her to hush up.

"Yeah. I guess there's some truth to the fact that I've always been a quiet quy."

Alice now interjected with, "Yeah, daddy, you've always been . . ." It was Kathleen who elbowed her quiet.

Francis saw Kathleen's movement.

"Yeah, like I was saying, I've probably always been too quiet. I guess I take after my father. Runs in the family."

I nodded, "I see."

"Yes, he was a quiet man, Mr. Whiting. But he was a strong man, too. People treated him with much respect."

"That's true," said Francis.

The implication in Kathleen's comment was that Francis was not strong, was not treated with respect by people. And, of course, his response, "That's true" rewarded her demeaning remark. I began to understand, then, that if Francis was weak, was the passive one in this marital relationship, it was because his emotional makeup permitted it and unconsciously he reinforced it.

There was a moment when no one spoke. I looked at them. "Well, now, what's the real reason we're all here?" There was a momentary pause and, predictably, it was Kathleen who answered.

"Judge O'Brien," she murmured, "He said we all had to come for family therapy. It was one of the conditions of John's probation. But you know that, Dr. Mansfield."

"Yes, I do. And, uh, call me Joe. I'm more comfortable in this kind of situation to be on a first name basis."

"Well, if you must know, I'm not. I've never, ever called a doctor by his first name. I know it's kind of the fashion today, but I'm not comfortable with it."

"O.K., suit yourself. Maybe as we get into our sessions you'll become more comfortable with it. Up to you. And you're right, I did know about O'Brien and the fact that he made family therapy a condition for John's probation. My point in asking was to know if you believe that that's the real problem in your family?"

"Why, what do you mean?" Kathleen asked with apparent sincerity.

"Well, only that I believe that adolescent delinquency is very much family related."

Kathleen nodded. "Judge O'Brien said something like that."

"Do you believe it?" I asked.

"I, I don't know. I guess my problem is I don't see it, I don't understand it," she said.

I glanced at John. He'd not uttered a word since arriving. There was a noncommittal expression on his face. But there was interest too.

"John, what do you think?"

"'Bout what?"

"'Bout your family. You think your family had something to do with your getting into trouble?"

"I dunno."

"What do you think the problems are in the family. I mean, what do you think the basic problem in the family is?"

"Nobody cares about nothin'."

"Do you care?"

He shrugged. "I care about as much as any of them do."

"Which isn't much, I gather."

"Yeah," he said tonelessly.

"Alice, what do you think?" I asked.

She nodded and smiled in a pleased way. "I never thought you'd ask me," she replied. Even as she glanced at her mother for approval, she seemed determined to talk. Her exuberance and motivation were a refreshing balance from John's inhibited, scarce comments.

"I don't agree with John about nobody caring. I think my mother cares and I know I do. My mother yells a lot at him and at me too. If she didn't care she wouldn't do that. It's John who doesn't care."

"How about you, Francis, do you care, about what happens and what's going on?"

Francis looked at me forlornly as if to speak but again, he was interrupted. This time by his twelve year old.

"Oh, daddy cares too, but he just doesn't know how to show it. He's a little bit, blah."

I looked at Francis, ignoring her comment. Quite apparently, Alice had acquired her mother's perceptual and interpersonal stance within the family. She took a condescending view of her father and was inhibited not at all about expressing it.

"What do you have to say to Alice about that, Francis?"

"Ah, she . . ."

"Tell her, not me, Francis."

He riveted his gaze on her. "Alice, you're still very much a little girl. You don't know, you . . ."

"Oh, Francis," Kathleen cried out. "Francis, Francis. If we don't do anything else here, let's be honest with each other. Alice is just telling Dr. Mansfield what she really believes. Don't put her down. The poor child is being as honest as she can."

"The poor child" beamed at her mother. A little satisfied grin played around her mouth.

"I wasn't going to put her down, Kath, I was just gonna' say that it's true that I'm quiet like you're so happy about telling everybody. She's learning to do that from you. That's all."

"What do you mean that I'm so happy about telling everybody," she queried, obviously embarrassed.

"Well, you do. I swear I've heard you say that I'm too quiet, I don't care. You even said something like that in front of Dalton. Oh, Kath, you want to be honest. Why, why don't you just admit it?"

Kathleen was obviously upset by these words. "I never said you didn't care. I never said that. I just said you couldn't help it. You couldn't, you've never been able to show how you really feel about things. So let's be honest, Francis, does it really matter if you do care, if you can't show it?"

"I think it does," he said, but without too much conviction.

It was Kathleen now who shrugged and who looked away. From the few exchanges so far it seemed clear that Kathleen was very much in control. Her self-assurance, her convictions, delivered so unequivocally, indicated pretty clearly that she dominated, if not the whole family scene, certainly the marital relationship.

At this point in the interview many thoughts kept nagging at me. Were John's delinquent acts a product of maternal domination? Was he acting out because he was rebelling against his mother?

Was he seeking to be independent of her? And, how much was all this related to Kathleen's apparent authority over his father? Or again, could John's alienation from his family be more a function of Francis' abdication of paternal role? Indeed, could John's apparent disillusionment be due to the fact that all his life he'd been denied a boy's traditional role model with whom to identify, i.e., his father. At any rate, these were the thoughts which buzzed through my mind.

I turned to John. "Do you think what Alice says is true, that your father cares but doesn't know how to show it, that he's, uh, 'blah'?"

"Yeah, he's like that, he's . . ."

"Tell your father, John, tell him, not me."

With obvious discomfort, he did turn to look at his father. "Yeah, dad, you're like that. I guess I always knew it but I . . ."

"Oh, for heavens sake," Kathleen began to impose something, but again, I signaled her to refrain.

John looked at her obviously much annoyed. "For Christ's sake, ma, I was gonna say that," now looking at her instead of his father, "if he had a chance to talk when he wanted to, maybe then . . ."

"But, John, that's all I've ever wanted him to . . ."

"Bullshit."

The expletive silenced the room. Kathleen blushed. Alice put her hand to her mouth in a sympathetic gesture for her mother. Francis just stared fixedly at his knees.

I tried to lighten the mood. Chuckling, I murmured, "I guess I've heard the word before, but, uh, I was wondering. What did you mean by it. Uh, what did you want to say?"

"Ma just runs things. She . . ."

"Tell her, John. Tell her." (In the initial session it's difficult getting members of the family to address their comments to each other.)

"O.K., ma, maybe you want him to talk and to run things but you sure don't show it. Every time he opens his mouth you jump in, shut him up or contradict him."

"Oh, John, how can you . . ."

"That's not true, John, mom is always telling him to take a stand with you, even with me."

"Yeah, but if he does ma hollers. She . . ."

"Do you hate me so much, John, do you," asked Kathleen.

"Oh, what's the use?" He shrugged and was silent.

Kathleen turned to me. "How can I make you understand?"

I smiled. "Honest, Kathleen. It's not so important for me to understand, as it is that you all, the four of you, understand what's happening."

She looked at me quizzically. "So, what's happening?"

"Well, the impression I get is that you've all of you, all four of you, developed patterns of relating to each other which very effectively block communication between and among . . ."

"What's all that double talk mean?" she asked. "I mean, be specific." Francis, John and Alice looked to be just as perplexed as Kathleen.

"Well, for example, several times you interrupted Francis. I signaled you to not do it but you tried again. Alice and you seem to have made an alliance to prevent him from becoming involved in family matters."

"An alliance, an alliance.   You make it sound like we're all of us in a war or something."

"Well, that might not be such a bad way to explain what's happening.   There's a war of sorts going on.   Alice is on your side, I think. Part of the trouble in this war is that Francis won't fight.   Maybe he doesn't want to, maybe it's because you won't let him. I don't know."

"Where's John fit in?" she asked.

"Where do you fit in, John," I asked.

"I don't fit," he replied without hesitation.

"Tell us what you mean, explain that for us," I said.

"Well, I'm like my father. I'm not fighting with anybody. I . . ."

"What do you mean, you're not fighting with anybody?" asked his mother. "We're all here because of you. I'm not here for myself. If it wasn't for you, John Whiting, we would none of us be here. And that's the plain truth."

"So you feel, Kathleen, that the reason you're here is because of John's offense?" I asked.

Without hesitation she responded, "Yes."

It was Francis now who volunteered. "Oh, Kath, let's be fair. How many times have I heard you say we're in trouble as a family?"

"Yes, that's true," she murmured.

"We probably all got problems, if we're in trouble as a family. Kath, you probably do yell too much and, and I buy that bit about alliance between you and Alice." He looked at Alice then, and said, "You know you and your mother have been taking sides against me." This was a quiet man but not a hapless one, I thought.

Alice turned a little pink. She said nothing.

John looked around as if he wanted to say something.

"Yes, John," I prompted.

"Eh, we're screwed-up. And I'm not the only one," he said with a kind of latent excitement in his tone. John seemed to be taking an interest. Maybe it was the fact that he was not turning out to be the scapegoat, the fall guy. Or maybe it was because his father had quasi-defended him.

There was a moment of silence. Our time was almost up. But I wasn't about to call a halt, even though this session had been more diagnostic than anything else. I wanted more from John. "John, a while ago I think you said something like, 'Nobody cares about nothin'."

"Yeah, I did."

"O.K. Tell me, *who*, specifically, who cares the least in the family? Take a moment and then tell that person, not me."

He sat there, I thought a little self-consciously, looked up and said, "I dunno and I'm not crappin' around, I dunno, no shit." He turned to his sister. "You're probably right, ma yells a lot and probably it's because she cares. But I think dad cares and he can't help a lot about how he is. And I don't believe that crap about if he don't show it then it doesn't matter. I think it matters. For all we know he's eatin' his guts out. And I don't know if that's true, but if it is, that's gotta' mean somethin'. I mean, for Christ's sake, he's here."

I've heard other teen-agers make comparably insightful statements but I never cease to marvel at the insightfulness some adolescents possess. It confirms what I've long believed, that insight is not so much a function of age or intellect as it is of emotional sensitivity, responsiveness.

"Alice, what do you think of all that?" I queried.

"I got to admit that he's probably right."

"You got to. You mean you got to but don't want to?" I said in a teasing tone.

She turned a little pink and chuckled, "I want to. But you know what's one of the first problems in this family?"

"Tell me."

"First problem is we never do nothing together."

I've never been a prime exponent of the idea that the family which plays together stays together. Some family outings involve activities which have little or no appeal to one or more members. The result often is not so much pleasant interactions as harsh clashes. At this point, however, I was not about to discourage any proposal by anyone in this troubled family.

"What did you have in mind, Alice?" I asked.

"Oh, I don't know. It just would be so nice to do something as a family. It'd be different."

"Sure be different," agreed John.

"Why don't you discuss it among yourselves." I got up and walked to the back of the room and poured myself a cup of coffee. I heard them discussing a picnic, a beach outing, finally, a movie. They settled on a movie. Kathleen, I observed, did most of the talking. Alice seemed unhappy with the decision.

"A movie. Oh, mother. A movie we can't even talk to each other."

"Daddy, what . . ."

"I think a movie's O.K., Alice," he observed.

I agreed with him. As a starting point it was probably the least threatening of any social evening. Togetherness. I thought the decision pretty good.

"What do you think, John?" I asked.

"I'll go along with it."

At this point we couldn't realistically ask for much more.

THE TEST RESULTS

Following this initial interview, Dr. Mansfield felt that an exploration of the Whitings' fantasy life would be helpful in assessing familial dynamics. Many psychologists, Mansfield among them, believe that an exploration of unconscious thoughts, feelings, and perceptions is an effective and an efficient way to come to understand how family members conflict, differ, and gibe with each other emotionally.

Accordingly, the Thematic Apperception Test and the Family Sentence Completion Test were administered to the four Whitings. The results follow.

Francis' T.A.T (Excerpts)

12 M.

Young man has dead pan expression, not really asleep. . . . He's drugged. . . . Older man who's in control coming at him. . . . The older man is really a detective who found out that this is a house of dope peddlers. . . . The detective has him locked up and put away . . . so he won't contaminate people.

9 B.M.

Buncha' hoboes . . . lazy bunch of guys who won't look for work. . . . They're all lying around sleeping, not doing anything. . . . Cop comes and moves them along.

18 B.M.

Man being mugged on the streets of New York City. . . . Respectable man too, you can tell by his clothes. . . . He's mugged. He was minding his own business. . . . He wanted to be alone. . . . He gets out of it all right. He's an expert in karate. . . . He's a peaceful man but since he's attacked he defends himself. . . . Police come and haul mugger away.

7 B.M.

A man thinking about his life, thinking about himself when he was younger, thinking about the dreams he had that never came off. . . . (Q. What's he thinking?) He's thinking he got mixed up with the wrong people, people who put him down. . . . but he snaps out of it. He figures his life could've been worse.

4

Man and woman fighting. He's very polite. . . . She's a tramp and a nag. . . . He hates fights, she seems to enjoy them. . . . Yeah, it's a husband and wife fight. . . . She nags him like always. . . . He's trying to get out to go for a walk . . . just to be alone for a while.

5

Man found his wife dead. . . . He doesn't feel good about it. . . . In fact, you might say he feels bad. . . . She had a long illness. . . . She suffered. . . . He was a dutiful husband, I mean he met all his commitments to her. . . . Now she's gone.

6 G.F.

A man talking to his secretary. . . . It isn't something he wants to do but he has to. He has to fire her. . . . He doesn't want to 'cause she's one of those birds with connections. . . . He catches hell from the big-wigs for firing her. . . . But he convinces them he can do the job cheaper and better without her. . . . In the end he gets praise from the boss.

2

Man doing his work on the farm. He's a real hard worker. He just finished gettin' one field ready for planting. Now he's gettin' ready for the next one. . . . That's a next door neighbor over on the right and here, that's a kid waitin' for the school bus.

6 B.M.

Man coming home after being away a long time. . . . He's talking to his mother. . . . He's come home after a long time to live with her again. . . . He's bankrupt. He wants to live with her 'cause he discovered he can't hack it alone. . . . She tells him he can stay for a little while anyway.

The Family Sentence Completion Test—Francis

1) *A mother is* very necessary in the home.
2) *A father should* be strong and do the best he can.
3) *A daughter is* someone who helps out.

4) *An unhappy father* is a man who's not appreciated.
5) *The worst thing a mother can do* is not love her kids.
6) *A mother who nags* is hell on earth.
7) *A happy mother is one who* gets her own way.
8) *A good son is one who* does like he's told.
9) *Parents who quarrel* have their reasons.
10) *Children who fight in a family* are a pain.
11) *A mother who kisses* is a rare thing.
12) *A good daughter is one who* helps out around the house.
13) *A father who kisses* is weird.
14) *A son is* something you got to put up with.
15) *Kissing in the family* [uncompleted]
16) *The worst thing a father can do* is desert.
17) *A son should* do as he's told.
18) *A father is* a hard thing to be.
19) *Family fights are* unnecessary and they're vulgar.
20) *A good mother is one who* does her work.
21) *A mother should* run her house right.
22) *A daughter should* be obedient.
23) *A happy father is one who* works hard for his family.
24) *An unhappy mother* doesn't bring up her kids right.
25) *A good father is one who* meets his commitments the best he knows how.

Francis Whiting is a man who is emotionally dissociated from people. An analysis of the projective tests indicates that people are threatening to him. He has learned that they impose emotional obligations. They expect him to emote, to express warmth, nurturance, and love. And it is precisely in the area of emotional expression that he feels threatened and thereby inadequate. Apparently Francis has never achieved even the most rudimentary levels in this area of personality development.

It is not surprising, then, that we find a strong narcissistic element complementing this emotional dissociation from people. As a child, Francis found that it was not rewarding to love others. Presumably, his first fumbling attempts to do so were rebuffed. Perhaps he never tried. Or again, perhaps he never learned. It matters not. Presently he prefers to love himself, to take care of himself only. And, if there isn't too much reward in this narcissistic approach to life, at least there is no threat.

Francis is a remarkably autonomous man. Up to now, anyway, he has relied upon himself alone. His paternity has not abated his jealous-like zeal to maintain his emotional independence. Even, perhaps especially, after twenty years of marriage his need to remain emotionally unfettered is very strong. An intense conflict between the need to be an emotionally autonomous man and the obligations imposed by paternity has resulted.

A major effect of this conflict is self-abasement. Most of his self-feelings are hypercritical and belittling. At this time he is cognitively and emotionally convinced that he is an inferior husband, father, and man. Much of Francis' fantasy life, then, involves a constant self-flagellation for what he perceives to be the interpersonal failures of a lifetime.

A second effect of this conflict is to be nurtured. Francis has a very strong need to be supported, to be consoled, to be taken care of. This need appears to be long buried and essentially unmet during most of his life. Francis is quite at a loss as to how he should go about trying to fill this need and even worse, he is stymied by the fact that he has learned to derive much reward from his emotional dissociation and autonomy.

Another effect of this conflict is to engender anger, at times even hatred. This hatred is directed at members of his family, since it is they who impose emotional obligations upon him, to be warm, to be nurturant, to be loving. As we have noted, he is threatened, he feels inadequate about meeting the needs of others and their existence is a perpetual reminder of his emotional inadequacies. It is they who have cast him into the role of husband and of father, both basically nurturant roles. And, when he cannot avoid their obligations, his constant response is hate.

Finally, Francis has a low sexual drive. He is not especially motivated to seek the company of either men or women. His fantasies reflect little or no concern for sexual encounter of any kind. Indeed, to a considerable extent, he denies his own masculinity. Quite probably, the overt manifestation of this denial is sexual impotence.

Kathleen's T.A.T. (Excerpts)

Card 8 G.F.

This woman dreaming about the parties she attended when she was very much the "belle of the ball." . . . Men flocked to her . . . not one dance did she sit out . . . women envied her . . .

Card 2

This is a girl going off to college—away from home—to seek her fortune. . . . (Q. What do you mean, fortune?) To escape from the drabness of the farm. . . . She doesn't make the mistake that her mother made (Q.) locked in—she (mother) is chained to the homestead. . . . The young girl escapes it all.

6 G.F.

This is a beautiful young woman—the man is her lover—He's older but sophisticated, attractive. . . . She's married, but the relationship is so fulfilling. . . . In fact she can be a better mother because of it.

9 G.F.

She's escaping her other self . . . escaping the miserable life she has to bear—she's escaping because she's unappreciated.

13 M.F.

The woman has just been sexually fulfilled. It's an affair, of course . . . the man feels a little guilty . . . she does, but only a little. She can live with it.

4

The woman's lover wants to leave her. . . . She desperately seeks to hold on. . . . But like so many men, he's cruel. . . . He used her. . . . She goes back to her family. . . . At least now she's got memories and not so much guilt 'cause the affair is over. . . . That's a relief that it's over. I mean. . . . The woman's gorgeous. Oh, I just saw the other woman in the background. Well, it's actually the same woman, just another view of the same woman, her sexy, other self. She's very attractive, like I said.

7 G.F.

A mother with her daughter. The daughter is a young, spitting image of the mother, except that the mother has let herself go, she gives me the impression of being sort of fat. The mother is talking to the daughter. They're very good friends, mother and daughter. The daughter wants her mother to have a baby. . . . That's a doll the daughter's holding, not a real baby. . . . Anyway, mother has no more kids. One's enough.

The Family Sentence Completion Test–Kathleen

1) *A mother is* unhappy when she is overworked.
2) *A father should* work hard and look out for his family.
3) *A daughter is* preferable and is to be loved.
4) *An unhappy father* is common.
5) *The worst thing a mother can do* is to have an affair.
6) *A mother who nags* is tiresome.
7) *A happy mother is one who* has time to herself.
8) *A good son is one who* obeys.
9) *Parents who quarrel* are better than parents who don't talk.
10) *Children who fight in a family are* upsetting.
11) *A mother who kisses* is one who feels loved.
12) *A good daughter is one who* has learned her manners.
13) *A father who kisses* is a father who cares.
14) *A son is* a father's responsibility first.
15) *Kissing in the family* is what we all want.
16) *The worst thing a father can do* is act like he doesn't care.
17) *A son should* love his mother.
18) *A father is* needed.
19) *Family fights are* depressing.
20) *A good mother is one who* puts up with her life.
21) *A mother should* love her family.
22) *A daughter should* love her mother.
23) *A happy father is one who* would be a joy to have around the house.
24) *An unhappy mother* is an unloved mother.
25) *A good father is one who* protects his family.

Kathleen's fantasy life indicates that she is both motivated and capable of relating to people outside her immediate family. Interaction with those outside the family does not impose obligations upon her which she feels she cannot meet. Why? Because they relate to the sexual her, the aspect in her personality makeup in which she feels the most secure. Thus, she is able to relate to both men and women equally well. Outside her family her role is simply "woman" and as she knows too well, a pretty and attractive one. In her relations with other people no threatening obligations are imposed upon her and equally important, her feminine sexuality is not ignored. Indeed, outside her family she feels positively enhanced. Within the family she feels demeaned. And so, in the same way that Francis was threatened by his roles of husband and father, so Kathleen is threatened by her roles of wife and mother. She feels inadequate as a mother and as a wife. It is interesting to note, however, that motherhood poses far more threat for her than does being a wife. The sexual aspects of the wifely role are still very much attractive to her. Any feelings of being demeaned or the many dissatisfactions she feels being a wife appear to be more a function of her relationship with Francis and not so much a function of the role, per se.

Kathleen's style of interaction with men and women is seductive and self-assured. Both these styles are a function of her narcissism, for Kathleen is narcissistic. Like her husband, she learned a long time ago that she can love herself without threat. Unlike him though, Kathleen developed another love. It stems from her self-love. It is her love of Alice. Alice, she views as an extension of herself, a kind of puerile feminine alter-ego. Alice provides her with an opportunity to give manifestly to another human being when in reality she continues to give to herself. She finds the other family members if not demeaning certainly not enhancing. They do not relate to the sexual Kathleen. She has discovered that it is only by shutting them out of her dynamic life, by focusing upon her own needs, that she can maintain a semblance of emotional balance.

Kathleen's most acute needs, then, are sexual. Her fantasy life is most rich in this area. Her desire for an extramarital affair is very strong. Her emotional view at this time is that such an affair would be emotionally supportive, enhancing, and rewarding. She feels she would be fulfilled as a woman. Even more, an affair would provide her with the consolation, the succorance she needs to mitigate the drabness and pain of her present life. As is true of most people, then, an aspect of Kathleen's sexual needs includes dependency.

She is inhibited from acting out in this desire for an affair by her conscience which is very strong. To date she has not become involved in any extramarital activity because she feels the guilt would be too much to bear. Indeed, the strength of her conscience is such that she already feels much guilt just because of her desire, still very much repressed.

Another factor which inhibits her from acting out sexually is her deep-seated belief that all men have a high capacity for cruelty and worse, that they want to use her, probably sexually. These projected fears work with her conscience to inhibit any sexual acting out.

The conflict between her desire for an affair and the inhibitory effects of her conscience and fears has engendered much hostility in her and this is directed toward her family. She is able to ventilate some of this hostility by criticizing, belittling and arguing with them. Much of this hostility, however, she represses. It continually nags at her unconscious. And the strain of keeping this anger in check keeps her in a state of discomfort, sometimes of downright unhappiness. At her deepest levels, then, Kathleen feels that her family, Francis especially, is the cause of her problems. If Francis and the children didn't exist she could become fulfilled as a woman.

Kathleen's problems, then, center on her inability, even resistance, to function in the role of wife and mother. Even after twenty years of marriage she is not emotionally equipped to deal with these roles. She is very unsure of what is involved in filling them and to some extent she is not interested in finding out.

John's T.A.T. (Excerpts)

9 B.M.

Bunch a' guys that all look alike. "Cool" guys, relaxed, independent. Can't think of any story.

18 B.M.

Could be either a guy being attacked from behind or could be a friend helpin' a guy on with a coat. (Q. Which one?) Probably a friend helpin' a guy on with his coat. After a party. Guy had a nice time. Maybe he's a little cocked. Yeah, he's a little cocked. He's goin' home now.

7 B.M.

Young guy and an old guy. Could be a father givin' his son like they say "words of wisdom." It's all crap. Son is tunin' him out. Old man's got nothin' to offer. Son's bein' very patient and very kind to him, only because he believes in that "honor thy father" crap.

13 B.

A little lonely kid, a little lonely kid who learned how to play alone. Just moved into a very poor section. He was very lonely at first 'cause no one would talk to him, no one would play with him. It was like he was livin' in his own little world. At first he was wicked lonely. Now he's gotten used to it.

13 M.F.

Guy just finished with his girl. He loves her too. I mean it wasn't just a "quick trick." No, he loves her. They're engaged and going to be married. He feels a little worse than she does 'cause he knows she secretly didn't wanta' until they were married like all proper. Anyway, they did. It's about the sixth or seventh time. They're getting used to it. They get married anyway, when he finishes school.

1

A little kid's gotta practice his violin. He don' wanna. His mother's makin' him. He hates her. He don' see any purpose to it.... He's not gonna' be a violinist. He's right, too. He turns out to be a bum.

8 B.M.

Kid dreamin' about his father havin' his operation. Kid's worried that he's gonna' die on the operatin' table. He was right to worry. He does.

6 B.M.

Guy goin' to visit his mother in the nut house. She's been there now for about six months ... she's not gonna' make it. Two years later he returns to see her.... She's worse ... then he starts visiting her regular-like. She gets a little better.

15

Guy—not the devil—countin' the souls he picked up in this cemetery. He got damn near everyone . . . ha! Place is full of screwed up dead souls! . . . He bought their souls. . . . But they lived it up while they were livin'.

2

Mother over there on the right. She's got another kid on the way. . . . Her daughter's going off to school. . . . Her son's workin' his ass off in the field. . . . The daughter's got it knocked. . . . She goes off to school. He works in the broiling sun. It's not fair. . . . So what else is new? . . . The mother's supervising to see he does his job right . . .

The Family Sentence Completion Test—John

1) *A mother is* a nag, bag, hag.
2) *A father should* be something.
3) *A daughter is* who knows?
4) *An unhappy father* is what I got.
5) *The worst thing a mother can do* is be a mother if she doesn't want to be.
6) *A mother who nags* is like all of them.
7) *A happy mother is one who* I'd like to meet.
8) *A good son is one who* puts up with his parents.
9) *Parents who quarrel* set a bad example.
10) *Children who fight in a family are* children who've got bad parents.
11) *A mother who kisses* is a good mother.
12) *A good daughter is one* who doesn't bug.
13) *A father who kisses* is cool.
14) *A son is* I don't know.
15) *Kissing in the family* would be embarrassing (in my family).
16) *The worst thing a father can do* is act like he don't want to be a father.
17) *A son should* be helped.
18) *A father is* a guy who you can look up to.
19) *Family fights are* not something I like.
20) *A good mother is one who* is happy.
21) *A mother should* love all her kids the same.
22) *A daughter should* [uncompleted]
23) *A happy father is one who* I'd like to meet.
24) *An unhappy mother* is one I got.
25) *A good father is one who* listens to you and talks to you when you want to talk.

John Whiting's fantasy life is permeated by many conflicts. On the one hand he seeks to be like his father, emotionally autonomous, and on the other he seeks to identify with others, to incorporate their personality characteristics. Compounding this most basic of conflicts is the fact that while he incorporates strong elements of narcissism he also has a very strong drive to relate to others sexually.

Within his family he has experienced few emotional rewards. However, outside the family he has experienced enough rewards to keep him from being totally disillusioned or dissociated from people. The effect of this has been to keep him in a state of anxiety about the worth of others, to vacillate in how he treats them, or to be unsure in evaluating others' treatment of him. John's confused perception of other people probably results in much inconsistent behavior.

As noted, he possesses strong elements of narcissism. This stems from his earliest years when he (like Kathleen and Francis before him) learned to love himself too well because not much love was forthcoming from his parents. His present strong feelings of inadequacy stem from the emotional deprivation of his earliest years.

His feelings of inadequacy clash with his budding feelings of sexual potency. This conflict precipitates much anger which is directed not only toward his parents but toward his sister, too. John resents Alice, even hates her. He feels that she's been loved, even doted upon by his parents, especially his mother. The fact that his parents starved him for affection has done much to feed and nurture his sense of worthlessness. For much of this he blames Alice. Her existence has prevented him from obtaining even little scraps of love from the paucity available in the Whiting household.

His feelings of hate toward the family are mitigated in part by a very strong, but unintegrated, conscience. In large measure John believes that it's wrong to hate. More than he would like, he is identified with heaven and hell. He is conflicted, then, about the hate which he feels toward his family. He is becoming increasingly impatient with his strong conscience. His latest delinquent acts may be understood, in part at least, as an unsuccessful attempt on his part to convince himself that he doesn't have a conscience.

Alice's T.A.T. (Excerpts)

7 G.F.

This is a mother and daughter. The mother wants the daughter to babysit for a neighbor. The daughter doesn't want to. The mother starts slow at first to convince her to do it. Then she starts yelling at her about it. The mother got a real thing about what the neighbors think.

12 F.

This is a mother up in front and that's her in the back too. The back part of the picture is the witch part of her, her evil, bad side of her. The mother's thinking about how bad she is and about how nobody loves and helps her. She's trying to be a better person. She works hard at it and in the end she gets rid of most of the witchy things in her.

2

This is a teacher going to school. She teaches the fifth grade. That's her mother over here and her father. They live on a farm. The mother has an unhappy look on her face and so does the daughter who's a teacher. They probably had a fight but it will be O.K. When she comes back from school it's all forgotten, what they fought about, I mean.

3 G.F.

That's a mother who's just going into her room. There's just been a real terrible fight downstairs. The mother started out yelling at her children and then the father got into it to smooth it over and instead of smoothing it over, it all got worse like it usually does when he butts in. She feels that the whole family's against her. And she spends the rest of the day in her bedroom trying to get over it. She does finally.

9 G.F.

That's a young woman running away from home. She wants to get away from home because her mother's nagging her to death. Her mother is coming up after her. She wants her to come back to the house because the mother, who's a real pain, needs her real bad. If the daughter goes back to her mother she'll never be independent. Well, she goes back for a little while because she loves her mother. She loves her a lot. Anyway, they do go back home and the daughter lives with her for one more year.

5

A mother who's coming in to her living room. She wants to talk to her husband who's there alone. She feels she's got to talk to someone because she feels very lonely and very unhappy. She's very worried about her children, two boys who are always in trouble. She's got a scared look on her face because she's afaraid they're going to end up fighting, like they usually do. This time they don't, however. They talk together and for once it all comes out all right.

The Family Sentence Completion Test—Alice

1) *A mother is* hard to take sometimes.
2) *A father should* take his family places.
3) *A daughter is* good, good, good, ugh! got to be, oh ugh!
4) *An unhappy father* is what we've got around the house.
5) *The worst thing a mother can do* is act sick.
6) *A mother who nags* makes everyone miserable.
7) *A happy mother is one who* makes a happy home.
8) *A good son is one who* doesn't sass his parents.
9) *Parents who quarrel* make an unhappy home.
10) *Children who fight in a family* are perfectly normal.
11) *A mother who kisses* is very good.
12) *A good daughter is one who* obeys her parents.
13) *A father who kisses* would be shocking, but "cool."
14) *A son is* a constant worry to his parents.
15) *Kissing in the family* is very rare.
16) *The worst thing a father can do* is not be part of the family.
17) *A son should* be more helpful and less worry.
18) *A father is* interested in his family.
19) *Family fights are* very embarrassing.
20) *A good mother is one who* doesn't complain all the time.
21) *A mother should* not nag.
22) *A daughter should* not be pushed around.
23) *A happy father is one who* does things with his family.
24) *An unhappy mother* is hard to live with.
25) *A good father is one who* you can talk to.

Alice's fantasy life reflects a major conflict between her need to identify with Kathleen and her need to be independent. She is very much mother-oriented. There is little doubt of that. Everyone of her T.A.T. excerpts has the mother as a central or supporting character. But this central character is not always one whom she seeks to be. Why? Because sometimes mother is one who is unhappy, who is to be pitied, and from whom one seeks to escape.

Alice's need to identify is characterized by a strong need for identity and for nurturance, typical in a child of twelve. Not so typical, however, is her considerable hostility toward this same person with whom she seeks to identify. The anger she feels is a function of the many inadequacies she perceives in her mother. Alice wants her mother to be more competent maternally and healthier emotionally. Thus, the themes running through both the T.A.T. stories and the Sentence Completion Test are that mother cries too much, nags too much, yells too much, etc. In short, Alice wants to be a mother, but not a Kathleen-type of mother.

What we can see, then, is that Alice lives with considerable unhappiness. Her parents quarrel a lot and she feels that, "Parents who quarrel make an unhappy home." Also, "Family fights are very embarrassing." She has little respect for her father who can't "Smooth things over," who indeed, makes things worse, "when he butts in." Her brother who "sasses" his parents and who is a "constant worry" only adds to the family tensions and her own personal woes.

However, despite her conflicts and unhappiness, Alice displays considerable health. This is seen in the optimistic outcome of each of her T.A.T. stories. Moreover, she sees herself as normal, "Children who fight in a family are perfectly normal." She also sees herself ultimately as being happy, ". . . in the end she gets rid of most of the witchy things in her."

Finally, this is a child with a conscience. To be good, to be helpful, to obey are values which she has incorporated into her emotional repertoire. A point to note, too, is that she has accomplished this with some measure of irony, even humor, i.e., "A daughter is good, good, good, ugh! got to be, oh ugh!"

A SYNTHESIS OF THE FANTASY LIVES

Narcissism is one of the emotional ingredients which transcends the Whiting family. Francis, Kathleen and John love themselves because each feels there is none forthcoming from the other. Alice, however, does love her mother and feels there is a little in return from Kathleen.

Both parents are acutely uncomfortable in their respective roles. Even worse, they both feel that the family, just because it exists, intrudes on their emotional serenity, even their health. Both have imbued much hate over the years because of this felt intrusion. The only difference between the two of them is that Kathleen ventilates it. Francis does not.

Sex is also a major problem between the parents. Kathleen has a strong sex drive which is frustrated by Francis' uninterest. The lack of interest by Francis may be a product of his hostility toward her and/or his own strong feelings of inadequacy as a husband and as a man. Kathleen, on the other hand, needs sex to reinforce her own self-image. This latter is strong only in this area of feminine sexuality. The parental dynamics, then, conflict sharply around this aspect of sex, viewed by many psychologists as an important criterion for a satisfactory marriage.

John harbors much hostility toward the other three members of the family. Some he ventilates at home, especially toward Alice, most of it is manifested in delinquent acts outside the home. The anger which John feels toward his family is derived from the Kathleen—Alice relationship. Alice, he feels, gets his share of maternal love. Most of it is derived from his deep-seated feelings that his parents have always rejected him. He feels strongly that they have not provided him with the emotional attention he deserves.

The littlest Whiting is probably the healthiest. Viewed as an extension of Kathleen, both by herself and Kathleen, she functions very satisfactorily. Her dynamics are inextricably interwoven with those of Kathleen. Whatever unhappiness she experiences she derives from the hostility in which she is steeped.

Finally, let us note that this is a family of conscience. It is conscience which has kept both Francis and Kathleen together. It is conscience which has kept them functioning as parents, albeit marginally. It is conscience which has inhibited John from more blatant acts of delinquency and it is conscience, in part at least, which has prevented his mother from becoming involved in an extramarital affair.

THERAPY WITH JOHN

P: C'mon in, John.

J: Hey, hi.

P: John, I'm glad you came this evening. I felt I needed to talk to you alone, you know, without your parents.

J: Yeah.

P: Well, what did you think about our first session?

J: I dunno. I dunno that it accomplished a lot.

P: Well, I met your family. I found out some things, like your mother's in charge of the family, sort of. Alice is much closer to your mother than you are, that your father's psychologically divorced from the family.

J: Humph. You found all that out, huh?

P: Yeah.

J: Well, I guess maybe it was worth it.

P: Yeah. But today I want to find out all I can about you. How you fit in to the family. You know as well as I do that the reason we all came together is 'cause of you, 'cause of Judge O'Brien's order.

J: Yeah.

P: All I know is that you were involved in an attempted burglary of a cassette radio.

J: Yeah. That's true.

P: Why? What was it all about.

J: I needed the money.

P: How much did you need?

J: $50 or $60.

P: Did you have to steal it?

J: I needed it fast.

P: You did?

J: Yeah. Well *I*, me, I didn't need it, my girl needed it.

P: What for?

J: Kinda' personal.

P: John, I'm . . .

J: She needed it. I mean I'm not a real crook, whatever else a lotta' people think about me.

P: I believe you.

J: She needed it for a doctor.

P: A doctor?

J: Yeah.

P: An operation?

J: Yeah.

P: She needed about $110.00 and you had to come up with half, right?

J: Yeah. [Pause] How'd you know?

P: John, you're not the first to come through here with that problem. You won't be the last either, I'm sure.

J: I guess.

P: You still like Dee?

J: Christ, yeah.

P: Why?

J: Why?

P: Yeah, why?

J: I only known her about six, no about eight months I guess. Why? 'Cause I always feel good when I'm with her.

P: How good?

J: Good, like when I was a little kid. Like when I was little kid I used to be real holy. Confession, Communion, Mass, every day. It all made me feel good, inside and outside. I felt like I was somethin', somebody, like I was, blessed. [Pause] You think I'm puttin' you on?

P: No, I don't.

J: Yeah, anyways, Dee makes me feel like that, like when I was a kid, an innocent, pure kid.

P: You don't feel like you're a pure innocent kid anymore?

J: Christ, no.

P: Why not?

J: Listen, Doc . . .

P: Call me Joe.

J: O.K., Joe. I ain't got my mother's hangups. Joe's O.K. with me. Anyways, Joe, I'm not innocent no more.

P: Why not?

J: Hey! I'm flunkin' in school. I been suspended, Sortino's on my ass the moment I walk in. I even deal in school.

P. Sell pot?

J: Yeah.

P: You been caught at it?

J: Yeah.

P: So now you feel because you've established the reputation you have you're sort of all done. You're not innocent anymore.

J: Well, I don't know if I'm sort of all done, but I sure ain't innocent anymore.

P: You're more sophisticated. You're grown up.

J: Yeah, but my head's not on straight. Let's tell it like it is.

P: O.K. Let's. How's your head not on straight?

J: [Pause] Well, I want money but I don't wanna work. I'm bored up to my ass in school. Teachers turn me off. They're all such phonies. They're all such shits. They screw off more'n the kids do. The only thing I like in school is creative writing. You believe that?

P: Yeah.

J: I had this English teacher in creative writing. She gave us three writing assignments during the whole year. Lazy bitch didn't want to read them. When I turned mine in early she read it in study and came up to me 'cause I was in study with her and she told me she had to give me an "A" but she didn't believe I wrote it. "It was too professional for me." That's what she said. "It was too professional for me."

P: You wrote it, though.

J: Betch' your ass I wrote it.

P: So how'd you make out for the rest of the year?

J: I flunked.

P: How come?

J: If I turned in anything else, if I turned in what I really can do, she'd tell me the same thing. Screw her.

P: I see. So you figure that by doing your best all that would happen is that you'd be put down. Nobody would believe that the notorious John Whiting, delinquent, pot seller and general nuisance of the school, could be a talented writer.

J: Something like that, yeah. [Pause] You got a way with words.

P: Thanks.

J: Anyway, Dee's my girl.

P: You known her long?

J: Nah, just since last Christmas.

P: When did she get pregnant.

J: February. I think.

P: How'd you feel when you found out?

J: Scared.

P: Scared?

J: Yeah, I didn't know what to do, where to go about it. I was scared.

P: She was too, I'll bet.

J: Yeah, but I didn't let on to her that I was. Anyway, we got it fixed. That's one of the things I learned out of it. All you need is money.

P: You both felt she should have an abortion?

J: Christ, yeah. What else could we do? How could I marry her? What would I do for a living? Become the number one pot seller of Middletown? Ha! That ain't no way to support a family. I know that much.

P: Who'd ya' learn it from?

J: Probably my old man. It's probably the only thing he believes in, hard work and being respected, I guess.

P: What else do you think of him?

J: He's not too much. I guess maybe that session we all had did accomplish something. I found out something. I found out that he cares in his own way. My mother's always been pretty rough on him.

P: She won't let him assert himself.

J: I don't know that he's ever wanted to but if he does now it's pretty rough on him.
[Pause]
Anyway, Dee's the only thing I got goin' for me.
P: She gives you a feeling of being important.
J: She does, yeah, she does.
P: Where do you spend your time together?
J: My house a lot. Her house a little.
P: Her mother doesn't approve of you?
J: She's a real bitch. She's even worse than my own mother. She just looks at me, her mother does, and I feel like shit.
P: She puts you down a lot.
J: Yeah. And a lot of the time it's not that she says anything, it's the looks. You know what I mean?
P: Yeah, I think so. She sends out real bad vibes.
J: Yeah. At least my mother yells. When ma's mad ya' know. 'Course most of the time she's mad about nothing. And me, she's always mad at me. [Pause] Anyway Dee's the only one I feel good with.
P: Yeah, you keep goin' back to Dee. You in love with her, would you say?
J: She's a real girl.
P: Did you have sex with anybody before Dee?
J: Not really, no.
P: How do you mean, "not really"?
J: Well, we just fooled around a little.
P: Did you have an orgasm with other girls before Dee?
J: Nah, Dee was my first. I'm not interested, I was never interested in anybody but her. Dee's my woman.
P: I take it she feels the same way.
J: Yeah. I never met anybody like Dee. She's not selfish.
P: You figure most people are?
J: Yeah, most people are out for themselves. They don't care about anybody. Look at my own family.
P: Your family are all selfish.
J: Well, I don't know if that's the fair word, but they're like all up tight about themselves, if ya' know what I mean. They're

so up tight about themselves they got no time for anybody else.

P: Like you, you mean.

J: Yeah. If ma was half as nice to me and dad and my brothers as she is with strangers, we wouldn't have half the problems we got. Like she'd be yellin' like hell at somebody and the phone would ring and she'd be just as sweet as sugar with her "hello and how are you"?

P: Yes, I believe that.

J: Yeah, she's good with other people. Yeah, and to be fair, sometimes she's O.K. at home. Mostly she's kinda' in bitchy moods. Seems for a long time.

P: John, we've been talking a little about a lot of things, but we really haven't gotten to what you said a little while ago, you know, when you said, "My head's not on straight."

J: Yeah, and I told you I don't wanna' work and I'm bored. I'm all screwed up.

P: You don't see any purpose in your life, uh, you don't know where you're going.

J: Yeah, and I don't think I can get there either.

P: Where?

J: Anywhere.

P: And that bothers you a lot.

J: 'Course it bothers me a lot.

P: All right, let's do it like this. What is it you know that you do want?

J: I'd like to be able to marry Dee, get a place to live alone with her and buy a motorcycle.

P: So you do have goals. You do have objectives.

J: If that's what you mean by goals. Yeah, I guess so.

P: Problem is you don't seem to know how to meet your goals.

J: You could say that and you know a big reason for that is that I got what Sortino calls a "bad rep." I got a bad rep in school, and I got a bad rep outa' school.

P: You mean nobody's willing to give you a chance.

J: Right.

P: The way you see it, even if you tried you couldn't make it.

J: Yeah.
P: But the reality is, John, you're only sixteen. You're very bright. Those are two real pluses if you're sincere in trying.
J: Problem is, oh, Christ, I don't know . . .
P: What?
J: It's people, people. People give me a pain in the ass.
P: You could do a lot if you didn't have to deal with people.
J: Yeah.
P: You're afraid of people.
J: I dunno. Maybe.
P: Or are you afraid of yourself?
J: What d'ya' mean by that?
P: The way I see it, and I'm not sure yet, the first problem here is, uh, here is you and how you feel about yourself.
J: Whaddya' mean?
P: You figure it like this, if I don't try I don't fail.
J: What?
P: John, you got it figured that there's no way you can be a winner. Somehow, and a lot of it has got to do with your family, you figure you're bound to lose, no matter what.
J: You think that I think I'm a zero?
P: Yeah. I think that you think that.
    [Pause]
    That's why, not the only reason but a big one, that you keep going back to Dee. Dee's got status for you. I imagine she's pretty, attractive, and a lotta' people envy you for having her as a girl.
J: Yeah, that's true.
P: She's the only success you can point to.
J: And I screwed that up too. I got her pregnant.
J: [Chuckle]   I suggest that was a mutual thing. I wouldn't beat myself over that.
J: Yeah, you're probably right. I come from a long line of losers.
P: You've believed that for a long time.
J: Never thought about it, but I guess that's so. My brothers aren't much. Tom got a girl gregnant, married her and he's divorced, and Frank, he's Tom's lap dog. Both of them

made a reputation for themselves that Sortino gave me before he even met me. Ha! I lived up to it and oh, what the hell's the point of talking about it? I'm like dad, Tom and Frank.

P: You don't figure you can break the mold.

J: What?

P: You figure you have to be like them.

J: Well, I don't gotta' be like them. But so what? I ended up like them. Right? Before you said something like "the reality is," well the reality is I'm like them. Christ, I'm worse! I'm on probation, they never got that far!

P: When I said, "the reality is" though, you didn't finish. I said "the reality is you're only sixteen." You talk about Christ. Christ, John, you're sixteen, you're not sixty-six!

J: Yeah, well, right now, Doc, I feel like I'm one hundred and sixty-six.

P: That's 'cause right now you're depressed. You're feeling real bad. You're on probation. You look back on a history of trouble, you feel like you're a zero and whatever good hopes you have, you don't know how to make them come true.

J: Yeah, I suppose.

P: One of the problems, big one, is you don't have anybody you feel you can look up to, anybody you feel you want to be like.

J: So?

P: So, maybe if you knew or saw people you wanted to be like, then maybe you'd know better what you yourself wanted to be.

J: I don't get what you mean.

P: I think a lot of your problem is like you say, you think, not think, you're convinced you come from a long line of zeros.

J: Yeah, my father and my brothers.

P: O.K. And you think you're just like them, even that you think you gotta' be just like them.

J: Yeah.

P: Why do you?

J: What?

P: Why do you have to be just like them?

J: I dunno'. I dunno, Doc, you got me all screwed up right now.

P: O.K., maybe I've moved too fast. Maybe we both have. Uh, today's Tuesday. When can you see me again?

J: Uh. Right now I'm all fuc-uh, screwed up.

P: How's Thursday? Give you a couple of days to think.

J: Yeah, O.K., Thursday.

P: Good. 'Cause Friday we're all gonna meet together. O.K., see you Thursday.

THURSDAY

P: Hey, hi!

J: 'Lo.

P: Been thinkin'?

J: Yeah.

P: What you been thinkin'?

J: A lot. You're right 'bout some stuff. But you don't got it all figured out. I mean, you make it all sound so neat and simple like it's all neat and simple. [Pause] And I don't think it is.

P: O.K. I'll buy that. Maybe I did make it, make you out to be . . .

J: Look, lemme talk. I don't want to forget nothin' that I wanted to say.

P: O.K.

J: See, there's a lot you don't know about. I don't feel like I gotta be like my old man and my brothers. I do sometimes, I do sometimes, but sometimes I don't. It's true I think they're zeros. A lot of it has got to do with my mother. She's always puttin' my father down. I hate her for that. She used to put Tom down an awful lot. I remember that, and Frank too. Then when they left the house she started on me, like, "You're just like your father," and Christ, do I ever know what she thinks of my father! [Pause] And you know what's real weird about all of this is that all of us guys in the family all came to believe it.

P: Believe what?

J: That we're all zeros. I mean we used to say it to each other and about each other. Like I remember Tom used to say it all the time about dad, and about Frank too. And then I used to say it about Tom and Frank and about dad too. Only we didn't use the word zero so much, we used another word, "nothin'." Like, "dad's a nothin'." Imagine that! "Dad's a nothin'," we'd say that all the time. Ma said it, Tom said it, Frank said it, so I said it. And now Alice says it. Only she don't say it like that. She's got her own word, "blah." But no matter how you add it all up it still comes out to zero.

P: Are you saying that it's all your mother's fault?

J: Nah. Well, I don't think so. If my mother puts my father down, then a lot of it's got to be his fault. That's why I hate him. He lets her dump on him.

P: Why do you think that?

J: Why? I dunno' except one thing my father said when we all met the last time. It stuck in my mind. He was talkin' about bein' too quiet and what he said was, "I guess I take after my father. Runs in the family."

P: Are you saying that your father lets himself be put down because it's sort of a Whiting family trait among the men to be quiet, uh, to meekly accept being put down?

J: Yeah.

P: But, John, you're hardly meek.

J: Yeah, but I'm pretty quiet.

P: Do you let yourself be put down by many people?

J: No. I guess not. [Pause] Well, what do you think?

P: I think you've done a lot of thinking in the past couple of days. That's good.

J: Yeah.

P: I think there's a lot of truth to the fact that probably your mother has been putting your father down over the years and you all learned to put him and each other down. The psychology of this is very . . .

For no apparent reason it was at this point that John exploded.

J: Down, down, down! I'm sick of all this psychology crap.

P: What?

J: You really wanta' know how I feel? I hate them all. Why do

I hate them? Because I'm the one who's the family shit. Not Tom. Not Frank. They're not even home anymore—and now I know why. They wanted to escape my crazy family. They wanted to escape being shit on.

P: You're the one everybody shits on.

J: You want the truth, the pure truth? There's so much hate in my house it comes outa the woodwork. My mother hates my father. My father hates my mother. Alice hates my father and they all of them, hate me. That's how it is.

P: And you hate them all back.

J: Yeah. [Pause]

P: And do you want to?

J: Who wants to hate?

[Pause]

You're right, I been doing a lot of thinkin'. About that, you're right. My mother and my father, they're screwed up. I know I am, but they're just as bad, maybe worse.

[Pause]

Somehow I ended up in the middle of the whole goddamned disaster.

[Pause]

P: I can understand how you'd feel this way from everything you've said and from what your family said last time we met. I'm glad we had these couple of sessions alone. I figured that there might be some things that you felt you needed to say to me alone first and the stuff about Dee I figured maybe you're not ready to discuss that with your family yet. But you know, John, your feelings about your parents and Alice, those you ought to share with them if things are gonna get better for you and for them.

J: Yeah. You been sayin' that. I know that. We all oughta' talk to each other. I know that.

P: That's why we're gonna meet as a family again.

JOE MANSFIELD'S REFLECTIONS

What's a delinquent? A bored, scared, bewildered kid who

doesn't know where he is, where he's going.

He's very unhappy and he's not at all sure about the why of it.

He's only sixteen, only sixteen, and he feels like the family scapegoat, a kind of emotional whipping boy.

Life has been unkind to him. No, not unkind, it's been positively cruel to him.

There's a lot of hate in him. A terrible lot of it quite rightly is directed toward those who engendered it into him, his mother and his father. There's hope here still, though, because the hate he feels toward them vacillates. I suspect it does because he feels that while they are the ones who gave birth to his problem, they are also the ones who gave birth to him.

He's aware at some level that he is the object of the displaced hostility and frustrations which over the years his parents have developed toward each other. And it is precisely this semiawareness which has led to a remarkable amount of understanding and, hopefully, will lead in time to a mitigation of his hostility.

The following session includes actually the three subsequent meetings with the Whitings. The tapes of these meetings were edited, abbreviated, and synthesized for readability.

THERAPY SESSION II WITH FAMILY

The next evening the four Whitings arrived promptly at 7:30 and at the second meeting took the same seats they had had at the first session, a typical familial procedure.

After the usual exchange of banalities, I looked at Alice and asked, "How was the movie?"

She shrugged, "Nothin' much."

"You didn't enjoy it."

"It was O.K. A movie's no way to get to talk. I think I said something like that. I mean . . ."

"Oh, Alice, stop being a wet blanket," piped in Kathleen.

"But mother, we didn't even go out for a snack after. All we did was go to a movie and go home. I mean, geez, who talked to who?"

"There was no talking, no interchange?" I asked.

"No. Nothing. It was, uh. It was, how can I put it, tense. Yeah, tense, embarrassing. Isn't that awful, we're all tense with each . . ."

"Alice!" Kathleen cried out. "What a terrible thing to say. To be embarrassed by your parents."

"For Christ's sakes, ma, she didn't say that she was embarrassed by you," John shot in.

"Oh, mother, how could I ever be embarrassed by you or because I'm with you. Everybody keeps telling me I look just like you. Everybody says I even act like you."

"How do you feel about that?" I asked.

Alice glanced, and not a little fearfully, at her mother.

"Don't look at your mother," I remonstrated. "Look at me. Tell me. How do you feel about people thinking that you look and act like your mother?"

"I don't know," she said in a soft, sincere tone.

"You don't know."

"No."

Kathleen was looking at her a little too intently. I looked at her and asked, "What are you thinking, Kathleen?"

"I'm thinking that that's a very embarrassing question to ask a twelve-year-old."

"Why?"

"Well, what twelve-year-old wants to be seen as her mother. After all, I'm forty . . ."

"Yeah, but you don't look it, Kath," Francis volunteered.

I continued to focus on Alice. "Alice? You must have some feelings about it."

"Yeah, mom is young looking."

"She's pretty," her father added.

Kathleen's intent look softened. A little smile tugged at the right corner of her mouth.

"Oh, Alice, tell us," she urged.

I was a mite irked. I knew Alice would tell us now. Her mother had given her permission. This was one of the problems I had already learned. Feelings and statements tended to come out only if Kathleen permitted it. I'd hoped that Alice would express herself sans the usual maternal O.K.

"Well, I like looking like you, mother. I guess that's true . . ."

"But," said Kathleen. Had her tone hardened?

"Kathleen, I'd appreciate it a lot if you'd let Alice tell it her own way," I interjected. Alice, I noticed, had edged over, more than a little bit over, to the other corner of the couch. Afraid of what she wanted to say? I thought so. She probably felt she needed support. I was determined to provide it.

"Well, you *are* pretty, mother, but I'm not you and you're not me." She was looking at her mother with what looked to be a little of Kathleen's own type of defiance.

"I know that you're not me, darling."

"Mother, you're too protective."

"Protective?" Kathleen looked genuinely puzzled.

"You still pick me up at school."

"Only when it's raining."

"Christ, ma, she won't melt," John quipped.

"Lots of times I want to be with my friends," added Alice.

"Well, why didn't you tell me. You've never told me that. You never tell me anything. I'm the only one in this family that ever does any talking."

"I tried a couple of times but you're always mad."

"I'm not mad always."

"You are too when you pick me up at school. You come pick me up and, and you do it like you don't want to. Why do you bother?"

"If what Alice says is true, why do you, Kathleen?" It was Francis who asked the question. There was only simple curiosity in his tone.

Kathleen seemed puzzled herself. "I don't know, I don't know."

"I think it's that you're just overprotective, I think it's all got to do with this, 'look like and be a baby bit,' that's why we fight about what I wear to school. Really, mother, I think I'm perfectly able to decide what to wear to school. Kids just don't wear dresses to school. They just don't."

"I think jeans are all right once in a while and you know perfectly well that . . ."

"Well, if they're all right once in a while, why aren't they all right whenever I want to . . ."

"It's just more sophisticated to vary your wardrobe. My God, Alice, you have a closet full of dresses . . ."

"And you bought them all," Alice replied with feeling.

"And she just said that none of the kids wear dresses. So what the hell good are the dresses that *you* bought." John said that almost sneeringly.

"You don't have to swear to make a point, John," she responded sarcastically.

"Oh, mother, don't be such a hypocrite. Look like a lady. Be a lady, blah, blah, blah. And you swear more than anybody in the family."

Kathleen was acutely embarrassed. She looked at Francis, almost beseechingly. And happily, he rose to the occasion. "Alice, it's none of your business if mother swears. It's not for you to tell her how to talk. Try hard to remember that you're twelve and she's your mother."

Alice looked to be nonplussed by her father's reprimand. She said nothing. I looked at them. The four of them were all talking to each other. It was hardly love flowing back and forth. But there certainly was a lot of pent-up emotion. Francis had shut Alice off. She edged even further away from her mother and curled up at the other corner of the couch like a pretty little kitten, I thought.

There was a momentary lull. I was determined not to lose the emotional and verbal interchange. I looked at the youngest Whiting. "You certainly looked surprised by your father's comment."

Alice looked at me and nodded.

"Why were you surprised?"

"He doesn't usually do that."

"What?"

"Defend mother."

"If you think he should do that, why don't you tell him."

Alice looked at her father with a little embarrassment, "Daddy, I "

Francis seemed upset. "Alice, I don't want compliments from my twelve year old daughter. I know what I'm supposed to and not supposed to do."

Quiet.

"Well, daddy," she asked gently, quietly, almost whisperedly, "why, why don't you?"

The question was a hard one, maybe a cruel one, but I'm sure it came from whatever affection Alice had for her father.

He looked at her with embarrassment, anger, confusion? I couldn't tell. He started slowly, looking down at the floor. "You know, you kids, are kids. You're kids who just don't know about me and your mother. You don't know what it was like for us. And why should you? We never told you much about what it was like growing up for us. I'm tired. I'm very tired. I'm goddamned tired [his voice had risen, cracked a little] of being told I'm quiet. That's how I am. I am what I am. Why can't I be respected for that? My father was quiet. Nobody criticized him for it. We all respected him for it. Everybody tells me I'm unemotional. My father and mother, they never showed me much emotion, love, whatever you want to call it." As I sat there listening to Francis I concluded that this supposedly quiet man was also very much a thinking person.

"Fran [I'd not heard Kathleen call him Fran until now], Fran," she repeated softly, "It worked for them, it doesn't for us."

"Damn it, Kathleen. My mother went along with him on it, on not being all emotional. She supported him. You don't. You're always yelling. So much you show me up. You yell. I don't, and the kids compare us and put me down 'cause I don't. I'm not mad at you, but Christ, let up on it."

"But Fran . . ."

"Let me finish, Kath. There's some truth to what Alice says." Francis was not looking at his knees anymore. He was looking directly at Kathleen. "You do swear more than all of us and you're always telling her to be a lady. It's not right for you to do that, but I don't think it's her place to tell you about it either."

"Whose place is it, Francis?" I asked.

"It's mine. It's mine," he said wearily.

There was a momentary lull. And it was I who broke it. "And if you don't, Francis, then what happens is that John or Alice take over and do tell her, and fights, resentment and a lot of hostility results."

"That's for sure. There's a lot of hate in this family," John said, aping his father's weary tone.

"But there is love too," said Kathleen.

"Ha! Christ, you gotta' be kiddin', ma."

There was a look of real shock on Kathleen's face as she cried out, "Oh, I am so tired of all this! I am, am just sick of this so-called therapy. Is this, all this, supposed to be good for us? To have our children, a twelve-year-old and a sixteen-year-old, feel perfectly free to speak so critically, so rudely. Is this supposed to be good for us."

The questions were addressed to me, but I didn't respond. I took them to be rhetorical. And I was right. She continued.

"I mean, ever since I came in here tonight all I've heard is how inadequate I am as a mother and this from a twelve-year-old! Now this sixteen-year-old who's still wet behind the ears tells me there's no love in me. I mean for heavens sakes!" She was looking at me now. I saw no need to respond. Kathleen was just beginning. That was obvious to all of us.

"A little while ago, Francis, you said something meaningful, very meaningful and very true and I don't think anybody but me here heard it. You said, 'I am what I am and why can't I be respected for that?' You said that and goddamn it all [she looked directly at her daughter as she cursed], that's really the point of everything. You are what you are and I am what I am and these two children can't seem to understand it. My father swore like a trooper. We accepted it. Just because he did that didn't mean that we had the right to do the same. I didn't dare swear, nor did anybody else in my family. And you, you Miss Alice goddy-little-two-shoes who doesn't like to be told what to wear, you have no conception what it is to be dictated to about clothes styles. My father . . ."

"Kath, Kath," now it was Francis who interrupted Kathleen, "when I was saying about 'I am what I am' it was you who pointed out something.   And I been thinkin' for the past five minutes, you were right.   It was you who pointed out, 'It worked for them,' it worked for our parents but it doesn't for us."

There was a pause.

"Maybe, Kath, maybe a little of it is because we're not the complete bastards they were."

"Why, what do you mean?" asked Kathleen.

She had been stopped in the middle of what we all thought was going to be a very long diatribe.   She looked at him with curiosity, puzzlement and was it, respect?   We waited for his reply.

"You told me and I knew about your house.   I remember you told me how you never had any privacy as a kid.   We give them that, maybe even too much.   Your father was cruel, he beat your mother.   Our kids never saw anything like that."

"So why are we here, then?" I asked.

"Search me," Francis sighed.   "All I know is I spent half my life trying to understand my father.   I always thought that was my responsibility.   Now I find myself spending the other half trying to understand my kids.   Christ!"   Francis was a reflective man, no doubt about it.

"Dad."   We all turned to John.   He'd moved over, to the chair right next to his father.   "Dad, what kind of a guy was he, your father, I mean."

Francis seemed a little what?   disconcerted? by John's move. He responded, though looking down again at his knees.

"He was a tough guy."

"Tough?"

"Tough guy to know.   Cold.   Like I told you before, very quiet."

"Did you like him?"

No response.

Again John asked, "Did you like him?"

"I liked him better than I liked my mother.   'Course I didn't like her at all, so that's not much of a comparison."

"So you didn't like him too much."

"I'll be honest with you, Johnny, I never talked to him much.

He wasn't, uh, approachable. Like to talk to him you sorta' talked to him on a dare, if you know what I mean."

John was looking at him intently. "I think I understand," he said with sympathy.

"Oh Johnny," his father looked up at him and not unkindly said, "No you don't, you can't. You just couldn't know what my house was like."

I didn't want John shut off. We had to continue on this vein. I asked, "You said you father wasn't approachable, was that because he was, uh, self-righteous, sanctimonious, arrogant, uh, what?"

"Best thing, most accurate way to put it is that he was very sure of himself. I swear to God I never met a guy like him. He never doubted himself or at least he never showed us kids that he thought he might be wrong. If he thought something was right, it was right, and if he thought it was wrong, it was wrong. That's what I meant, Johnny, when I said you couldn't know. How could you know? It was like livin' with God."

"But it wasn't exactly heaven," Kathleen interjected.

"No, it wasn't heaven. It was hell."

"Why was it hell?" asked Alice, seemingly confused.

"It was hell because I was never right. I always seemed to want or to do the wrong thing. Christ! When I was in high school I wanted to get out of that house."

"See, you kids with all your silly, piddly complaints, you don't know what hard parents are really like," Kathleen chimed in.

There was another pause. I looked at John. "You think your mother's right, John?"

"Maybe she's right. I think my father's right, I . . ."

"Don't tell me. Tell them." I nodded toward Kathleen and Francis.

"What I was gonna say," he was looking at Kathleen, "was no, mom, you're not like what you describe your parents were. Me and Alice have a lotta privacy. But I don't think it's because you respect us, our privacy. I think it's 'cause you guys just don't care. And dad certainly isn't like his father, he sure don't act like God, but for a long time now I got the same ideas he used to have about wanting to get outa' the house. Christ, ma, that's exactly what Tom and Frank already did! So maybe you guys are better parents than your parents were, but we feel turned off by you like you guys felt turned off by them. Maybe it's like dad says, it runs in the family.

I looked at Kathleen, whose legs were crossed and whose arms were folded across her bosom. She had positioned herself like an impregnable emotional fortress. It was I who asked, "Do you think it runs in the family, Kathleen?"

"I'm not sure what it is you're asking me about," she replied with not a little defiance.

"What do you think runs in the family, John?"

"Kids gettin' turned off by their parents," he responded.

"Oh, every family's like that," she quipped, "Haven't you heard about the generation gap?"

"Yeah, but in our family it's not a gap. It's the Grand Canyon," he shot back.

"Oh, mother, why can't you just admit some things," Alice blurted out.

"What things?" she asked frostily.

"Oh, mother, supper every night is such an up-tight time. I'm always either a nervous wreck or embarrassed 'cause you're either nagging daddy, or complaining about John or me or if it's not one of us three, then it's about yourself and one of your headaches that you're always complaining about. And speaking of headaches, you get one every time there's a little work to be done."

"Oh, Alice, how unfair. How utterly unfair. That's just not true."

"You do, mother. You do, too. You always seem to get a headache after supper or you run upstairs crying so I have to end up doing the dishes. That's how you get me or John to do things, by always pretending to be sick so you can be waited on. Do you want to know what John and I call you behind your back? You know what?" Alice didn't wait for a reply. "We call you 'Your Majesty' 'cause you always want to be waited on, like a queen."

"Yeah, ma, you rule the house like a real tough queen," said John bitterly.

Kathleen's anger was transparent, but she did not speak. It was Francis who broke the tension. With positive wonderment, he said, "Listening to the kids reminded me I used to call my mother Queen Victoria."

"Christ," John reiterated, "It does run in the family."

"Oh, I am so sick of all this. Is all this supposed to be therapy session or is it a pick-on-mother time?" Kathleen looked at me. Her legs were uncrossed, her arms hung limply at her sides, the impregnable fortress had crumbled. She was no longer angry. She was bewildered and genuinely distressed. She looked at me, "Please tell me what's going on."

"What's going on is simply that the rest of the family, John and Francis, see parallels between this family and the ones you and he were reared in. His house was dominated by a Queen Victoria type and Alice and John feel that you function like a, a 'tough queen,' I think John called you."

"Well, my own house certainly wasn't run like that! My father ran my house like a despot."

"What was your mother like?" I asked.

"She was a nothing. She was beaten down to a nothing by my father."

"Nothing. You just called your mother a nothing," John said tonelessly.

"Well, she was. So what?"

John turned embarrassedly toward his father. "No offense, dad, but that's what I got used to calling you."

"So what?" Kathleen repeated.

"Well geez, ma, I'm just trying to show you that what we're talking about, about problems running in families, there's a lot of truth to that."

"But I called my *mother* a 'nothing'. You call your father a 'nothing'. There's a little difference there." She looked at me for corroboration.

"I was just thinking about some of the things you've said here today. You didn't admire your mother at all. Apparently you didn't want to be like her. But your father, I guess, was the strong person in the family and he swore a lot in the family and he put your mother down.   I think you said, 'he beat her down to a nothing.' Now what . . .''

"And that's what you do to daddy," Alice cried out. "Honest, mother, sometimes you act like a, a, ogre.''

"Oh, my God.   Are you saying that I act like my father in this family?''

"Well, I wanted . . .''

"Oh, I'm leaving.   I've had enough of this, this psychological garbage.''   Kathleen got up and headed toward the door. Francis and Alice rose to follow her. Neither John nor I got up.

"Mother," Alice called plaintively, "Please come, sit down.''

Francis called to her, "Please Kath, come back.''

Kathleen turned.   She was crying and was searching frantically but unsuccessfully for a handkerchief or tissue.   She stood near the door.   Her husband handed her his handkerchief and in the process of taking it from him she dropped her pocketbook and what looked like a basketful of feminine ware spilled all over the floor.   Kathleen sank to her knees and bawled like a young child.   "Oh damn, damn, damn," she cried.   Francis and Alice got down beside her and picked up and refilled the purse. Francis helped her up and led her over to a couch where they sat together. His arm was on her shoulder.   She had her head down and dabbed at her eyes with the hankie.   Alice sat next to me.

There was what seemed like a long pause while we all regained our composures.   At that moment I felt I'd let things go too far, too fast.   I should have been more protective of Kathleen, more supportive, perhaps shutting off her children who had been pretty harsh, I now realized.   An awful lot had been said.   I wasn't sure *I* could digest it.   I doubted strongly that the others could.   I wanted to end the session but not like this.

"Uh, let me say a few things then we'll close.   Kathleen, you have indeed put up with a lot.   We've all, excepting Francis perhaps, been less than kind.   John and Alice can be excused on the basis of being honest in what they said and, perhaps, being a little thoughtless and, I think, sometimes genuinely interested and curious about all the emotional history of their grandparents. *I* want to apologize.   I should have been gentler, more supportive and just plain kinder. I wasn't, let's say, at my therapeutic best. I think we could have arrived at the same point we did a few minutes ago as far as understanding, insight or whatever, without the scene which I unkindly and stupidly let happen. I'm sorry. We all need time to reflect on the past hour, especially the past ten minutes or so, reflect on it and digest it. I'm going to, I'm sure you'll all be thinking about it. Let's end it for tonight. We'll meet next Tuesday, same time, same station.

MANSFIELD'S REFLECTIONS ON THE SESSION

Kathleen's needs for dominance and dependence were well exemplified in this session. She controlled the initial moments with her interruptions and via her looks, her words, even deigned to give Alice permission to emote.* Kathleen's dominance, however, dissipated rapidly as the session proceeded, and the hostility toward her increased. Her dependency needs began to be manifest when she asked Francis for support. They became blatant with her realization that she had identified in considerable measure with her father and little at all with her mother. The realization was sudden and, indeed, harsh. But it was not devastating for she returned to the session. For a moment when she turned to us and I saw her tears, I wondered if her behavior wasn't just another emotional ploy, another version of the passive-aggressive histrionics which Alice had described, ". . . speaking of headaches, you get one every time there's a little work to be done." I'm convinced now that her reaction was emotionally genuine.

One item is already very clear. Kathleen structured her life so she wouldn't have to play the role which her own mother played, passive, dependent and the constant object of displaced hostility. Kathleen wasn't going to let happen to her what happened to her mother. Her determination in this regard is apparent.

---

*I'm convinced Alice doesn't need too much attention. Dynamically, she's the least needy member of the family. As she matures she'll become healthily independent. I noticed, too, that she has a remarkable amount of understanding and insight for a twelve-year-old.

On reflection, could part of Kathleen's tearful reaction at the close of the session, could that have been motivated a little bit by the fact that she saw some of her own mother in herself, for momentarily at least, she was the member of the family who was "beaten down to a nothing."

And the irony and the tragedy of Kathleen Whiting's emotional life is that she identified too well with the worst qualities of both her mother and her father. It is for this reason that within her own family Kathleen has become not only her mother, but her father, too. Thus, not only do her children try to beat her down like her mother was "beaten down," but she is perceived in the same light as was her father—the family "ogre."

Despite all of this, and despite their narcissism, there is affection among the Whitings. Francis and Alice got up to bring Kathleen back. They both helped to pick up the contents of the purse. Francis led her back, sat with his arm on her shoulder. I'm convinced that all these behaviors were a function of love. John has learned to communicate his affection least, probably because he has received the least. Francis, for all the comments about his quietness, spoke up and at times, I thought, insightfully. One of his more profound comments was, ". . . we're not the complete bastards they were." I took this to mean that, unlike their own parents, he and Kathleen love their children, if not a lot, then certainly in some measure. And it's that "some measure," together with the fact that he and Kathleen have never been emotionally equipped to communicate love, which has gotten them both into familial difficulty.

There are some positive outcomes from this session. One is that John and Alice learned that Francis and Kathleen had problems with their parents. They learned that their grandparents inflicted pain upon their parents, inculcated "hang-ups." They learned, I believe, that there are emotional radii that transcend the generations.

What they have not learned is that most of the familial problems, including John's delinquency, is a function of parental incompatibility. I suspect also that Kathleen and Francis are experiencing sexual problems. My best judgment is that Francis' expectations concerning a wife and Kathleen's expectations about a husband do not now, perhaps never did, gibe. These problems of role expectation need to be explored.

I need to see the two of them alone. I will do that before the next all-family session.

THERAPY WITH FRANCIS AND KATHLEEN

Mansfield's original thought was to have no more than one meeting with Francis and Kathleen alone. The breadth and the depth of the dynamics discovered and covered, however, necessitated three. The tapes of these three sessions were edited, abbreviated, and synthesized for readability.

"Come on in, c'mon in, Kathleen, Francis. Uh, I wanted to see both of you alone."

Kathleen and Francis came in, he a little sheepishly, she, I thought, a little embarrassedly. They sat down together on the couch opposite me.

"Like I said, I wanted to see you both alone, for one session."

"Why?" Kathleen asked. She spoke a little sharply, or at least there was a defiant edge to her tone. She probably felt that maybe this was going to be another pick-on-mother time.

I replied, and not a little self-consciously, "Uh, I wanted to see you both alone, without the kids 'cause I believe there may well be problems that are personal, that you just wouldn't want to bring up or discuss with John or Alice present."

It was Kathleen again who responded, "Yeah, well, I'm rapidly getting to the point real fast where I'd just as soon chuck this whole family therapy. I mean who needs . . ."

"Kath, Kath, c'mon now, let's not . . ." said Francis.

"I mean it. I mean who needs to be humiliated and be put through . . ."

Kathleen was getting back at me. She knew I felt I'd been wrong to let the last session go as far and fast as it did and consciously or unconsciously, she was letting me know I'd have to *woo* her into cooperating. I was willing to.

"I appreciate how you feel, Kathleen. If I were you I'd probably feel the same way. The last session certainly had to be embarrassing, at least embarrassing for you." But I had to be honest with her too. "This one may well be the same. That's one, perhaps the major reason I thought it would be better if the kids weren't present."

If nothing else, her curiosity was piqued. "Well, what was it you wanted to know?"

"Well, I've seen, uh, we've talked enough and the testing told me enough now, so I think I'm getting to know the Whiting family pretty well. Most of the problems which exist, I think, stem from . . ."

"Me?" asked Kathleen nervously. She was twisting a handkerchief in her hands.

"No, no, Kathleen, not you, per se. From both of you, uh, more accurately from the kind of relationship you and Francis have created. Let me make this real clear to you. Any problems which exist in your family do not come from you alone. Francis has contributed to the making of them, too. For that matter, the kids have, too. Your interaction with Francis, uh, the expectations you had for him and he had for you and how you both met each other's expectations, all that . . ." I knew I sounded garbled.

"I don't think I understand."

"O.K. Try to think. What did you expect of Francis when he married you?"

"What do you mean, expect of him?"

"Well, did you expect him to be the provider, and how did he meet your expectations? Did you expect him to be strong, dominant or weak and dependent? What did you expect of him?"

"Well, of course I expected him to be the provider. I was pregnant."

"So you expected him to fill the role of provider."

"Well, of course. Is that wrong?"

"No, no. And you need not be defensive. There's no right or wrong, I'm just trying to show . . ."

"If we both acted like the other one expected us to."

Francis completed his first comment. He was obviously interested in this.

"Yes. Exactly."

"Well, Francis has been a provider. He's provided O.K. I mean it could be better, but I don't think that not having enough money is why we're here."

I didn't want to focus all my attention on Kathleen. "What about you, Francis, what expectations did you have for Kathleen?"

"I dunno. I never thought about it. She was pregnant when we got married. She was gonna' be a mother. She's always been a mother and a housewife. I don't guess I expected much else."

"Well, has she been an adequate mother, an adequate house-wife. Let's take housewife first."

He looked at her. A little fearfully? I wasn't sure. "Ah, she's O.K."

"No. I'm not. You used to complain that I didn't always make the bed, iron, that supper wasn't ready."

"Yeah, but that was a long time ago. I don't anymore."

"He doesn't anymore 'cause he knows it won't do much good. I hate housework. And the truth is I'm not the best housewife."

"How do you feel about that now, Francis?"

"I dunno." He sounded sincere. "I never think about it."

"Well, think about it now. Your mother, what kind of a housewife was she?"

"Very efficient," Kathleen chimed in.

"How was she, Francis?"

"Yeah, she was very neat."

"Do you resent Kathleen's, uh, admitted inefficiency?"

"Yeah, I s'pose I do. I used to a lot more'n I do now."

"Did you ever speak to her about it?"

"Nah."

"I don't know that we ever fought about it," said Kathleen. "At least he," she turned to Francis, "You didn't ever make an issue out of it, did you, dear?"

"No."

"Did you want to?" I asked. "Let's be honest, Francis."

"Well, I guess there were times I sorta' got mad about it, but I couldn't see makin' a big deal, a big hassle over an unironed shirt or something."

"Are you trying to start another scene here, Dr. Mansfield?" Kathleen asked this a little heatedly.

"No, Kathleen, I'm not. Let me point something out. A few moments ago you said that Francis never made any issue out of your lack of enthusiasm for housework, that a shirt was unironed, or what-have-you. What I want to point out is that just because, or maybe precisely because he did not make an issue out of something that bothered him about you in the early stages of your marriage, that wasn't necessarily healthy. In fact, it might have been better if he had."

"Why?" she asked.

"Just wait," I said. "How much did it bother you, Kahtleen's unwillingness to do housework?" I asked.

"Oh, I dunno."

"Did you care about it a lot, once in a while?"

"Yeah, once in a while it might've bugged me. If I was late gettin' to work and I couldn't find a clean shirt then I . . ."

"Oh, come now," Kathleen cried impatiently, "marriages don't go sour because of a dirty shirt."

As gently as I could I said, "Kathleen, you interrupted him. Let's hear what Francis has to say."

"Yeah, I was gonna' say I'd get a little mad if I was in a hurry and I couldn't get a shirt."

"Why didn't you tell her?"

"'Cause it would start a fight."

"And you preferred to wear a dirty one to asking her to have a clean one ready for you."

"Yeah."

"What's the point of all this, anyway?" asked Kathleen irritably.

"The point is that right here on something as common, maybe even silly as a clean shirt, we can see an important pattern of your marriage being laid down. Francis didn't like something. You, Kathleen, were not meeting his expectations but because of the kind of person you are, Francis, and apparently still are, you preferred to not say anything than express how you felt. Quite rightly, Kathleen, you concluded it wasn't that important to him. But at home, Kath, when your own father didn't like something your mother knew about it, right?"

"Damned right," she nodded.

"So you learned quickly that Francis wasn't like your father. Maybe even you've thought often that Francis didn't care about too many things 'cause he never complained about anything."

"Yeah," she nodded. "I've thought that."

"But what we're learning now is that Francis just didn't want to start a fight. Or maybe you really didn't care. Which was it, Francis?"

He looked perplexed. "I dunno. Kathleen sure can yell. She always could."

"And you weren't used to yelling."

"No, I wasn't. There wasn't any yelling in my house ever."

"And you didn't know how to handle it."

"I guess that's right, yeah."

"The easiest thing was simply to give in and put up with a dirty shirt, or a late supper or whatever."

"Yeah," he affirmed.

"And so, in not confronting Kathleen about how you felt, you gave up a lot of your rights as a husband, as a partner in the marriage. You led her to believe that her way was O.K. with you." There was a pause. "See Kathleen, that's what I meant when I said that a lot of the problem here was not just you but came out of your interaction with Francis. What about Kathleen as a mother, have you let her know how she's done in your eyes, as a mother?"

"No, I guess not."

"Well, tell us now. How do you feel about it?"

Francis was nonplussed. This confrontation method was diametrically opposite his own style. In his usual embarrassed way he was looking down at his knees.

"I don't know what to say," he replied desolately.

"Well, I'm sure Francis doesn't think too much of me as a mother or for that matter as anything else."

"Oh, Christ, Kath, that's not true, not true."

I didn't want to get into the "anything else." I wanted to focus on the mother role. "What's a mother supposed to be like, Francis?"

"She's s'posta' take care of her kids," he mumbled.

"Does Kathleen do that?"

"Oh, she tries," he said too softly.

"Oh for God's sakes, Francis, will you for once be honest with me and with yourself. You think, no, you're sure, that I'm a lousy mother. I've known that for a long time and you think that I think you're a lousy father. I think I'm beginning to understand something, something, now." She looked directly at me. "You think that most of our problems come from the fact that we don't talk to each other about how we feel about each other. Right?"

"Right. And what each of you thinks about how the other's doing in his role as a parent. Like I'm sure that you, Francis, had certain expectations about how a mother and wife is supposed to perform and you never let Kathleen know. Maybe it ate away at you too, I don't know. 'Course this may have fit in with your own needs too, Kath."

"How so?"

"Well, we touched on this at the last session. It made you upset."

"Yeah," she replied. "You think I act like my father..."

"Well, you did incorporate some of your father's way into your own personality. We all do take on some of both parents' ways, not just the like-sexed parent. Francis, you have some of your mother's ideas about some things, I'm sure."

He nodded. "Yeah, I guess I admire efficiency in a woman. I was doing some repairs over at the Watsons'. That Watson lady, lemme tell you, runs a tight ship as a mother."

Kathleen shot him a dirty look. "And our own ship is sinking, eh?"

"And so you're disappointed, maybe even angry with Kathleen," I said.

"And you think if Francis is angry he ought to let me know."

"Yeah, especially if it's eating away at you, Francis. I think you should let Kathleen know. It's better to let each other know what's bugging you about the other. Otherwise, what happens often is that you become more distant from each other or you become irritated, angry, upset about trivial things."

"What do you do if you're just not the angry type?" asked Francis, with a kind of baleful but terribly honest look.

"He's not talking about being angry, Francis, he's talking about being honest."

"Yeah, that's right, Kath. I am. But it's not a moral honesty, so much as an emotional honesty. See, Francis, a basic problem here is that as a child growing up you got the idea that getting angry was wrong."

"I guess that's so.   Both my parents were very controlled people. They never got mad. If they were mad they controlled it very well. Looking back, I suppose they overdid it. But I don't think that they were completely wrong either. I mean, Jesus, supper in our house is more yelling time than eating time."

"Yeah, but I'll bet that a lot of the reason for that is precisely because Kathleen feels you never talk to her about how you feel about things, important things," I suggested. The look on his face suggested that this thought had never occurred to him, that in a real sense he was the cause for the yelling he detested so.

Kathleen nodded. "Yeah, but I'm the one who's guilty of the yelling. *I* do it. Alice mentioned that last time. I've thought about it a lot. She's right. What's funny about it all is the fact that I remember dinner in my father's house. It was hell for us kids. I should know better."

"Knowing with your head and knowing with your emotions are two different things."

"What do you mean by that?"

"Well, just because you know something's wrong doesn't mean you can stop doing it, even if you know it might hurt you or somebody you love. You grew up in a house with a strong, domineering and even cruel father. O.K. And you may well have hated many things about him. Your mother was, as I understand it, weak, passive and dependent. For whatever reason, your emotional choice was to be more like him than her. It was preferable as you saw it to be dominant than passive, to be strong than to be weak."

"God, I find that hard to accept, that I'd rather be like my father than my mother."

"I appreciate that, Kath, but I think it's true. I don't think it's all your fault. I don't know if that makes you feel any better to say that, but I also think that it's better to tell you than not to. Francis, you fed into the whole thing, just by choosing not to confront Kathleen when she bugged you doing and not doing things that you didn't like. Francis, tell me, you think I'm wrong in how I see it?"

"Sounds pretty right," he said meekly.

"Is it right?" I asked sharply.

"Guess so," he said looking down. There was a pause. "You got it all diagnosed, I guess."

"Francis, how do you see your relationship with . . . No, how do you see your marriage? What do you think of your marriage?"

He looked surprised by the question. So did Kathleen.

"I love my wife," he answered simply.

"Why?" I asked.

"Why?" he was really perplexed by the question.

"Yeah, why. She hasn't measured up very well as an efficient housewife or mother."

"Yeah, well maybe I'd just as soon not have, uh, an efficient woman living in my house. I hated my mother."

I was the one a little perplexed now. It was a damned good point and one that frankly had not occurred to me. Quite understandably Francis could well prefer *not* having an efficient woman around. The price of efficiency, as he saw it in his mother anyway, was rejection. Efficient women didn't have time for loving. Francis, I concluded, was a very astute guy.

"Uh, good point," I responded. "Yes, perhaps that's true. May well be. So you love Kathleen."

"Yeah, I do."

"But hon, maybe you do, but you never show it. You don't tell me."

"Do you act it?" I asked.

"Act?"

"How do you show it?"

"Guess I don't," was his glum response.

"No, you don't, Francis. I mean even in the privacy of . . ." She stopped.

Francis was reddening.

"Of the bedroom," I finished the sentence.

Kathleen nodded.

I didn't know how far we would go or how willing they were to discuss it. I was convinced that Kathleen wanted to. I glanced at Francis. He was stony faced now but I'm sure he was more than a little rattled.

"Tell me if you want to, Kathleen."

"I won't if Francis doesn't want to."   She looked at him.

"Christ, Kath, how can I say no now?"

Francis was, if nothing else, I concluded, a very honest guy. He was too embarrassed to say "no" was what he was telling us.

"Well yes, we're having our problems."

"Francis doesn't, uh, want to have relations?" I asked.

"I want to," he said.

"You can't," I responded.

"Yeah," he muttered with a long sigh.

"Well," I sighed back, "I'm not surprised."

"You're not?" Kathleen asked interestedly.

"No.   All the indications are . . . but wait, tell me how long's it been like this, that you can't, Francis."

"Uh, I don't know, couple of months maybe."

"And before that how often did you have relations?"

"Not too often. I don't know. What's often?"

"Typical, they tell me, is once, twice a week maybe."

He looked at her.   "Well, we never did it that much.   Maybe three, four times a month.   Kath's a Catholic."

"We practiced rhythm for the longest time," she added.

"I see. Anyway, now it's been two months or so since there's been any sex, right?"

Francis nodded, "Yeah."

"O.K.," I nodded back. "You didn't want to, you couldn't, uh, what?"

"Both," he answered, "both. Christ, don't ask me, I mean, I don't understand it, I don't."

Francis was mortified by the discussion, so much so, I felt myself becoming uncomfortable. However, I felt or saw no alternative but to continue.

With all the sympathy I could inject into my tone I said, "I know you don't understand it, Francis, I'm positive of that but maybe, just maybe if we can even touch on the emotions of it all, you might just find it really helpful."

"Whaddya' mean?"

"Well, as I understand it, you'd like to be able to get together with Kathleen. Is that right?"

"Yeah," he said with a mite of impatience.

"Well, impotence isn't caused ordinarily by your conscious awareness but it's a product of emotions, feelings, uh, how to . . ."

"You mean I can't with Kath because I don't feel right toward her?"

He'd said it simply and easily, better than I.

"Yeah," I said a little weakly. "You don't feel right toward her."

Kathleen had been quiet but apparently more than interested. She'd edged forward on the couch and was looking intently back and forth to each of us. For the past few moments she seemed to have focused upon her husband.

Now she broke in. "How does he feel?" she asked me.

"I don't know for sure how you feel, Francis. But one thing I do know is that sex, in marriage especially, is just another way of expressing how spouses feel toward one another. Now as I understand it, you, Kathleen, are willing but you, Francis, are . . ."

"I'm willing," he cried.

"But for whatever reason you, uh, can't."

"Yeah," he replied ashamedly.

"Which brings me to my point. You've got a lot of negative feelings toward Kathleen that you won't or better, can't seem to admit to yourself. And these feelings are preventing you from performing sexually."

"Sounds awful complicated," he said.

"It isn't really. Your body's telling Kathleen more accurately how you feel than what you've been telling us."

"Are you trying to say that I don't love my wife." He said this in a choked, shaking voice.

"I think the truth is you do and at the same time you've got a lot of hostility toward her, a lot of very negative feelings, almost none of which you've ever let yourself express toward her. And they're coming out now in this way. You're unable to love her sexually."

"You mean Francis hates me?" Kathleen asked this in a kind of shocked way.

"Oh, come now. Few people just plain love their spouses. Most married people have some negative, even a lot of negative feelings, dissatisfactions with their spouse. Thing is, most of them express some of those feelings."

Short pause.

I turned to Francis and asked, "When was the last time you expressed any dissatisfaction with Kathleen?"

He looked at me sheepishly. "I dunno," he replied.

Kathleen looked at him and not unkindly said, "Oh, Francis, you never complain about anything. You know you don't."

"Yeah, I guess I don't."

"And because he doesn't you think that, that's why he can't do anything with me?" Although a question, it came out more like a statement.

"Well, there could be a lot of reasons. That's for sure. But I think a big one has to do with a lot of repressed hostility you have toward Kath, Francis."

Francis sat next to his wife, a little woodenly, I noticed, but surprisingly composed.

I asked curiously, "Francis, you ever get mad inside?"

"Yeah."

"Well, what do you do about it?"

He looked at me. "I dunno, not much. It goes away, I get over it."

"What about at work?"

"I work alone."

"What about the kids when they were young. They must've got on your nerves. Didn't you ever get after them, you know, spank or yell at them?"

"I raised the kids when they were small," said Kathleen.

"That's true. I always figured it was her job." He paused and almost as an afterthought added, "I worked."

Kathleen corroborated his statement. "Francis was almost never around when they were small. He even worked Sundays, moonlighting. If I complained a lot, and I guess I did, he'd answer always with such honesty that, how did you put it, Fran, 'I'm committed to my work,' something like that."

"Yeah, that's true," he nodded.

"You still feel that way?" I asked.

"Look, I guess I done a lotta things wrong. One of them was not taking, uh, not helping to take care of the kids. You know what I realize? That Watson woman, she runs a tight ship, but you know, Kath, I was planing down a door upstairs and I heard her and her husband with their kids. You know, they seem to be able to do something we never been able to do."

"What's that?"

"Enjoy the kids. We never enjoyed the kids. Be honest with you," and he looked at me, "and with you, doc. I guess I always found them more a pain than anything else." He said all of this in a kind of choked-up way. If one had never heard him speak before he would have concluded that Francis Whiting had a cold. The truth was, however, that Francis Whiting was emoting. I really thought for a moment that he might cry.

Kathleen looked at him. "Fran, I always suspected that. Why didn't you ever tell me?"

"Christ, Kath, how could I? You were always bitching about them. What was the point of both of us doing it?"

"But damnit, Fran, I did bitch a lot, an awful lot, but I did 'cause you never did a damned thing to help. Just like even take them off my hands for a couple of hours on Sunday. I mean, God, Fran, there was no help." Kathleen's voice had risen sharply on the last couple of sentences.

Francis shrugged, "I know, I see that. I do see that," pause, "now."

There was silence for almost a minute. I looked from one to the other. They both were looking down apparently engrossed in thought. It was Francis who broke the silence. "We never should have had kids. Neither one of us was cut out to be a parent. We don't, we never had the constitution for it."

I was inclined to agree. Neither was emotionally equipped to deal with, to meet the infinite demands and obligations which children, just by their existence, impose upon their parents. Yet the reality is, I thought, the kids are here. They have to deal with them. But the problem was not only the children. Their lack of relationship with them was an extension, a symptom of their problems with each other and with themselves.

It seemed as if Kathleen had been reading my thoughts or at least we were on the same wave length for her next words were, "I think you're right, Fran, we probably should never have been parents. I never wanted any either, if you must know. But what could we do with them, once I was pregnant? But what I'm starting to see is that the kids aren't the problem, it's not them, it's us."

He nodded.

"We're so different, you and I. Yet we're so much alike."

"What do you mean by that?" he asked.

"We're both such private people. Maybe you're a little more private than me. You could be perfectly happy living alone, so could I, that's how we're alike, but I have to see people, you don't."

Fran nodded again.

And, simply, almost detachedly, Kathleen continued, "Neither one seems to be able to give. My excuse, maybe it is and maybe it isn't, is that I've spent twenty years giving to you and the kids. I can't anymore, that's how I feel, that's why I went to the hospital. Lord, Fran, you can't give, and I'm just realizing now you never could. It's not that you're selfish, it's . . ."

Francis jumped up. He was angry. My thought was 'Christ, finally!'

"That's not true, that I can't give. It's just not true. I'm just different than you. We're two different people. Listening to your goddamned complaining for twenty years, worrying sick every month if I'd make enough money, then every day comin' home dead tired to squallin' kids and a naggin' wife, a wife that put me down in front of everybody. I met my commitments in spite of everything."

Kathleen had started to get angry when Francis started but the anger melted away as he proceeded and was replaced by surprise.

There was quiet again. I broke it. "What do you say to that, Kath?"

"Francis, you always end up with your little speech about commitment. Life is nothing but one big bloody duty. A wife wants more than a dutiful husband. Kids need more than a dutiful father. I mean, what about affection, what about love."

"Kath," I said, "we each of us love in our own way. If I read you right, Francis, what you're saying is that your love was expressed by working, supporting the family and putting up with frustrations that you didn't know how to cope with, is that right?"

"Yeah, that's right," he nodded.

"But what's all this got to do with the fact that Francis can't make love to me?"

"A lot, I think," I replied.

"I wouldn't be surprised if Francis doesn't feel emotionally castrated by you."

"What?" she cried incredulously.

Francis too looked astonished.

"You see, Francis understands that love for him is expressed not with words, hugs, or kisses, but with meeting his conscience obligations to his family. I'd bet anything he's done that scrupulously. You, Kathleen, don't and apparently can't understand it. I do appreciate it. Your understanding of love is the more common one, with words, a kiss, a pinch, a little present for no special reason, helping with the kids and so on."

She nodded in agreement.

I continued, "Well, Francis feels rejected by you, probably has for a very long time. Not only does he feel rejected, he feels demeaned. He offers love as he sees it and you put him down for it. He says he's been putting up with it for years and years. Now his emotions are rebelling unconsciously and via his body are telling him something like, 'To hell with her, shut her off, you don't need her.' "

"You mean Francis is unconsciously punishing me?"

"Honestly, I'm not sure, but it's a good possibility. There's a lot of anger in Francis toward you, about twenty years of it."

"Twenty years!" Kathleen echoed. "Twenty years, oh, wow!"

"But Christ, you pointed out before yourself there's more than just anger in me. I think I love her, I know I love her."

"And I'm sure you do too," I chuckled, "Kathleen, physically is very easy to love."

"Why would I want to punish her? For Christ's sakes why?" Francis asked this with sincere bewilderment.

"I think that has to do with how well you know her, and with the fact you've never learned how to express your anger."

"What do you mean by that?" he asked.

"Well, what you've probably felt, all unconscious too, mind you, is that where you can hurt her the most is in her femininity. Kathleen is very strong here and much aware of her femininity. Depriving her of sex, attacking her in her most precious concern, her feminine self-esteem, you figure that's one way to really get to her."

"Well, if she's so strong, why should it bother her so much? How can I hurt her if she's so strong?"

"Because sex is probably the most effective way to communicate 'you're really something as a woman,' by not doing it and when she wants to, you're saying, 'you're not too much as a woman.' That would hurt any woman and a lot, after a while."

"Yeah, I can see that," he assented.

Throughout this exchange between me and Francis, Kathleen had remained quiet. Her interest in what I had to say was transparent. Now she spoke, "I've been listening. A lot of this is like a revelation. And I must admit, I gotta agree." She chuckled. "And it isn't that I got to, I want to. I suppose what you're saying here is that Francis isn't able to with me because I don't make him feel like much of a man."

She had said it easily, accurately, and succinctly.

"Yes, I'm saying that. I'm saying exactly that."

"I see." She sat back, crossed her pretty legs demurely and sighed.

We all paused, looked at each other and I said a little hesitantly, "Kath, how can you help Francis to feel more like a man?"

"What?" she asked.

I repeated my question.

"Why I guess generally, not to put him down, not to nag him, not to embarrass him in front of the kids, not to . . ."

"Can't you think of anything positive, Kath?" Francis asked.

"What?"

"Everything you said began with 'not to.'"

"Like what were you thinking about?" she inquired.

"I guess this is both your problem, Francis. I think you're being a little harsh. You'll find it just as difficult, I'm sure. I mean I have to ask you a comparable question, how can you help Kathleen be a more competent wife and mother, a more effective woman in the house?"

"Show my love more," he answered simply.

"O.K., your answer is easier to come up. However, I suspect it's gonna be a bitch to implement for you."

"Yeah," he nodded, "I'll bet."

I turned to Kathleen. "Any thoughts on how to help Francis?"

She shook her head. "No, you know the problem is like you said a while ago. It's me and him together and how we act toward each other. I feel it sometimes. I feel like I'm in control and you seem to want it like that, Francis." She had turned to look at him. What do you think?"

"Yeah. There's truth to that. And I think that's why we, I can't make it with you in bed." He turned to me and said, "Oh, what the hell, let's get it all out. I started to get turned off about six or eight months ago."

"How so? Why?"

"Why?" echoed Kathleen.

"That's when you started to get, uh, aggressive in bed. Up to that time, I was calling the shots.   That's when I got turned off."

I glanced at Kathleen.   She had turned a little pink, her head was down.

"So that, uh, turned you off.   You felt that Kath was trying to dominate the bed scene as well as everything else."

"I guess so, yeah.   And she wanted to start trying different things, that, uh, I didn't want to."

"Why not?"

"I just didn't think it was proper for a wife.   I mean, geez, it was the kind of stuff I used to hear about when I was in the service."   There was a pause.   "I guess I never let myself think about it too much, but it was 'cause like you say she was trying to take over in bed."

"And that's where you drew the line."

"I think that's what happened, yeah."

Kathleen's pink face had turned red.   Francis had noticed. He was becoming increasingly embarrassed too.   He lowered his head.

Kathleen spoke.   "You know, maybe this is all proper in therapy but I think it's awful personal business.   I . . ."

"Oh, Kath," Francis responded with irritation, "It's you who started it, who brought it up.   Maybe you're embarrassed.   Christ, how do you think it makes me feel?   You bringin' up the fact I can't get an erection.   What do think that does for me.   Talk about bein' put down.   Jesus!"

Kathleen's redness had vanished.   "But you're talking like that about me makes me feel like some kind of a nymphomaniac or at least a sexual pervert.   Heaven sakes, you are my husband. It's not like I was with another man."

I felt Kathleen needed a little support.   "Yeah," I nodded, "but more important even, we might ask, why did Kathleen act like this?"

"Why?" Fran looked puzzled.

"Yeah, why was Kathleen being aggressive?   You know, sexual behavior in the bedroom, like I said before, can be symptomatic. How spouses behave in bed is pretty consistent with how they behave out of bed. So, if Kathleen was starting to behave aggressively in bed she wanted some behavioral expression of your love since it was the only way you were showing her any. After all, Fran, among other things sexual intercourse can be a way to demonstrate real affection."

Francis was quiet. So was Kathleen. I had the feeling that for a while now she was comparing me to Francis. This made me a little bit, but just a little bit, uncomfortable. I had to be very careful not to let Francis feel put down, I had to be even more careful not to let myself be emotionally seduced.

Francis, meanwhile, was becoming very threatened. "I know," he said archly, "that sex is a way to show love. Geez, doc, I'm not a kid. But Kathleen here wanted to . . ." He stopped again, too embarrassed.

"So she wanted to stimulate you because by not having sex with her you were, she felt anyway, rejecting her in the last way, in the only way you were still demonstrating your love for her."

"Yeah, maybe."

"You're unconvinced."

"Yeah."

"My problem at this point is that I don't have all the details. I suspect but I'm not sure of what . . ."

It was Kathleen who said it. "I tried to use my mouth."

"And you were repelled by that, Francis," I said without emotion.

"Yeah, I was."

"Well, symbolically, especially between marrieds, there are those who view the act of fellatio as putting the man in the dominant role. Maybe Kathleen was trying to say to you, 'You're my master and I'll do anything you want. That's how much I love you.'"

"Oh, that's bullshit," Francis' voice crackled with disgust.

I continued, ignoring his expletive. "Maybe you were repelled, Francis, because it was too threatening to have Kathleen in what you felt was a servile position precisely because she's your emotional support and she wants you to be hers."

"I don't know if I got all that," he said honestly.

"Both of you have a need to be dependent on the other. A little while ago I asked Kath how she could help you to be more of a man and you pointed out to her that she was saying all the negative things, you know, she was 'not gonna' do this and she was not gonna' do that, she wasn't gonna' nag or put you down', well this approach of oral sex by her, some might see this as an attempt to make you feel that she's not the dominant one in your relationship, that you are."

Francis turned to Kathleen. "Is he right?" he asked curiously. "I, I don't know," she said again turning a little pink. "I, I don't know why, I guess I just felt like it."

"That's what I think," he replied.

Even though I believed my interpretation was accurate I didn't press it. Neither, I felt, was emotionally ready to accept it. I had learned a long time ago that a person's emotional life can't be reordered via intellect only. I had expressed my view. It was their choice to accept and utilize it. Time would tell.

"One thing I got out of this," Kathleen said, "is the point you made about how you act in bed is consistent with how you act out of bed, so I suppose if we're sensitive to each other . . ."

I don't know why she stopped. She seemed to be thinking. "Yes, I said if you're both sensitive to each other's needs outside of bed, bed shouldn't be threatening to either of you. Anything you feel you can do to enhance Francis has got to be good. And anything, Francis, you can do to enhance Kathleen, obviously that's gonna be good too. Neither one of you needs to list or go over now what to do, how to act with each other."

Francis had been nodding while I'd been talking. He'd been looking at his wife.

"I'm convinced you both do have negative feelings toward each other. You have to. Both of you. Both of you feel put down a lot by the other. In a real sense John's delinquency is a symptom of the delinquent feelings you two have toward each other."

"Are we gonna go back to that hate we got . . ."

"No, Fran, all he's saying is that we do have hateful feelings but that doesn't have to matter that much 'cause we also have positive feelings toward each other."

"Exactly.   And if you both talk and express to each other, and constantly, about how you feel, both the negative and the positive feelings, well then . . ."

"Things oughta' get better," said Francis.

"Yes," I said.

"The talking and expressing is going to be especially hard at first for you, Francis."

"Yeah."

"Although I've heard again and again about how quiet you are. Admittedly there've been moments like that here, but you certainly haven't come off like the original quiet man."

"Yeah."

"And Kath, there's a lot you haven't said but you must be aware of where you've put Fran down and . . ."

She nodded as I spoke and raised her hand to hush me up. "I know," she said with a smile.

I turned to Francis. He, too, had a little grin on his face. I grinned back. I'd never seen him smile before. "I got a lot of thinkin' and talkin' to do. A lot of thinkin' first."

I was tired, but pleasantly so. Over the years I'd learned to gauge the effectiveness of a session by how I felt at its close. I felt good about this one. Real good.

EPILOGUE: KATHLEEN AND FRANCIS

The following account was pieced together by Joseph Mansfield. It's derived from a chance meeting he had with Francis on the street (they decided to have coffee and chat), from a couple of phone conversations with Kathleen and from a letter which she sent him several weeks after the last family meeting.

Kathleen and Francis were returning home from a shopping stint in a nearby town. It had been a relaxing day and both felt pretty good. "Let's eat out," Francis suggested crisply. "I wanna' eat out."

Kathleen looked at him with unveiled surprise. "Eat out? We haven't done that in . . ."

"I know," he interrupted, "I know. I wanna' eat out."

"But, but, can we afford . . .?"

"Screw it. I wanna' eat out."

"Fine," she replied happily and a little demurely.

Francis drove to a local eating place which billed itself as a "family restaurant."

She ordered a Tom Collins, he a beer, and both the special entree for that day, deviled pork chops. And then, quoting from Kathleen's letter, "We talked and talked and shared and loved with our eyes. It was the first time ever that Francis suggested going out to eat. We just never did it. Well, maybe it was the setting and being served instead of making and serving the dinner myself, I don't know. All I know is I was excited as a bride. I felt like I'd just met Francis and as you'd put it, doctor, I *related* to him like that, I guess. 'Cause he seemed different, I suppose like he was many years ago."

"Whaddya' think," he asked, sipping his beer.

" 'Bout Mansfield?"

"Yeah and what he said and what we said when we were alone."

"I have to think about it. There's probably a lot of truth to so much he said."

"Yeah, I gotta talk more. I believe that."

"You talk."

"Yeah, but not enough."

"You think a lot. You're not a talker."

"I worry more'n I think. Worrying's bad."

She touched his hand. "What do you worry about. Tell me."

"That I'm gonna' get work. Every month I worry about that."

"Oh, darling, you get work every month. Some of your jobs last two or three months. We've been married twenty years. We've made out O.K. We will. I have confidence in you about that. You know I do. I always have."

"Yeah, I believe that, Kath. It's not really the money, I s'pose, it's us. I think he was right about that business of whatever problems we got, we got because of both of us."

She nodded, "Yeah."

"And I been wrong not to tell you when I thought you were wrong."

"And I been wrong to yell. Especially at dinner. I remember my house, my father, ugh!" Kathleen laughed. "I don't believe this."

"What?"

"This whole scene. Me and you and dinner here. We've never gone out to dinner on the spur of the moment since we been married. And you talking and apologizing and me. I just don't believe it. If I'm dreaming, Fran, don't, don't wake me up!"

"Well, I been makin' resolutions for an hour now and I'm gonna really . . ."

"I'll help you keep them. I will. You watch." And she squeezed his hand. And he squeezed back. "Fran, you've never done that."

"I know."

Their food arrived. "Darling, I'm not hungry but I think I'd like another drink. And I'm feeling high."

Francis ordered another round.

"Kath, you know I love you?"

"Yes," she breathed loudly, "I know."

"How much truth do you think there is in this stuff about me not being able to 'cause I want to shut you off 'cause I really hate you."

"I don't know," she answered honestly and became serious. Her brow wrinkled. It always did when she was just serious, not angry. Francis knew that. "But, Fran, you know there could be a lot of truth 'cause I must have made you real mad over the years. Sometimes I suspected it, even, but I never knew. I never knew. Think about that, hon."

"Yeah, yeah."

"You're worried about not, not being able to with me, aren't you?"

"Christ, am I! And Jesus, I want to."

"Well, don't worry, it'll come."

"That's all I wanta do, come!"

Kathleen roared and Fran managed his best grin. She had started her second drink. She felt a mite dizzy. But oh, she felt so very good! Her husband had just cracked his first joke in twenty years! And a risqué one at that! Mansfield, the restaurant, circumstances or maybe God, had made it happen. Right now she could care less about the who, what or why. It was a dream come true.

Francis put on his usual serious expression. "I don't like that in myself, if it's true," he said.

"What?"

"That I want to shut you off from me, from sex 'cause I hate you, 'cause I wanta punish you."

"Oh, Fran, to hell with what's happened. Right now I feel so great. I feel so close to you. Don't you feel that way?"

His unaccustomed grin returned and Francis nodded.

"Funny, I don't understand it." He shrugged and asked hesitantly, "Kath, you been charged up for a long time now, huh?"

"Yeah," she nodded back sheepishly and turned a little pink. "Yeah, oh Fran, if you only knew!" Kathleen put her hand over her mouth.

"You know my mother and father, they were such goddamn prudes," Francis said that slowly and took a long sip of his nearly empty glass. He refilled it from his second bottle.

She watched him in amazement. Francis almost never discussed his parents with her. Certainly he never spoke of them like this. Kathleen uttered her thought, "You never said anything like that to me before either."

"Yeah," he nodded.

I don't know how long this is going to last, she thought. 'Oh Lord, don't let this mood, these feelings, this moment end, don't let them ever end.

"Yeah, we gotta be less private and more public with each other," Francis said.

She sipped her drink and licked the edge of the glass in a way she knew instinctively had to be seductive.

"Whaddya' mean before when you said 'If you only knew' about how charged up you been?"

"I'm embarrassed," she answered honestly.

"Good, that makes me feel good," he said, returning the sincerity.

"I'll tell you later, in bed," she said provocatively.

Francis for the first time in too long felt in control. She'd turned a darker shade of pink.

"Tell me now."

"You'll be disgusted with me."

"So what? We gotta be honest, public, not private, with each other," he said teasingly.

She looked at him and thought this is like an affair! No, it's better than an affair because if nothing else she could trust him, she could trust him more, she realized in that moment, than she could trust anybody in the whole world.

The thought which Francis had was simpler: She's so fuckin' beautiful and she's my wife!

She lowered her voice and looking into his eyes she said, "Darling, that night I tried to, you know, use my mouth I think it's just 'cause I wanted to so much. Maybe it was selfish as well as like Mansfield said, to tell you that I want you to be my master."

"I don't believe that shit about the 'master' bit."

"I just wanted to. I've wanted to for a long time. Are you disgusted?"

"Yeah, a little, but you know what?" he said grinning again.

"What?"

"I'm interested too." They both laughed again, too loudly, and everyone in the local family restaurant turned to look at the pretty auburn-haired woman and the balding man who were obviously enjoying themselves.

FINAL SESSION

As was their habit, the Whitings arrived promptly at 7:30 for their last session. Kathleen entered first followed by Alice, Francis and John, in that order. I heard Kathleen murmur something unintelligible to Francis about where to sit. He nodded to the couch and both sat down, she gracefully, he heavily. Alice took a chair to her father's right and John sat next to her. I sat down facing the four of them.

Kathleen per usual opened the session. "Is this really going to be our last meeting?"

"I think so," I answered, "We'll have a follow-up session in about a month. You see, I don't think there's too much we've got left to cover that we haven't. If changes for the better haven't begun to show up by now, I doubt that they would."

"Well, there have been changes in these past couple of months, that's for sure," she nodded with a smile.

"Yeah, that's what I'd like to do this evening is to review how you all feel with what's happened, with what's going on in your family."

Alice piped up. "I'll tell you this. Supper time is much better. Sometimes it's even fun."

"Your mother isn't yelling so much."

"Yeah. I mean no, only once in a while," she answered.

"That's one resolution I'm still working hard on," Kathleen volunteered.

"To cut out the yelling?" I asked.

"Well, yes. I suppose. But I was thinking more about supper time, you know, to make that, well a pleasant time. I still remember that as a horror in my father's house. There's no reason why we can't at least have a good . . ."

"Man, that's killing you, ma," John chipped in with a smile.

"If you mean by that that it's not easy, you're right, Johnny," she admitted. She turned to me. "You know, one thing you said back when we started had to do with expressing how we felt, that it was good to do that. I don't believe that it's necessarily good to express how you feel. Sometimes I just feel like yelling at John and Alice, especially for not picking up after themselves. But I don't 'cause it'll just start more haranguing back and forth."

I nodded in agreement. "Yeah, sometimes it's better to overlook or ignore little problems." There was a pause. I glanced at both of the younger Whitings. "What do you guys figure are your mother's rights?"

Alice looked puzzled by the question. "Why, what do you mean?"

"This is one of the things I wanted to bring up with all of

you tonight," I said, perhaps too slowly, "what are each of your rights in the family? Each of you has them. And the idea is, if each of you respect each other's things ought to change even more for the better, at least that's the idea."

There was a pause.

"So, what are mother's rights?" I asked again.

Another pause.

Kathleen spoke. "Maybe I could explain what I think they ought to be."

"Sure," I said.

"Privacy," she replied.

"What?" I asked.

"Privacy. My rights," she said thoughtfully, almost dreamily, "center around privacy. There was a time that all I wanted was a hot meal. I used to complain regularly about that."

"Yeah," nodded Francis in agreement. I noted that he still retained some quietness. This was his first utterance. No, Francis would never be outspoken, I though wryly. "Yeah," he repeated, "when Tom and Frank were still little and John here was born, that's the main thing you complained about, having a hot meal. I remember you'd get the supper for the family but by the time you sat down to eat it, yours was cold."

Kathleen sighed, "That's all over, thank God. But my need is privacy. I guess it's always been that."

"What do you mean by privacy," I asked.

"Well, I don't mean to be, be, uh, isolated from the rest of the family. I mean the right to be alone, moments to myself."

"Christ, ma, you got all day to yourself."

"Yeah," chirped in Alice.

Francis said nothing. He was listening. He looked at his wife with curiosity.

"What I mean," she said rather loudly, "is the right to talk on the phone without being interrupted by who's that, mother, what did they want, etc., etc., or, I like to sit down and read after supper, sometimes I like to read right up to supper if I'm into a good book and I'm constantly badgered about the supper." She turned to Francis. "You see that, hon?"

He nodded slowly. "Yeah, yeah, I see that. You got a right to have time to yourself. I think we all got that. But where does it end?"

"What? What do you mean?" she asked.

"Like, Kath, you got a right to read or be alone after supper, but that's askin' a lot before supper," he said.

"Why?"

"'Cause sometimes you really get into a book and you don't want to leave it and get the supper so we're all standin' around waitin' and I just don't think that's right. Sure, you got a right to your privacy but we all got obligations to each other too. You know what I mean?" He said all of this in his quiet, even-tempered way.

Maybe Francis wasn't exactly outspoken but he made sense when he talked. His family listened. I observed that John and Alice, too, had what? satisfied or were they merely contented looks on their faces? I couldn't be sure. Francis will never be a dominating man, I remembered thinking, but certainly he was making his presence felt. He was a part of the family scene.

Kathleen looked at him. "I know what you mean, Fran, I know perfectly well what you mean," her tone was impatient, "but honestly, I feel put upon when you all nag me about supper not being ready. I just don't think it's fair."

"Geez, ma, what do you expect, what do you expect? You expect dad to get supper?" John asked testily.

"Well, no, I don't expect that," she answered, "but why couldn't I get more help, let's say for getting the dinners on weekends? Or why can't we all go out to dinner as a family once in a while? We've never gone out to eat as a family." She was looking at John when she started but at her husband when she finished.

Francis nodded, "Yeah, I haven't taken the family out to dinner, that's true, but Kath," he added gently, "I do barbecue for the family on weekends. I do that a lot."

"Yes, that's so. I guess I was complaining about never eating out."

"Yeah, but to get you back to the point. You think you got the right not to have dinner when we expect it?"

Kathleen smiled. "No, you're right. What I got to learn is not to get involved in a book before dinner."

I was finding the conversation a trifle too specific, perhaps even banal. I said, "I think the point here is the one which Francis made a while ago. You each of you has obligations to each other. You should all reach some kind of an agreement on what those obligations are. I think that's what's really important because we're not going to deal with every specific irritation which each of you may have."

"Yeah, but there are some major ones," said Kathleen.

"A supper not ready when you expect it sets a bad mood for the whole night," added Francis.

"Yeah," chimed in John.

"O.K.," I said, backing off a little lamely.

"I'll work at not reading before supper."

I sighed. Actually it was all going pretty well. They were talking to each other and even more, resolving issues. I was hoping that they could come to grips with principles. There was a pause and I jumped in, "What's the major obligation each of you has toward the other?"

"Not to bug each other," said Alice quickly and simply.

"What do you mean by that?" asked her mother.

"Just not to bug, sort of like your privacy." She looked at me for clarification.

"You mean not to intrude on each other's lives. Like Kath, you want time to yourself after supper, say, and everybody agrees to it, then they should not bug you during that period," I said, explaining what I thought Alice had in mind.

"I agree with that," said Kathleen.

Francis nodded.

It was John who said, "Well, speaking of rights, have kids got rights?"

"Of course you've got rights," said his mother.

"Yeah, but I figure I got the right not to be bugged, not to be hassled. And I think I'm the one in this family who's hassled the most."

"Maybe, John, but that's probably 'cause you're the one

who intrudes on our lives the most," said his father.

"Yeah, but if I did that's cause like we've been saying here for a long time, that's 'cause you and ma weren't exactly acting right."

Francis nodded. "I know, Johnny."

"Well, what do you figure your rights are?" I asked.

"Well, I like that privacy bit that ma came up with."

"Privacy is not secrecy," said Kathleen with perhaps a little pomposity.

"Whaddya mean?" he asked.

Francis surprised all of us by answering for her. "You want your privacy. That's fine and O.K. and you're certainly entitled to it and I understand you don't wanna' be hassled. That's fine and O.K. You're no different than me. I don't wanna' be hassled either. But, Johnny, when you're being private, doing what you like, that don't give you the right to do something or not do something that's going to hurt me or your mother. You understand what I mean?"

"No," he answered. He looked honestly puzzled.

"O.K. You got a right to your privacy. But that don't give you the right to do things secret that are gonna get you into trouble."

"Why not? Everybody's got a right to make mistakes," he answered with some defiance.

His father nodded. "You're right there. We all gotta' make our own mistakes, but Johnny, if you get into trouble I'm hassled just as much as you are."

"I know, 'cause you're responsible."

"Yeah, that and . . ."

"And what else?"

" 'Cause I'm nervous about you."

"You're nervous?"

"Yeah."

"Christ, dad, you never show it."

"I am, though." And he said it in his usual awfully quiet tone. None of us doubted the truth of it.

"Why you nervous?"

There was a little pause and in a strained, almost whisper-like tone, Francis said, " 'Cause I love ya', that's why."

Kathleen's hand went to her mouth in surprise. John was too astonished to reply. His response, however, was more dramatic. He turned a deep shade of pink and he looked down at his knees, sort of like Francis had done often at past sessions. But it was Alice, with her childlike candor, who summed up the feelings of all of us. "Geez, dad, that was nice. I never heard you say that. That was so-o-o nice." She jumped to her feet and kissed her father on the cheek. Now Francis turned a little pink, but he smiled.

"That *was* nice," I contributed.

"Yes," Kathleen murmured, "There have been changes." She turned to me. "Have you any idea how hard that must've been?"

I looked at Francis. For a moment I thought about asking Francis to discuss how he felt. But then, I thought, What purpose? What purpose would be served? Kathleen's observation had reinforced the fact that changes, emotional as well as behavioral, had indeed occurred.

I turned to John. He was still looking down. "John, what do you think about what your father said about your right to privacy doesn't give you the right to get involved in activities so that you intrude on his life?"

"Yeah, he's right there," he nodded.

Alice piped up with, "Daddy's right. What he's really saying is that we're a family and . . ."

"We've got obligations to each other," her mother finished the sentence for her.

There was a momentary lull. All four seemed to be in deep thought. John broke the lull. "Ya' know I used to complain that there wasn't any love in our family. I guess there is, but ya' know what I'm thinkin' here?"

"What?" I asked.

"I was thinkin', love is a bitch."

Both Kathleen and Alice looked at him, astounded. Francis, however, seemed only curious.

"Whaddya' mean by that, John?" he asked.

"Just what I said," he replied. "You said I made you nervous. I buy that. And you said I make you nervous 'cause you love me. I buy that, too. I guess if you didn't love me you wouldn't get nervous."

"That's about the size of it," Francis responded, nodding.

"Trouble is," John continued, "trouble is whenever I want to do anything now I'm gonna' feel guilty."

"Only if it's gonna' hurt me, or your mother or Alice. And me and ma and Alice, we got the same pressure on us, if you want to call it a pressure."

"That's a pressure," John said.

"I hadn't really thought about it in just this way," I volunteered, "but I suppose the pressure you're talking about, Francis, is the price you pay for family support." I turned to John, "Yeah, I see what you mean, love can be a bitch."

"Maybe, maybe," Kathleen said, "but it's an awful lot better than feeling like nobody cares, I'd rather be pressured to do what I know my family expects than to feel like I can do whatever I want 'cause nobody cares about me."

"Yeah, ma, that's easy for you to say 'cause you're the mother here," he said a little heatedly.

"What's that mean?" she asked.

"Well, you and dad, you're over forty. I still gotta' learn a lotta' things. I'm still learnin'. I know I screw up. I want to, uh, experiment. Now what I'm hearin' is I gotta' watch it. I gotta' watch it a lot how I experiment. That's a down. That's a put-down."

Francis nodded sympathetically. "Yeah, I can see that, son. Like you say, love's a bitch. But I bet growing up without it has gotta' be more of a bitch." He paused. "You want to experiment. Sounds good. I guess what you mean is you figure you got the right to make mistakes, right?"

"Yeah, guess so," his son nodded.

"I think we talked about that already and I don't wanna' beat a dead horse, son, but I agree you got the right to experiment, make mistakes or whatever you wanna' call it, but you don't got the right to abuse yourself."

"Whaddya' mean, 'abuse yourself'?' "

Francis looked a trifle perplexed. "I'm not sure I can explain what I mean," he said honestly.

"Well," Kathleen suggested, "if he abuses himself, he's abusing our love for him, isn't he?"

"Yeah, yeah, that's what I was trying to get at," said Francis with expression.

"See, John, if we love you, your mother and me, and you experiment as you call it with trouble, then you're abusing what we got in you, our love, our, our faith."

"Well, I don't see that at all. 'Cause I'm a separate person. I got my own life to lead, I got a right to do, to live my own life."

"Well, that's true too," said his father agreeably, "but what's also true, like it or not, that when you got a family your life isn't your own life completely."

I'd been sitting quietly for a while now very much taken with Francis' exchange with his son. No doubt about it, Francis had changed. He continued to be a generally silent man, I supposed, but where several months ago he projected the image of a hapless, helpless, hopeless man who was silent because he had nothing to offer, now his silence enhanced a man who exuded a quiet confidence. Moreover, I had come to learn at each session and especially at this one, that Francis was a man who used his silent moments to enjoy a very good mind.

"You mean my life's not my own?" asked John incredulously.

"No, not completely, just like mine is not, and your mother's isn't. We all belong a little bit to each other."

"Well, how can we have rights, then, if we belong to each other?"

"We all of us got all the rights in the world," said Francis thoughtfully, "just so long as we don't abuse the love we got for each other and just so long as we don't intrude, that's a nice word, intrude on each other's privacy."

"No offense, dad, but it sounds like a put-down, well not a put-down, but it sounds, uh, well stifling."

"How do you figure that?" asked Francis.

"Well, how do I get to know what *I* want, me, if I always gotta' worry about the family?"

"You got me all wrong. It's not all one way. I didn't mean like you just give and worry about the family. I didn't mean that your mother and Alice and me too, that each of us just lives to give to the family, I believe we all got our own lives too.

"I think what you mean here, Francis, is that each person has his own identity," I suggested.

"Exactly, that's what I mean. We all of us got our own identity. We're all different and we all of us got a responsibility to make each other better. There, that's what I mean. And when any one of us screws up we all got a responsibility to help out because all of us are hurt a little bit."

"How do you figure we're all hurt if one of us screws up?" asked John.

" 'Cause we all got a commitment to each other," said Francis simply.

John smiled wryly. "There you go with the commitment bit. I'm startin' to understand better some of the things you been sayin'. It all comes down to this commitment thing."

His father grinned a little and replied, "I been thinkin' a lot about this. A lot. Yeah, it all comes down to this commitment business. I guess that's so. I started out my thinkin' about me and the family there at my commitment and that's right where I ended up, at my commitment, and because I am whatever I am I ended up with that idea of commitment. I realize now and maybe it's too late that my responsibility to you and to Alice is to help you understand by my example what a total commitment is. I made it, I think, when I married your mother. But the problem was nobody knew, not even your mother. Nobody knew it except me. My problem, and it became a problem for all of us, look at your trouble, look at Tom and Frank, they're not even here to hear this, my problem was I never let anybody know. I never said nothing to nobody. See, John, I screwed up. I did. And a lot of people suffered. You and ma and Alice and me and your brothers who don't even wanna' be here. For all of that I am heartily sorry."

The three other Whitings sat there quite apparently magnatized by the sincerity and the contrition of Francis' statement. The emotional climate and their expressions told me that he was expressing their contrition too. I couldn't help thinking that now it remained for all of them to translate the talk, the contrition, the sincerity, and the commitment into the reality of their life-style. At this point there was nothing which I could add. Certainly there was nothing to clarify, explain or amend. We ended.

OUTCOMES

We never had a follow-up session. Francis telephoned me several days before the scheduled date to cancel for his family. He and Kathleen were going away for a two week vacation. His succinct explanation was, "First vacation we've had alone since Tom was born."

Cancellation of the follow-up session is not unique. In fact, it's common both for those families which have profited from the therapy and for those families which have not. All the reports from Kathleen, who phones me periodically to chat, are that the Whitings profited much from the sessions.

I haven't seen or heard from John himself since our last session. All the reports about him, however, are very encouraging. He completed his probation without undue incident. He's presently in his last year of high school and according to Mr. Dalton, "obtaining very respectable grades." Of even more significance, he's working part-time with his father, "The boy's good with wood," was the laconic comment from Francis.

If John's progress is any barometer for forecasting the Whiting domestic climate, and I believe it is, then the prognosis for the Whitings is good. According to his wife, Francis continues to be relatively quiet, unemotional, and uninvolved outside the family circle. Within the family, however, Francis has modified his behavior markedly. For one thing, he confronts Kathleen when he feels that she behaves inappropriately. In her last call she had implied that Francis' bout with impotence had dissipated. I had suspected this. His comments at out last session were those of a competent man, a man with strong feelings of adequacy. His ability to be sexually attentive in turn has rewarded Kathleen's strong sexual needs, which she continues to interpret as womanly and feminine. The effect upon Kathleen is to make her feel more adequate as a person. The maternal role has become very tolerable, since her children are grown and her role as a wife, never threatening, has become positively rewarding. It is for this reason that whatever need Francis may have had for nurturance, Kathleen is highly motivated to reciprocate. My best judgment is that both parents now have little need to hold on to their narcissism.

Alice was from the beginning the healthiest of the Whitings. If anything, her good health has increased since her major concern, the family's disintegration, has been alleviated.   In addition, because Kathleen functions better, it is highly probable that Alice identifies even more with her.

I'm convinced that one reason for the realtively speedy and continuing success of the Whitings has been the family conscience. It is strong in all of them. What this means, of course, is that they are all very much identified not only with the social and moral taboos, but with each other, too. It is conscience which arouses feelings of guilt. And it is precisely conscience and the fear of the guilt it precipitates which has inhibited John from more violent acting out. It is conscience which has kept Kathleen from becoming involved in an affair and thereby becoming further, perhaps permanently, alienated from her family. And it is conscience, too, which forms the foundation for the commitment which Francis is so fond to explain. I learned a long time ago that people without a conscience are not capable of loving. The Whitings, I have learned, are very loving people.

THE LOOSE ENDS

Is John's improvement profound and real or only a veneer? I don't know. It's too early to tell. There is little doubt that on the surface, anyway, he is healthier. His academic self-esteem would appear to have risen as evidenced by the reports about his grades from the principal, Mr. Dalton. A memo about his conduct from Mr. Sortino, the assistant principal, indicates that John is functioning successfully with all his peers and with most of his teachers.

John's family life is ameliorated, of that there is little doubt. The effect would seem to be a general decline in his anxiety level and an increase in his feelings of adequacy. Perhaps, but only perhaps, there's been some decline in his narcissism.

How does he feel about Alice? Does he still hate her? Will he ever be close to her or to his brothers?

And what about his brothers? Will he, his sister and his parents ever become close to them? I have no answers to these questions. These are some of the loose ends with which the Whiting therapy ended.

The major loose end in the Whiting story, however, has to be the effect of Diane Henessey. John is still very much involved with her. I met the two of them coming out of a movie a few weeks ago. John introduced me to her. They continue to see each other and frequently, at the Whiting home. Indeed, she has dinner there, Kathleen told me, several times a week. Mrs. Henessey, it seems, does not approve of John and continues to treat him shabbily. This news comes from Kathleen too. The effect this will have upon John is purely speculative as is the outcome of John's and Diane's romance. Another loose end.

Fin

Discussion Questions

1. In what ways do the fantasy lives of the Whitings conflict? How do they jibe?
2. Do any of their behaviors reflect their fantasies? How?
3. Do you agree with Mansfield's reflections that John is scared, bewildered, and very hostile? Why?
4. In what ways are Kathleen and Francis stronger, weaker than their own respective parents? What unfortunate qualities did the two of them pass on to their children?
5. Why is Francis unable, unwilling to have sex with his wife?
6. Is their poor sex life symptomatic of their relationship? Is so, how?

7. Mansfield believes that the Whiting family conscience has kept the family together. Do you agree or disagree? Why?
8. Do you think John will continue to improve now? Why? Why not?
9. In what ways is the Whiting family typical, atypical?

DATE DUE